Libraries in the Information Age

Library and Information Science Text Series

The Academic Library: Its Context, Its Purpose, and Its Operation. By John M. Budd.

The Collection Program in Schools: Concepts, Practices, and Information Services. 3d ed. By Phyllis Van Orden and Kay Bishop, with the assistance of Patricia Pawelak-Kort.

Developing Library and Information Center Collections. 4th ed. By G. Edward Evans with the assistance of Margaret R. Zarnosky.

The Economics of Information: A Guide to Economic and Cost-Benefit Analysis for Information Professionals. By Bruce R. Kingma.

A Guide to the Library of Congress Classification. 5th ed. By Lois Mai Chan.

The Humanities: A Selective Guide to Information Sources. 5th ed. By Ron Blazek and Elizabeth Aversa.

Information Sources in Science and Technology. 3d ed. By C. D. Hurt.

Introduction to Libraries and Information Centers. By Denise K. Fourie and David R. Dowell.

Introduction to Library Public Services. 6th ed. By G. Edward Evans, Anthony J. Amodeo, and Thomas L. Carter.

Introduction to Technical Services. 6th ed. By G. Edward Evans and Sandra M. Heft.

Introduction to United States Government Information Sources. 6th ed. By Joseph Morehead.

Libraries in the Information Age. By Denise K. Fourie and David R. Dowell.

Library and Information Center Management. 5th ed. By Robert D. Stueart and Barbara B. Moran.

The Organization of Information. By Arlene G. Taylor.

Reference and Information Services: An Introduction. 3d ed. Richard E. Bopp and Linda C. Smith, General Editors.

The School Library Media Center. 5th ed. By Emanuel T. Prostano and Joyce S. Prostano.

The School Library Media Manager. 2d ed. By Blanche Woolls.

The Social Sciences: A Cross-Disciplinary Guide to Selected Sources. 2d ed. Nancy L. Herron, General Editor.

Systems Analysis for Librarians and Information Professionals. 2d ed. By Larry N. Osborne and Margaret Nakamura.

Wynar's Introduction to Cataloging and Classification. 9th ed. By Arlene G. Taylor.

Libraries in the Information Age
An Introduction and Career Exploration

Denise K. Fourie

David R. Dowell

Cuesta College

2002
LIBRARIES UNLIMITED
A Division of Greenwood Publishing Group, Inc.
Greenwood Village, Colorado

Libraries Unlimited
A Division of Greenwood Publishing Group, Inc.
7730 East Belleview Avenue, Suite A200
Greenwood Village, CO 80111
1-800-237-6124
www.lu.com

Library of Congress Cataloging-in-Publication Data

Fourie, Denise K.
    Libraries in the information age : an introduction and career exploration / Denise K.
Fourie, David R. Dowell.
        p. cm. -- (Library and information science text series)
    Includes bibliographical references and index.
    ISBN 1-56308-635-2 -- 1-56108-634-4 (pbk.)
        1. Library science. 2. Library science--Vocational guidance. I. Dowell, David R. II.
Title. III. Series.

Z665 .F74 2002
020--dc21
                                                                              2001050745

P

In order to keep this title in print and available to the academic community, this edition
was produced using digital reprint technology in a relatively short print run. This would
not have been attainable using traditional methods. Although the cover has been changed
from its original appearance, the text remains the same and all materials and methods
used still conform to the highest book-making standards.

To our students at Cuesta College,
to our colleagues,
and to our spouses.

Thanks for your ideas, inspiration,
and patience!

Contents

List of Figures

Preface

Ongoing change is the constant for today's library or information center. And for staff at all levels, welcoming and embracing the ongoing excitement and introduction of new services, products, and the ever-expanding boundaries of information access present both an inspiration and a challenge. The electronic information era has directly impacted libraries, archives, and information and media centers, making the promise of instant information a reality.

This textbook is designed for students and others interested in an overview of the world of modern libraries and information centers. It is especially useful for those beginning a course of study as a library/media technician in a community college curriculum, or graduate library and information school students. The book is also versatile enough to accompany continuing education courses for staff or to be used for on-the-job reference.

Libraries in the Information Age: An Introduction and Career Exploration, begins by examining the redefined role of libraries in the era of electronic information, then provides historical background on the evolution of libraries. Job opportunities in a variety of library and information center settings are discussed, followed by a detailed look at the typical major library activities of collections, processing, circulation, and reference. The critical role of resource sharing networks is examined, along with the ethical issues surrounding information access, and an overview of basic job-hunting skills. The text concludes with a brief discussion of the impact of the Internet on library services.

Overall, the book introduces the novice to trends and issues affecting the current library agency. At the end of each chapter, references to print and electronic resources are provided to help the reader further in learning and information gathering. A good textbook represents the first step in assimilating knowledge about a course of study or, in this case, a potential career path. But going beyond the text is an enriching second step. Especially helpful to students is the opportunity to communicate electronically with practitioners via e-mail, listservs, and World Wide Web sites.

Acknowledgments

The authors wish to give a special acknowledgment to the late Barbara E. Chernik, whose *Introduction to Library Services* (Libraries Unlimited 1992) was the trailblazer that *Libraries in the Information Age* is attempting to replace. Chernik's work forms the foundation for Chapter 3, "Types of Library Job Opportunities."

The authors further wish to acknowledge the following persons and entities for their valuable support toward the publication of this book.

The ALA Reference Desk

Kevin Bontenbal

Joanne Britton

Johanna Brown

Richard Brumley

Del Chausse

Oscar Chavez

Cuesta College

Deana Cook

Jennifer Cooper

Jennifer Correa

Hiram Davis

Kathy DeCou

Denise Dowell

Sohair W. Elbaz

Joan Foster

Mary Gamewell

Martha Greene

Nancy Guidry

Kathy Headtke

Ruth Jordan

Tina Lau

Mary Ann Laun

Mike Line

Nancy Loe

Dominik Muggli

Mike Multari

Nancy P. O'Neill

Joan Olseen

Betty Stout

Arlene Taylor

Rebecca True

Catherine Trujillo

Mary Lou Wilhelm

Chapter 1

Introduction

Redefining the Role of Libraries

The 1990s ushered in a new era for libraries and information centers because of the incredible growth seen in the electronic dissemination of information. This trend was most clearly seen in the explosion in use of the World Wide Web (WWW). Although considered by many to be synonymous with the Internet, the global network of networks, the Web is the multimedia portion of the Internet that, because of its ease of use and graphics, has made earlier protocols, such as Gopher and Telnet, obsolete.

In addition to the impact of the Internet, the maturity and widespread use of electronic periodical indexes and full-text databases, and of automated holdings catalogs have reached to the far corners of the globe, greatly impacting library agencies, whether they are rural or urban, small or large. No longer are libraries defined by the size of their physical collections but rather by the amount of information to which they can provide access.

Along with this new standard of electronically disseminating and accessing information, libraries of all sizes have found themselves redefining their role. Will the printed book become obsolete? Will physical library buildings become unneeded? Will salaries rise with the increased need for technological know-how? And, ultimately, what does all of this mean for people employed in the library and information science profession in the twenty-first century?

Although there is no crystal ball to give us definite answers, we can discern some trends in the profession. As we enter the new century, information services personnel have a higher profile and increased status among both the general public and their co-workers because they are often the Internet trainers in school, academic, special, and public library settings. They are expected to be knowledgeable and to help lead their organizations in planning for new technologies. Patrons view both technology and libraries as vital services. In a 1998 Gallup survey conducted for the American Library Association, nearly all the respondents indicated that they "expected libraries to be needed in the future, despite the information available via computer."[1] Whether in an elementary school media center or in a university research library, the job environment is faster-paced than in the past, with continual retraining needed as the newest information-storage media become mainstream. Few libraries or information centers are tied to any single medium of information storage anymore. Rather, multiple formats are in use simultaneously: microforms, paper, optical discs, and digital data. There is a continuous learning curve for staff and, correspondingly, for patrons and researchers. Increasingly, the role of librarians and technicians is that of trainer and navigator—instructing customers on the use of tools and recommending relevant resources among the welter of available information.

Computer Skills Essential

For library and information center personnel, the emphasis on computer skills cannot be stressed enough. Although a knowledge of and reverence for books is still valued, these alone are insufficient background for entering a field that increasingly depends on computer resources and applications.

This does not mean that hard-core programming skills and in-depth knowledge of mainframe computer operations are necessary. Although some understanding of these areas is often useful, the emphasis must be on using the computer as a tool to unlock the world of electronic information and to transmit the appropriate information to patrons whether or not they are physically present in the library. It also means skillful use of productivity tools (e.g., word processing programs, spreadsheets, databases, e-mail) that enable the internal operations of libraries to function quickly and effectively. In addition, library staff are now being called upon to provide basic computer instruction to library users.

The World Wide Web is but the most recent manifestation of the impact of computers on the working conditions in libraries. For the past three decades, automation of behind-the-scenes processes in libraries has been gaining speed. Repetitive (translate that as "boring") routines gradually have been reduced to a set of programmable instructions that a computer can execute. These tasks have included card filing, the physical formatting of catalog cards, generation of overdue notices, and so on. More recently, these advances have allowed library catalogs to be searched from remote locations—either within the same organization or from far greater distances. With each step of this process the tasks of library staff members have become less routine and more reliant on the ability to manipulate computers.

In addition to changing the day-to-day activities of library staff, automation increasingly has added value for library users. For example, after libraries had automated both their catalog and circulation records, the two records for an item could be linked together. As a result, library catalog users not only could determine whether the library owned a particular item but also could learn if it was checked out. If it was checked out, then they could see when it was due. Other internal library records once reserved for staff use could also be made available to the public. Examples of this are on-order files, in-process files, and periodicals check-in files.

Although at each step along the way library staff have feared that automation would reduce jobs, these fears have not been justified. No libraries, to the authors' knowledge, have reduced staff because of increased automation. In a few isolated cases, automation has been used as a justification for staff reductions, but in each of these cases the real motivation was to reduce the budget—automation was just a convenient excuse. In fact, it is often possible for staff to process a greater volume of transactions since automation. And the list of benefits to patrons continues to grow. Increasingly, it is the information itself, rather than just brief summaries of the desired information, that is available. With this shift, the role of library staff in assisting library users is changing with accelerating speed. The increasing pervasiveness of the World Wide Web in the 1990s accelerated the trend toward electronic information resources that gained momentum throughout the last one-third of the twentieth century.

New Paradigm for Evaluating Information

The rising challenge is to help library users become skillful in evaluating the usefulness and reliability of the wide array of information now available. Until the advent of the World Wide Web, information available through libraries had gone through two separate refinement processes before reaching readers.

The first process was the publishing process. As uneven as this process was, at the very least it ensured that a second set of eyes, and sometimes multiple sets of eyes, passed over the information before it found its way into print. The process of writing and publishing a book often requires two years or more. The author carefully crafts the text so that the editor and the publisher will accept it. The editor often makes suggestions about the content and accuracy. The publisher has to be concerned about potential litigation. This process does not ensure the accuracy or the relevance of the information, but it does improve the likelihood of a credible product. In addition, readers had the opportunity to consider the reputation of the publishers who were willing to market the author's product.

The second refinement process was the decision to add a title to a library's collection. This decision was based on selecting a resource—from all of the many resources competing for the library's scarce acquisitions dollars—that appeared to best meet the customers' unique information needs for that specific library.

Web-based information is not required to meet such scrutiny. The electronic page shares at least one characteristic with the paper page. A favorite history professor used to remark, "Paper is a very neutral medium. It will record any nonsense any fool writes down." Within the professor's context, today any "fool" can write any nonsense that pops into his or her head and, using the power of computer word processing and automatic Web page creation, publish it on the Internet in a couple of hours without the review of another human. The same tool that allows brilliant insight to be communicated worldwide at near the speed of light also allows any fool to broadcast lesser thoughts just as effectively.

The greatest challenge facing information professionals in the twenty-first century is the evaluation of online information. Many patrons will require assistance and training in how to gain access to electronic data, but this task will pale in comparison to the daunting task of training patrons in evaluating the information they find. Critical thinking skills are not easily transmitted. In school and academic libraries, this responsibility is shared with classroom teachers. Staff in special libraries have a responsibility to sift through and evaluate such data for other professional colleagues within their organizations. The role of the public library is less clear and more of a double-edged sword: the general public they serve deserves as much assistance as the patrons of other types of libraries, but balancing access to information with the frequent demand to mediate offensive materials often leaves public library staff walking a tightrope.

Characteristics of Library Personnel

A wide variety of job knowledge and skills are required for any library to operate smoothly. In a small, one-person location, the solo staff member must possess a wide array of these skills. In a large library, these attributes may be spread among literally hundreds of different individuals.

In one-person libraries, staff members must do everything. At certain times, they may perform tasks that would generally be considered professional. At other times, the tasks may often be purely clerical or, in emergency situations, even janitorial. Whatever needs to be done *is* done by that single person. Such staff members must be Jacks (or Jills) of all trades and perhaps masters of none.

Solo Librarian or Part of a Larger Team

If a person likes a wide variety of very different tasks during the work-day, then the small library offers such an opportunity. Such a person must be a self-starter who can see what needs to be done, can organize and prioritize the tasks at hand, and can work through them until they are completed. No supervisor is physically close at hand to advise on difficult situations. In fact, no colleague is nearby to assist with any technical matter. Flexibility is an important attribute because the arrival of a single customer can cause the reordering of the work plan. The main priority is helping the customer, whether that customer is a student or teacher using a school library, a professional in a firm or organization using a special library, or a member of the general public using a small public library.

Even if the location is part of a larger library agency, a certain amount of physical processing of materials and of database maintenance will be required. Other staff members at that location may provide assistance with peripheral tasks such as janitorial, computer, and bookkeeping support. They may also be available to assist with difficult-to-please patrons and to provide general moral support and camaraderie. However, they cannot be relied upon to advise on library technical matters. If the small library is a branch of a larger system, then advice may be readily available by telephone, e-mail, or a visit. If the site is not part of a larger organization, then there is the danger of a sense of isolation becoming a morale issue. The solo librarian, in this case, must become a skilled advocate and protector of the library turf as well as a highly skilled technician. This kind of assignment makes good use of general skills but does not allow the luxury of specialization.

A large library, on the other hand, requires a certain amount of specialization of function. The larger the library, the more compartmentalized each position becomes. In the largest libraries with hundreds of staff members, tasks are carefully defined and everyone is a specialist of sorts. In such libraries, it is often hard to keep track of the big picture of what the entire organization is trying to achieve. Each person is important to achieving the desired outcome, but sometimes that fact is forgotten in the stress of everyday life. In such larger libraries, many levels of staff are employed with different sets of specialized knowledge and skills required throughout the organization.

Each person performs a part of the entire process and must depend on other staff members to do their part of the work. Working as part of a team is critical in providing good service to the customer. One staff member may decide which items to purchase for a subject area of the collection, another may verify the bibliographic information needed to complete the order, another may select the vendor and place the order, another may receive the order, and yet another pay the invoice. Then the creation of the bibliographic record begins to intensify.

In some libraries, the physical description of the item (i.e., descriptive cataloging) may be performed by one person and the subject analysis (i.e., subject cataloging) by another. In very large libraries, the descriptive work may be divided among foreign language specialists, and the subject headings and classification work may be performed by subject specialists. Physical processing such as bar coding, "tattle taping," and ownership marking will likely be performed by yet another person. Serials and government documents, manuscripts, and other special collections are likely to have separate but parallel assembly lines in which information necessary to establish and maintain bibliographic control over the item is accumulated. All of these staff members are involved before an item is ready to be offered to the public.

No attempt is made here to list all the possible specialties within libraries. Rather, the point is that the size of the library will determine whether staff members are primarily specialists or generalists.

Public Service Versus Behind the Scenes

The tasks described in the previous paragraphs have something in common. They are performed behind the scenes. These tasks require attention to detail, extreme accuracy, and the ability to follow through on long complex procedures, and they are often best performed away from the distracting interruptions of customers arriving and telephones ringing. People who thrive in this environment are similar to those who do well in jobs such as computer programming and accounting or bookkeeping.

Other types of individuals are also needed in libraries though. Public service staff members require the same attributes that lead to success in other jobs that either flourish or fail depending on how well the needs of individual customers are satisfied—one customer at a time. Great oral communication skills—especially intuitive listening ability—tops the list of required characteristics. Ability to function without getting frustrated when three customers are competing for attention and two phones are ringing is also important. Juggling multiple priorities, which change from minute to minute, often becomes the order of the day at a busy library public service desk. Variety can be great; but many of the service requests can be repetitive and seemingly mundane. However, all customers believe that their requests are very important, and the customers must be treated with courtesy, speed, and skill. Successful experience as a sales or waitperson may be excellent preparation for this kind of library assignment. No single background, aptitude, or personality is best for all library work. A variety of individual attributes is needed to staff today's libraries and information centers.

Staff Categories

To the general public, anyone who sits at a desk in a room where a substantial number of books are shelved is a librarian. Even supposedly sophisticated university faculty have often approached a library administrator with some emotion and stated, "Your librarian told me . . . !" In reality, the staff member with whom the professor had just had an unfortunate encounter was a new part-time student assistant with less than two weeks of experience. Such a casual use of the term *librarian* is akin to calling anyone who works in a medical clinic a doctor. To more knowledgeable individuals the term librarian has a much more precise definition.

Within the knowledge and skill sets required for efficient delivery of quality services, there are at least two different career ladders, each with multiple rungs. In the small library discussed previously, as many of these as possible need to be packaged into one person. As the size of the library increases, a narrowing of focus and a corresponding depth of specialization of knowledge and skills become increasingly necessary.

Library Education and Personnel Utilization
Staffing Recommendations

The following discussion of staff roles in libraries is based on *Library and Information Studies and Human Resource Utilization* (LISHRU) (formerly known as the *Library Education and Personnel Utilization* [LEPU]), a policy statement of the American Library Association. This statement has survived the test of time and remains an excellent framework for understanding the division of labor in libraries. The full document is included in this book as Appendix A.

A word of caution is in order. Libraries are not compelled to follow ALA policy. Library staff are not certified and regulated to the extent that medical staff are. For example, most states regulate and mandate the exact education and experience required for physicians, physician associates, registered nurses, licensed practical nurses, pharmacists, pharmacist assistants, and so on. Although most states prescribe the minimum requirements for certification as a school librarian, other categories and types of libraries are generally ignored. As a result, each employer generally is free to deviate from the concepts espoused by the national professional association. Therefore, for any concept expressed herein, it will not be difficult to discover libraries that are organized in ways that deviate from this model. This model, however, has shown that it generally will balance the needs of the organization to operate in a cost-effective manner with the needs of employees to be treated realistically and fairly and the interests of the profession to provide good library services to all.

Basic to the understanding of LISHRU is the appreciation of various groups of tasks within libraries. These levels are summarized here into three categories: (1) clerical, (2) paraprofessional, and (3) professional. Another term in common usage is library support staff. The term *support staff* refers to all non-librarians, whether they are clerical or paraprofessional, full-time or part-time.

Clerical Staff

Libraries are not only a place where books are stored and made available but also are organizations that must maintain themselves in the same manner as do other types of bureaucratic organizations. In this aspect of their activities, libraries have many tasks that are similar to all such organizations.

Some of these maintenance tasks are primarily clerical in nature. Clerical tasks are the same as those performed by office workers in most any kind of organization. Keyboarding, filing, greeting customers, and paying bills are a few examples of clerical tasks needed in libraries. In large libraries, some positions will be almost exclusively for such tasks. This does not mean that the positions are all entry level. Within larger libraries, there can be several levels of clerical positions, depending on the responsibility level of the position (e.g., Secretary I, Secretary II, Secretary III, or Account Clerk I, Account Clerk II).

Entry into such positions generally will be through clerical training, clerical experience, or both. Knowledge of basic library terminology and concepts that may be required can be learned on the job. For such positions, it is almost incidental that the position is located in a library.

Paraprofessional Staff

Paraprofessional positions in libraries are generally called Library Technical Assistants (LTAs), Library Assistants, or Library Technicians. The LISHRU statement also envisions another category: Library Associates. Only the very largest of libraries would have both categories in use. However, it is not unusual for even medium-sized libraries to have three or four levels of library assistants or library technicians. These positions are differentiated from the clerical positions in that they require library education, training, or experience, or all three, before they can fulfill the requirements of their positions.

In actual practice, the demarcation between all of these titles is blurred. The title, Library Associate, as used in LISHRU, describes a position for which a bachelor's degree is required and general education is more important than library knowledge. Sometimes foreign language capability or knowledge of a specific subject discipline may be required. On the other hand, the LTA classifications as used in LISHRU "assume certain kinds of specific technical skills,"[2] but they are not meant simply to accommodate advanced clerks. Although clerical duties may be required, the emphasis is on special technical skills specifically associated with library work, such as handling multimedia equipment or bibliographic searching. Small to medium libraries tend to combine these categories into one hierarchical series of position classifications (e.g., LTA I, LTA II, LTA III or Library Assistant I, Library Assistant II).

The ideal preparation for an LTA is an associate's degree or a certificate in library technology from a community college program. However, there are not currently enough such programs in the United States to train the number of paraprofessionals needed by libraries. As a result, many libraries are forced to hire candidates with general education and then provide them with on-the-job training so they can gain the knowledge and skills needed to perform their duties.

LISHRU differentiates between the kind of training appropriate for LTAs and that needed for those who want to become professionals in libraries: "Emphasis in the two-year Technical Assistant programs should be more on skills training than on general library concepts and procedures."[3] This is a conceptual starting point. "Training courses for Library Technical Assistants at the junior or community college level should be recognized as essentially terminal in intent, designed for the preparation of supportive rather than professional staff."[4] On the other hand, LISHRU states, "Students interested in librarianship as a career should be counseled to take the general four-year college course rather than the specific two-year program, with its inevitable loss of time and transferable content."[5] To keep future career doors open, most students seeking a certificate in library technology and who do not have a college degree should not get their associate's degree in library science; rather, they should major in a subject that has a related four-year degree that will facilitate the transition if and when the time is right.

However, astute students of career development are learning that there is not one correct path of career progression. Now, instead of the employer defining how careers should develop, employees increasingly are fitting their careers around other priorities in their lives.[6] Likewise, one cookie cutter approach does not provide the single, correct way to enter a career in librarianship. Library work is a career choice often made by individuals in their late twenties and those in their thirties, forties, and even older. For such persons, it often is an easier transition for them to explore a career by investing in an LTA degree or certificate.

In fact, in many LTA programs the typical student already has a college degree and perhaps considerable work experience in another field before entering the program. A student may already hold an associate's degree, a bachelor's degree, even a graduate degree. In this case, the student is seeking a certificate (essentially the core of courses of the LTA associate degree) just to have vocational credibility. For many such individuals, the paraprofessional level is their desired final goal. For others it is a careful first step that may lead to experience as a paraprofessional and, subsequently, to a Master of Library Science (M.L.S.) and a position as a librarian.

Librarians

Librarians are responsible for looking at the information needs of the primary customers of a particular library. Then they look at the information and library resources that are available to meet those needs. Finally, they plan strategies that will make the most relevant information sources available to their primary clientele in ways that will be most useful to those individuals.

"The title 'librarian' carries with it the connotation of 'professional' in the sense that professional tasks are those which require a special background and education on the basis of which library needs are identified, problems are analyzed, goals are set, and original and creative solutions are formulated for them. Theory is integrated into the practice and planning, organizing, communicating, and administering of successful service programs to users. In defining services to users, the professional person recognizes potential users as well as current ones and designs services which will reach all who could benefit from them."[7]

Normally, to qualify for the title *librarian* one must have a master's degree in library and information science. Often this degree must be from a graduate program accredited by the American Library Association. Some states stipulate this requirement for such a designation in school and public libraries. A teaching credential with a specialization in school library and media services may suffice for entry-level school library assignments in other states. However, individuals wanting to have the flexibility to move from one type of library to another as their career unfolds would do well to secure a master's of library science and to attain their degree from an ALA accredited institution.

"Positions that are primarily devoted solely to the routine application of established rules and techniques, however useful and essential to the effective operation of a library's ongoing services, should not carry the word 'Librarian' in the job title."[8]

Both librarians and LTAs carry out duties that are fairly routine applications of established rules and techniques. The librarian, though, also has a fundamental responsibility to constantly review those established rules and techniques and replace them when they no longer provide the most effective means of delivering services for the unique clientele served by that library. At the Cuesta College library, a librarian was the project manager responsible for implementing the current automation system. After the system stabilized, day-to-day administration of it was turned over to an LTA. However, the librarian still takes the lead in implementing upgrades and new modules.

As anyone who has observed the operation of libraries knows, the distinction between professional and paraprofessional responsibilities is not always as clear in practice as in theory. The degree alone does not a good librarian make.

Background Research

Nevertheless, research has provided support for the value of the M.L.S. Four little-known dissertations completed in the 1960s relate to this issue. John McCrossan found that M.L.S. holders were likely to perform better in collection development than others.[9] Charles Bunge showed that although the end result might not differ, library school graduates were more efficient in performing reference searches than those with similar library experience.[10] Lucille Wert's study showed that school librarians holding an M.L.S. offered more services and spent less time in housekeeping tasks than did those with similar experience and responsibilities who had an undergraduate minor in library science.[11] In a slightly different exploration, Gordon Baillie found a positive correlation between library school grade point average and successful performance on the job.[12] Since this research, library education has changed, libraries have changed, and the tasks performed by librarians have changed. Similar research needs to be conducted today to see if these results still hold.

Specialists

One other category in LISHRU that deserves brief mention is that of *specialist*. Specialists in LISHRU are a professional parallel to librarians in education and in function. Their education, however, is not librarianship. They work primarily in larger libraries as systems analysts, personnel experts, accountants, or a specialist of another type.

Such specialists may even hold an M.L.S. degree. One of the authors had a running discourse of several years with a top administrator of the Library of Congress that went something like the following:

* * *

Library of Congress administrator (upon sighting the author at a library conference)*:* I'm surprised to see you. I thought you would be in jail. I saw your name in *American Libraries* in an advertisement requiring an ALA-accredited M.L.S. for a librarian position. You know that we have proved at the Library of Congress that an M.L.S. is not required to be a librarian. Therefore, it is illegal to require an ALA-accredited M.L.S.

Author: You don't operate a library. You operate a factory. You don't hire librarians at Library of Congress. You hire specialists—language specialists and content specialists. If any of them tried to act as a librarian in the manner in which I expect librarians to operate, you would fire them or severely discipline them for not following established routines. You don't want them to be looking at ultimate users and be making judgments about how best to serve them. You just want them to keep production up.

* * *

Specialists meet a valid need, particularly in very large libraries. Some libraries try to find individuals who have both an M.L.S. and a relevant specialty degree. Others just seek the specialty. Whatever other strengths may be brought to an organization by a specialist, the expectations for them should not be the same as that for librarians, unless the person is also trained as a librarian.

Librarians alone have responsibility for moving library services forward. As the LISHRU states:

> The objective of the Masters programs in librarianship should be to prepare librarians capable of anticipating and engineering the change and improvement required to move the profession constantly forward. The curriculum and teaching methods should be designed to serve this kind of education for the future rather than to train for the practice of the present.[13]

There is a myth about a great medical controversy that allegedly took place a couple of centuries ago. The principle under discussion was whether anyone other than the physician should be allowed to touch the patient. The function in question was who should be allowed to empty bedpans. Speculate for a moment what our medical care today would be like if this argument had been resolved in a different way.

Today libraries must resolve many similar issues. For both the profession and library services to move forward, more of today's practice needs to be routine and delegated to supporting staff. A couple of decades ago, copy cataloging was an issue.[14] Today it is original cataloging and reference work. We can only speculate what the "bedpan" issues of this new century will be.

As we move into that great future, librarians will need some of the same characteristics that lead to success in other professions—analytical ability, communication skills, intellectual curiosity, and service orientation. In addition, the librarian must be committed to continuous improvement of services to the patrons of their library.

Colleague Brian Nielson described it slightly differently:

> I think it would be nice to be able to hire a fresh M.L.S. grad who knew how to build a hypercard stack, or a Gopher server, or a series of scripts to make using an online catalog easier. Better yet, to hire a student who knew how to teach herself how to pick up the next new information tool which will come along next year.

Available Resources

The following two online glossaries of library-related terms are recommended to students for immediate use as they read this textbook, and also for later reference as they seek employment or work in the field.

Pepperdine University Libraries maintains "Library Vocabulary: Common Terms Defined," a brief listing of the most common vocabulary terms that library users may encounter. See http://rigel.pepperdine.edu/instruction /libterms.html.

A more comprehensive and much larger listing (and it may load slowly), was developed by Joan M. Reitz, a librarian at Western Connecticut State University. ODLIS: Online Dictionary of Library and Information Science is a glossary containing words and concepts dealing with instruction, computer usage and programming, library and print history, and more. See http://vax .wcsu.edu/library/odlis.html.

Notes

1. Gallup Organization for the American Library Association. *Usage and Perception Study*. Lincoln, NE: Gallup Organization, 1998.

2. American Library Association. "Library and Information Studies and Human Resource Utilization: A Statement of Policy." Adopted January 23, 2002. Paragraph 15. Available: http://www.ala.org/hrdr/lepu.html (Accessed January 27, 2002).

3. Ibid. Paragraph 15.

4. Ibid. Paragraph 25.

5. Ibid. Paragraph 26.

6. Douglas T. Hall and Associates. *The Career is Dead—Long Live the Career: A Relational Approach to Careers*. San Francisco, CA: Jossey-Bass, 1996.

7. American Library Association. Ibid. Paragraph 8.

8. Ibid. Paragraph 9.

9. John Anthony McCrossan. "Library Service Education and Its Relationship to Competence in Adult Book Selection in Public Libraries." Ph.D. diss., University of Illinois, 1966.

10. Charles Albert Bunge. "Professional Education and Reference Efficiency." Ph.D. diss., University of Illinois, 1967.

11. Lucille Mathena Wert. "Library Education and High School Library Services." Ph.D. diss., University of Illinois, 1970.

12. Gordon Stuart Baillie. "An Investigation of Objective Admission Variables As They Relate to Academic and Job Success in One Graduate Library Education Program." Ph.D. diss., Washington University of Illinois, 1961.

13. American Library Association. Ibid. Paragraph 29.

14. David R. Dowell. "From Cataloger to Catalog Librarian." In "Catalogs and Catalogers: Evolution Through Revolution," ed. Tillie Krieger, *Journal of Academic Librarianship*, 2 (1976):173–74.

Chapter 2

A Brief History of Libraries

The story of libraries begins with the history of the written record. The oral tradition, which relied on the memorization of history, legends, and folklore, was the earliest form of preserving and transmitting data among people. As humans developed methods of recording data on cave walls, stones, tree bark, and in other forms, the era of written communication began. Whether using pictures, symbols, letters, or languages to express themselves, humans made the transition from using human memory as the predominant storage device to using the written record, some 5,000 years ago. As we transition into the twenty-first century, data are increasingly recorded in electronic formats. In addition to storing data, the computer also gives us amazing means for composing, transmitting, and publishing information.

With the accumulation of written records—whether clay tablets, papyrus rolls, parchment leaves, paper, and now digital format—arose the need to store, access, and preserve them.

The Ancient World

By surveying some of the major inventions, institutions, and technologies of ancient civilizations, we can glimpse the issues surrounding the development of early libraries. In addition, it is insightful to think about certain common information needs that historians have identified that helped drive the collecting of written materials, then and now. These information needs fall into the following broad categories: government records, religious records, business records, and household records. Tax receipts, property ownership, laws of the land, military intelligence and campaigns, and population censuses are typical examples of government data. Sacred laws, songs and rituals, creation stories, and legends of gods and goddesses illustrate vital religious records. Successful commerce depends on sales records, accounts, inventories of goods, employee records and salaries, trade routes and explorations, inventions, formulas, and trade secrets. Individual families collect and pass on their genealogical and marriage information, land and property records, personal correspondence, culinary information and recipes, family legends, history, and literature.

Middle East

The oldest form of writing that survives today is known as cuneiform. This significant contribution to civilization was developed in the Middle East by the ancient Sumerians. They occupied an area once called the Fertile Crescent, a valley bounded by the Tigris and Euphrates rivers, now within the present-day country of Iraq. Very little stone or wood was available for building in the arid environment, so they fashioned houses and structures out of native clay and sticks. Around 3100 B.C., the Sumerians began using a sharpened reed called a stylus to make wedge-shaped marks in damp clay to keep track of grain and other agricultural products. The clay tablets were then dried and baked, leaving a permanent written record.

Contemporary scientists continue to uncover buried collections of these cuneiform tablets. In 1987, archaeologists unearthed a cache of more than 1,000 clay tablets, dating back to about 1740 B.C., that inventoried the royal wine supply, tracked the deployment of spies in warfare, calculated taxes, and contained correspondence between regional kings.[1] Not surprisingly, these are all topics that are still vital to humans today.

Throughout the Middle East libraries arose to house the tablets of the Sumerians by about 2700 B.C., as well as those of later civilizations, such as the Babylonians and Assyrians. Historians have evidence of significant official libraries at Telloh (southern Iraq) and Nineveh (northern Iraq), each with thousands of clay tablets.

The Ancient Egyptians

At the same time in a different part of the ancient world, the Egyptians made use of the native papyrus plant to develop their writing medium. Sheets of the beaten and pressed plant material were joined to make long and fragile scrolls. Although easily damaged by dampness or torn because of its brittleness when dry, papyrus paper was economical to produce and easily transported. With a brush-like reed pen, Egyptians recorded information in a hieroglyphic style of writing. For more than 4,000 years, papyrus remained the standard writing medium in Egypt and along the Mediterranean shore. Use of papyrus continued until about A.D. 300 in parts of Europe and as late as A.D. 1022 in Egypt.[2]

A few scroll fragments are held at the Bibliotechque Nationale and other major museums. Libraries of papyrus scrolls have long disappeared, and the descriptions of their existence are based on second-hand accounts.

Thus, historians know that by about 2500 B.C., large governmental libraries of papyrus scrolls existed, including one at Gizeh near the great pyramids. By 1250 B.C., ruler Ramses II developed an extensive library at Thebes, an ancient Egyptian capital, that stored rolls of papyrus in clay jars with keywords visible on the end of each scroll to denote the contents.

The Greeks

As with many aspects of European civilization, libraries and knowledge reached a pinnacle during the time of the ancient Greeks. Socrates, Sophocles, and Herodotus, great writers and thinkers, were just a few of the scholars active during the period known as the Golden Age (fifth century B.C.).

The noted playwright and scholar Aristotle had one of the great private libraries of the ancient world housed at his school, The Lyceum. His collection was coveted and changed hands many times after his death. Governmental and royal libraries were commonplace throughout the Greek world.

Among the great cultural accomplishments of the Greeks was the founding of the ancient library in Alexandria, Egypt, by Ptolemy I, circa 300 B.C. A scholarly facility, its purpose was to collect every book in the world and to translate it into Greek so that the expanding empire could better understand the cultures they ruled. The Alexandrian library flourished for approximately 600 years and by all accounts was the greatest, richest library of the ancient world, with an estimated 700,000 papyrus scrolls.

This academic community functioned like a university with noted scholars, librarians, and historians being responsible for inventions such as the first encyclopedia and dictionary.[3]

Scribes went to great lengths to copy everything to enlarge the Greeks' knowledge and power base. No trace of the fabled library remains today. There are differing opinions among historians as to the degree of destruction sustained by the facility at the time of the Roman conquest in the fourth century A.D. Egyptian officials and the United Nations Educational, Scientific, and Cultural Organization (UNESCO) are reported to be partnering in an ambitious interpretive center at the library site.

In about the second century A.D., the Greeks devised the codex, a forerunner of the book as we know it today. This storage format used parchment (i.e., sheep's skin) or vellum (i.e., calf's skin), rather than papyrus. Both sides of the parchment could be used, and then the leaves were bound or fastened together, forming pages that could be opened flat and read in sequence. Although both papyrus and parchment were used in various places for centuries throughout the ancient world, the eventual displacement of papyrus as the standard writing medium was fueled by a rivalry.

As Alexandria was accumulating volumes and copies of documents, so was the library in Pergamum. Another important center of scholarship, the Greek kingdom of Pergamum was located in present-day Turkey and was founded in the second century B.C. Not to be outdone by a competitor, Egypt placed an embargo on the export of the native papyrus, thus preventing Pergamum from obtaining the needed writing medium. Cutting off the supplies only led the scholars in Pergamum to improve parchment and to rely on it as their main writing material. By the waning of the Roman Empire in A.D. 476, the parchment codex had become the predominant form of the book, replacing the papyrus roll.

The Romans

As the Roman civilization flourished, from 650 B.C. to A.D. 476, it was greatly influenced by the Greeks and continued that society's emphasis on learning and literature, science, mathematics, and technology. Throughout the expansion of the Roman Empire, libraries were considered important spoils of war, and Roman army leaders routinely pillaged the contents from collections in fallen cities.

The library as an institution for the general public was a new concept that emerged from the golden days of the Roman Empire. Enumerated on a census of noteworthy buildings in Rome circa 40 B.C. was the first public library, which was based on the private collection of a wealthy donor.[4] Almost 400 years later, the number of libraries increased to 28. Library facilities were part of the Romans' extensive municipal building program, with reading rooms a component of the lavish public baths. As such, they were available to all literate people, whether slaves or free, not exclusively a resource for the wealthy and privileged.

Asia

Although histories of libraries often focus on the evolution of technologies in Europe, many innovations took place at an earlier date in Asian civilizations. During the time of the creative Han dynasty, paper was invented (A.D. 105), some 1,000 years before its introduction to European countries.

Wooden block printing was in use throughout Eastern Asia about 700 years before the German Gutenberg was credited with the invention of movable type printing in 1456. First used in China, block printing then spread to neighboring Korea and Japan and became a standard for several hundred years. Baked clay blocks were used from A.D. 1045 forward in China, and in A.D. 1403 printing with movable metal type was invented in Korea.

The appearance of pictographic writing on bone and other natural materials dates from the Shang period, 1766–1122 B.C., sometime after the advent of the Sumerian cuneiform. This early Chinese script persisted and formed the basis for modern written Chinese.

Mexico

Although little information survives about whether written works were gathered and organized in libraries in what is now Mexico, a vast array of literature existed in the New World before the arrival of the Spanish. Unfortunately, most of the evidence of these writings soon disappeared "owing to the diligence of church and government officials who rooted out any manifestations of this visible symbol of 'paganism.' "[5] Bishop Diego de Landa described some of that destruction and the Indian reaction: "We found a large number of books in these characters and, as they contained nothing in which there were not to be seen superstition and lies of the devil, we burned them all, which they regretted to an amazing degree, and which caused them much affliction."[6] Among the few surviving specimens shipped to Europe by early colonists, three survive today. The information in these books was recorded by painting glyphs (pictographs) on paper made from the bark of fig trees.

Fragments of a variety of forms of recorded information have survived indicating that many of the pre-Colombian Indians had a high degree of culture. These include myths, hymns, poetry, drama, history, and other forms of expression. Carbon-dating tests have established that by 600 B.C. sophisticated writing and calendar systems existed. In fact, the calendar of that era was so accurate that it appeared to have evolved over a long period of time.

Libraries in the Western World

Dark Ages

With the decline of the Roman Empire and subsequent collapse in A.D. 476, Western Europe entered a dark period between A.D. 500 and A.D. 1000, when libraries, learning, and scholarship slumbered. Although many Roman libraries were sacked in the fall of the Empire, some collections had been moved east to Byzantium (present-day Turkey) when Emperor Constantine relocated there. Thus, it is believed that part of Aristotle's renowned private collection survived. Meanwhile, a continuous stream of barbarians invaded Western Europe, seeking land and resources. During the upheaval of the early Middle Ages, Christian monasteries were the only protectors of books, culture, and education in the region.

In the monasteries of continental Europe, Ireland, England, parts of Asia, and Northern Africa, scribes toiled in their copy rooms or scriptoriums, laboriously hand copying any written document made available to them—whether secular or religious in nature. Because of the labor-intensive effort in producing additional copies of each text, books were very valuable and were literally chained to the shelves. Libraries in the monasteries contained literature on parchment scrolls and codexes. The great works of antiquity—the Bible, Homer's writings, Greek plays, and Roman law—were preserved for humanity through the dedicated copying efforts of the monastic centers. Figure 2.1 depicts such a monk of that time at his desk.

Figure 2.1. During Europe's dark ages, the task of preserving written works fell to the scribes in monasteries. Reprinted by permission of Dover Pictorial Archives, Mineola, New York.

Early Renaissance

Monasteries remained the primary centers of learning and study until the rise of the modern universities began during the twelfth century. The Crusades had brought the West in touch with ideas and literature from Asia, and increasing economic stability led to a revival of interest in education.

Among the early universities were those in Bologna, Oxford, Cambridge, and Paris—still major institutions of learning today. Book dealers and professional scribes provided an important service to the university community. They copied and then rented authorized textbooks to the students. Eventually, the number of students increased, and libraries were formed, with each college of the university maintaining a separate collection to support its scholars.

By the fourteenth century, the Renaissance, or the rebirth of learning and the classical influences, was stirring in Italy. This marked the emergence of Western Europe from the Middle Ages into a period of incredible discovery, artistic brilliance, technological inventions, and cultural development. With the renewed emphasis on learning, art, and study, the demand for books—books written not only in the scripts of the clergy but also in the vernacular languages of the people, such as Italian, French, and German—was great.

Ownership of books was a mark of status, and the ownership of personal libraries among wealthy individuals expanded during this period. But the multiplication of manuscripts by hand copying was too inefficient and unable to keep up with the burgeoning demand. With the fertile climate of the Renaissance as a backdrop, the introduction of a new technology for more easily producing books was imminent and would revolutionize the world.

Invention of Movable Type

As with many major inventions, several parties were hard at work on perfecting the movable-type printing press, but Johann Gutenberg of Mainz, Germany, is credited as the first European printer to use the new technology. This was not the birth of the art of printing—wooden blocks and other molds had been used in China since the ninth century. Paper was discovered by the Chinese in A.D. 105, eventually making its way to Europe, where it was readily available by the mid-fifteenth century. The convergence of cheap paper and the invention of the printing press combined to make Gutenberg's technology revolutionary.

The *Gutenberg Bible*, also known as the 42-line Bible, was the first Western full-length book produced using movable metal typeface. Historical evidence suggests that 180 copies of the work were produced around the year 1455. Large, handsomely illustrated, and written in Latin, the bibles were hand finished with colorful illumination and underlining. Extant copies of the rare bibles are held today by the Library of Congress, Bibliotheque Nationale, the National Library of Scotland, and other major research facilities, as well as in private collections.

The significance of Gutenberg's invention was that the mass printing of documents, broadsides, and books became much faster, cheaper, and more accurate. Compared to the previous method for the multiplication of books—laborious hand copying—the printing press was an incredible advancement. With this new technique, printers were able to produce a wider variety of reading material, including texts, romances, poetry, travel books, histories, and religious works, for a general audience.

Early examples of books printed after the seminal Gutenberg Bible until 1501 are referred to as incunabula. Today, a major project to publish the full text of classic works in the public domain on the Internet is appropriately titled Project Gutenberg. (See Resources section at end of this chapter for the Web site address.)

Post-Renaissance Europe

During the 1600s and 1700s libraries and literacy thrived, with a diverse array of facilities being established or expanded. Great university libraries continued to grow throughout Europe, as did the leading national libraries, such as France's Bibliotheque Nationale, the British Library, Germany's state library in Berlin, and Catherine the Great's state library in Leningrad. Earlier collections, such as the incredible Vatican Library of the Roman Catholic Church, developed during the 15th century, were joined by flourishing Italian state and private libraries. Periodicals and newspapers appeared during this time.

City and town libraries were popular throughout Germany during the eighteenth and nineteenth centuries. And in 1850, England instituted the Public Libraries Act, giving official sanction to the concept of tax-supported institutions that had been evolving in Britain since 1653.

North American Libraries

Books were highly cherished possessions brought from their homelands to the New World by the first settlers. During the early decades of the colonies, these private book collections were a mark of intelligence and property. Because few printers existed in America, anyone desiring to obtain a book had to purchase it from England. Today, genealogists and other researchers perusing historical insurance policies and estate inventories often note the estimated worth of book collections listed alongside the house, livestock, silverware, china, piano, and other valuables.

The largest private holdings in the colonies formed the nucleus for official research libraries at Harvard, Yale, and Princeton. In addition, lending libraries were common among church ministers during the 1600s and 1700s, as they sought to provide appropriate spiritual reading to members of their congregations.

Early College Libraries

Today academic libraries pride themselves on their student-centered policies and learning resources, with extended operating hours, computer labs, special collections, and remote access to electronic holdings, all considered basic to a library. Such offerings are in stark contrast to the limited services to be found in early American colonial colleges.

Harvard was the site of the earliest college library, founded in 1638. The library was based on the donated theological book collection of clergyman John Harvard. This was typical of many early colonial colleges, which were established with the donation of a private collection of books by one of the founders.

However, these cherished volumes were hardly available to the toiling students because college libraries were open only an hour or two a day at best, and the books were chained to tables and shelves in poorly lit, cold buildings. Preservation, accumulation, and storage of books, not service to students, were the primary tasks of the academic library. That philosophy did not change much until 1877, when Boston Public Library administrator Justin Winsor became head of Harvard University Library. He brought with him a new philosophy that caused academic libraries to shift to a more customer-service orientation, offering expanded hours, reserve collections, and early interlibrary loaning.

Subscription Libraries

Benjamin Franklin—printer, scholar, diplomat, and inventor—at 25 years of age, was responsible for starting up one of the first American subscription libraries. Precursors to the concept of a community-funded public library, subscription or social libraries were similar to clubs. In the case of the Library Company of Philadelphia, Franklin gathered together 50 men who shared with him an interest in obtaining significant books on history, political science, agriculture, and other topics of interest. With an initial contribution of 40 shillings each, the association was formed in 1731 as an effort to provide a resource for the self-education of its members.

Books were purchased with the collected dues and members then borrowed the titles at no charge; the association retained ownership of the books. The concept of forming subscription libraries was a popular one until the mid-1800s. Many different types of readers founded such library associations. Women's groups often formed general reading libraries. Merchants and clerks formed mercantile libraries, and tradesmen and apprentices formed mechanics' institute libraries.

Today, serious researchers can study the fine collection of seventeenth-, eighteenth-, and nineteenth-century volumes that are housed in the Library Company of Philadelphia's special collection. The Mechanics' Institute of San Francisco, formed as an early subscription library in post-gold rush days, is another extant example of a membership library.

National Libraries Established

By 1800, leaders of the new nation realized the need for a designated library collection in the capital to serve their information needs. Thus, the Library of Congress—now the largest library in the world with more than 120 million items—came into being with a start-up budget of $5,000.[7] During the War of 1812, the British burned Washington, D.C., and the fledgling legislative collection of 3,000 tomes was destroyed. In 1815, former president Thomas Jefferson sold his private collection of 6,487 books to Congress for $23,940, as a nucleus from which to rebuild the collection.[8] Figure 2.2 shows the Library of Congress, Jefferson Building. In rebuilding the library around Jefferson's volumes, they also adopted his classification system for the collection, which formed the basis for the first Library of Congress (LC) classification scheme. Figure 2.3 shows the modern-day Library of Congress Web page.

Figure 2.2. Library of Congress, Jefferson Building

At the bequest of British scientist James Smithson, the Smithsonian Institution was founded in 1846 to serve the United States as a scholarly institution. Soon to be included in the research facility were art galleries, lecture halls, and a library. Charles Coffin Jewett was hired as librarian. As part of his start-up efforts, he advocated the concept of centralized cataloging and conducted a census of libraries. His census count, though probably conservative, indicated that there were 10,015 libraries in the United States in 1850.

Earliest Public Libraries

Two important events, which occurred in New England during the early decades of the nineteenth century, are evidence of the grassroots momentum that was building in support of public education and for free public libraries in the young nation.

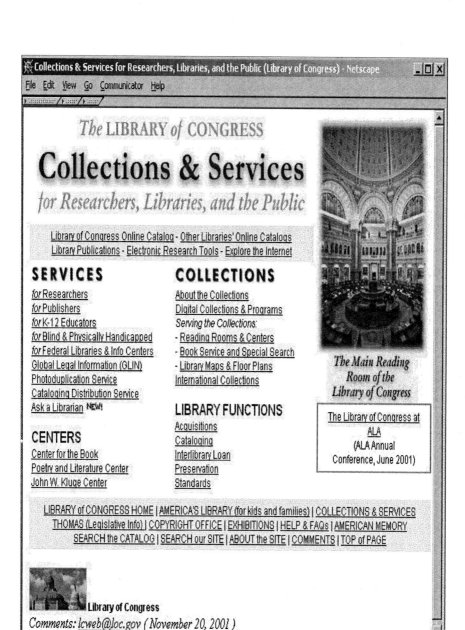

Figure 2.3. The Library of Congress provides access to a wealth of information through its sophisticated Web site.

In 1803, educator and bookseller Caleb Bingham established a free library for local youths in his hometown of Salisbury, Connecticut, in an attempt to provide enrichment opportunities and improve the use of the youths' leisure time. After his initial donation of books, the municipality voted to provide some ongoing funds for the purchase of more titles. Then, 30 years later in Peterborough, New Hampshire, the first free, tax-supported public library was established by a vote of the citizens.

Eventually, with Massachusetts leading the way, each state had to pass legislation giving cities and other jurisdictions legal authority to collect taxes for library support.

Melvil Dewey

The single most significant contributor to the development of library science in the nineteenth century, arguably, was Melvil Dewey. A leader and innovator in the emerging profession, he initiated many tools that are still viable today. Most famous for devising his library organizational scheme known as the Dewey Decimal classification, he also co-founded the first periodical devoted to the library field, *Library Journal*. He also helped establish the ALA in 1876 and started the Library Bureau, a supply and furnishings company still in existence today.

His decimal system tackled the major problem of organizing the knowledge that libraries had been accumulating over the centuries, and it remains the standard in K–12 schools and public libraries. Realizing the importance of education for the field, he established the School of Library Economy while serving as librarian at Columbia University in 1887. This program was the first organized training curriculum for library workers.

Dewey encouraged women to enter the fledgling profession at a time when many of his colleagues opposed women's entry into the field. Efficiency, organization, and time management were his mantras. As a child, he allegedly found delight in arranging the contents of his mother's pantry.[9] Along with Teddy Roosevelt and Andrew Carnegie, he was a proponent of the failed phonetic, reformed spelling movement.

Dewey's life was not without controversy. He was accused of sexual improprieties against young women at an ALA outing and of financial irregularities involving several business ventures. His fervor for new ideas coupled with his sometimes questionable personal behavior resulted in his resignations from library positions during his career.

Despite his faults, Dewey had a major impact on American librarianship with his standardization of library systems and staff education. In addition, he showed great foresight in advocating active library promotion, the consideration of user needs, and the development of new outreach services. The previous passive role of merely warehousing books was insufficient.

John Cotton Dana

Another leader in these formative years of the library profession was a man of many talents, John Cotton Dana. His 44-year career bridged the end of the nineteenth century with the twentieth century. Today, he is best known for his advocacy of library promotion. His name graces the annual public relations award co-sponsored by the H. W. Wilson Company and the American Library Association. During his nearly half century in the field, he advocated many other new ideas, including separate children's departments, open stacks, and the use of displays. He also founded the Special Libraries Association in 1909 and established a separate business collection at the Newark Public Library during his tenure as its director. A prolific writer, Dana's essays have been reprinted and still make for thoughtful reading today.[10]

Era of Philanthropy

By the last quarter of the nineteenth century, American libraries and librarianship were gaining momentum and acceptance. The Boston Public Library, often considered the institution that launched the modern library movement in the United States, opened in 1854. During the 1860s and 1870s, many major cities, including San Francisco, Detroit, Cleveland, and Chicago followed Boston's lead in opening their own public libraries. The many ideas of Dewey were taking root, and tangible support for the institutions came in the form of contributions from wealthy philanthropists.

In 1882, Baltimore merchant Enoch Pratt provided land, a new library building, and $833,000 for library development. A condition of the bequest was that the city set up a $50,000 endowment fund to generate income for annual operating costs and to build four branch facilities. In gratitude, the city named their system the Enoch Pratt Free Library of Baltimore.

Phoebe Apperson Hearst, widow of the senator and mining magnate George Hearst, selected a variety of educational causes to support; among them early kindergartens, the Parent-Teacher Association (PTA), the University of California, and libraries. At the turn of the century, she outfitted free libraries to serve miners and their families in the mining communities of her husband's big mining strikes in Lead, South Dakota, and Anaconda, Montana. The library in Lead was unveiled to the residents as a Christmas gift in 1894 and came fully stocked with materials in English and in foreign languages to serve the many immigrant workers.[11] In addition, Hearst supported the founding of various local subscription libraries in areas where she lived.

Andrew Carnegie

To date, the greatest philanthropist to libraries has been Scottish-born steel millionaire Andrew Carnegie. Born in 1835, Carnegie was the son of a handloom weaver. As the weaving trade became mechanized, his family followed relatives and emigrated to the United States in 1848, searching for improved economic opportunity. They settled in Allegheny, Pennsylvania, near Pittsburgh, where 13-year-old Andrew went to work as a bobbin boy and studied at night. Then Andrew worked a string of increasingly more responsible jobs, with the young man eventually working for the Pennsylvania Railroad. Shrewd investments in the Pullman sleeping car made him wealthy and were followed by further investments in railroad bridges, iron mills, and oil fields. By the 1870s, the demand for steel to expand the country's infrastructure was high, so he formed the Carnegie Steel Company. Immensely successful by 1901, when he sold his steel firm for a profit of $40 million, Carnegie was dubbed the richest man in the world. Known as a hard, aggressive businessman among his former partners, he was very unpopular among labor and trade unions.

From his own rags-to-riches success story, Carnegie valued the notion of self-improvement and lifelong learning. He also had a theory of philanthropy, which he detailed in essays published in 1889. In Carnegie's "Gospel of Wealth," he speaks of the moral obligation of the rich to distribute their wealth for benevolent purposes.[12] Among his many philanthropic projects were providing funding for public gardens in Scotland and pipe organs for churches, erecting Carnegie Hall and several museums, and creating educational endowments. But the richest legacy is his library construction program.

Beginning in 1881, through the Carnegie Corporation, Andrew Carnegie gave more than $56 million for the construction of public library buildings in the English-speaking world. Starting with his birthplace, Dunfermline, Scotland, Carnegie launched a unique effort to help communities construct public libraries. The first city in the United States to benefit from his philanthropy was his adopted hometown, Allegheny, Pennsylvania, where a new facility was built in 1886.

More than $41 million was distributed to American libraries, both urban and rural, during a 32-year period.[13] By the conclusion of the Carnegie program in 1917, communities representing every state except Rhode Island received grants for a total of 1,679 library buildings.[14] Figures 2.4, 2.5, 2.6, and 2.7 are photographs of four Carnegie libraries built in California. Note the ornate architectural styles commonly seen in the Carnegie libraries.

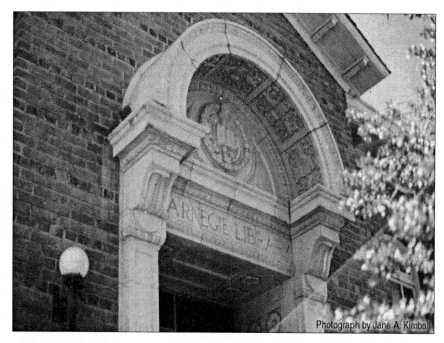

Figure 2.4. Carnegie Library in Willets, California. Reprinted by permission of Jane Kimball.

Figure 2.5. Carnegie Library in Gilroy, California. Reprinted by permission of Jane Kimball.

Figure 2.6. Carnegie Library in Monterey, California. Reprinted by permission of Jane Kimball.

Figure 2.7. Carnegie Library in Petaluma, California (interior detail). Reprinted by permission of Jane Kimball.

Impact of Carnegie's Program

Carnegie's unique program had a lasting impact on American communities. Until this time, early free public libraries were limited primarily to larger, urban areas. Many communities had a subscription library but not a tax-supported resource. Because of Carnegie's largess, within a couple of decades public libraries for smaller communities became commonplace in the United States. In addition to the educational resources the libraries provided to residents, the surviving edifices themselves are often extraordinary examples of American architecture at the beginning of the twentieth century.

In supporting individual communities, he was attempting to stimulate the movement for more free, public libraries. Carnegie's donation to a town was the building only, thus forming a cooperative venture with the city that would then need to stock the building with books, staff it, and provide ongoing fiscal support. Carnegie's grants ranged from $5.2 million for the city of New York to $3,000 for smaller, rural towns. A grand total of 1,412 communities received Carnegie library funds.[15]

Today, many areas have outgrown their small, historic Carnegie buildings. As new library facilities are constructed, some communities such as Newberg Public Library, south of Portland, Oregon, cleverly find ways to incorporate the original facade into an otherwise modern-day building. Another trend is for the turn-of-the century Carnegie buildings to be converted to new community buildings, such as local history museums, galleries, city halls, or chamber of commerce offices. Figure 2.8 shows how a community proudly announced its Carnegie library grant.

The Twentieth Century

Special Populations

Library services for special populations including children, the visually impaired, rural citizens, and new immigrants began to develop in the twentieth century. Children's departments first appeared in urban public libraries in the 1890s and became a mainstay in the twentieth century. The Library of Congress's National Library Services for the Blind and Physically Handicapped (1931) and Braille Institute collections (1934) were originally developed to provide reading materials for the blind and visually impaired population.

Washington County Free Library in Maryland operated the first traveling library service to rural citizens with the advent of its bookmobile wagon in 1905; similar services developed in rural areas throughout the United States.[16] City libraries responded to the wave of immigrants in the early decades of the twentieth century by providing magazines and book collections in foreign languages.

CONTRACT FOR CONSTRUCTION OF CARNEGIE LIBRARY IS LET.

Stevens & Maino of This City Take the Job at $8,900---Building to be Done Within 120 Days--Materials Are the Very Best.

The Library Trustees met yesterday according to advertisement and opened bids on the proposition to build a new public library building. The lowest bidders were found to be Stevens & Maino of this city, and the contract was let to them at the price of $8,900. The contractors have 120 days from today to complete the work and it is expected that the building will be occupied by the first of the year.

The library trustees have worked very hard and feel that they have accomplished the most that was possible with the $10,000 donation of Andrew Carnegie. The contract as let does not include electric lighting and some other items which it is expected the balance of the money will provide.

The building will be of one story on a basement of Bishop's Peak blue granite laid in pitch face random rubble. The superstructure will be of the finest stock brick, trimmed in Caen stone from the Los Berros quarries. The roof will be of the finest black slate, and the specifications call for the very best material.

The entrance will be especially fine and will consist of double doors six feet wide. The main floor rooms will be a 12,000 volume stack room, large reading room, committee room, librarian's

The library is thoroughly up-to-date in every particular and will be a perfect institution as near as can be built at the present time. Convenience, utility, light and ventilation are the things which the trustees have kept especially in mind and believe they have incorporated in this structure.

Unless they should be disposed of, the stacks, shelving, tables, chairs, etc., of the old library will be used in the new building. The library has paid in advance a nine year lease on the present quarters which has not as yet been disposed of. This of course can be made a source of considerable revenue to the new library.

The contract for the new building was signed yesterday and the work will be commenced breaking ground on the site at the northwest corner of north Broad and Monterey streets as soon as the contractors can get their preliminary arrangements made.

A. P. FITZGERALD

Life Insurance. Fire Insurance. Accident Insurance. Plate Glass Insurance. Surety Bonds. Notary Public. Money to Loan, and last but not least, Real Estate. If you want any of the above call on the old reliable. No monkey business and no

Figure 2.8. The construction of a Carnegie library was often headline news in communities that were awarded a grant. From the San Luis Obispo, California, Morning Tribune, *July 7, 1904. Reprinted by permission of Kennedy Library, Cal Poly State University, San Luis Obispo.*

Nonstop New Technologies

Movable-type printing was the dominant method of printing for 400 years. A major improvement came with the invention of linotype, or machine movable printing, in 1884. Today, the revolution of digital publishing is transforming the authoring, dissemination, and access to information as we have known it. The venerable printed book is facing serious competition as the dominant format in distributing the written word. However, for many purposes it remains the most cost-effective container for distributing information content.

Microform technology became commonly used in libraries just before World War II. Today, it is primarily microfiche and microfilm that are still viable media for the preservation of periodical back files and other historical materials. Prior to the advent of electronic information storage, microforms were hailed as the solution to the never-ending library-space dilemma. Currently, the National Archives and the Genealogical Society of Utah's vast family history facility in Salt Lake City are almost exclusively microform-based collections. Future plans for transferring these extensive collections into digital format are beginning to unfold.

The Library of Congress developed the MARC (Machine Readable Cataloging) record in 1966, which became the world's standard format for the communication of bibliographic information between libraries via computer. With the establishment of the MARC standard, computer use and cooperation among libraries has grown tremendously. Most early computer use in libraries was for circulation systems or inventories, in-house functions such as database building and word processing, and for union catalogs or cooperative bibliographic databases of library holdings.

OCLC has been and remains one of the largest databases of library cataloging and holdings data, with more than 40,000 users as of 2001.[17] Total bibliographic records number more than 40,000,000, with a new record added every 15 seconds, totaling about 2.1 million new records annually.[18] Originally, OCLC was the acronym for the Ohio College Library Center, but it now stands for Online Computer Library Center.

Computers and libraries make a worthwhile match, with large amounts of data needing to be stored, sorted, retrieved, viewed, and printed. The first generation of automated library catalogs showed up in academic facilities in the 1970s. As we enter the twenty-first century, the majority of libraries have automated Online Public Access Catalogs (OPACs). Although no one source comprehensively tracks automation for all types of libraries, the following statistics provide a representative picture. An estimated 95.9 percent of public libraries had OPACs in 1998, according to the ALA.[19] Peterson's, the well-known publisher of academic guides, reported in their 1997 annual survey of undergraduate institutions that an OPAC was available in 83 percent of two-year public, 37 percent of two-year private, 69 percent of four-year public, and 77 percent of four-year private institutions.[20] School libraries (both public and private) seem to be the area most behind in adopting some kind of automated catalog, specifically because of funding and other issues.

Thus, the use of computers is now pervasive in all library tasks, with the online ordering of materials, full-text retrieval of periodicals, and Web-based OPACs and job postings just a sampling of the automated functions in widespread use, in addition to traditional cataloging and circulation tasks.

In the early 1990s, another technical advance was realized. Although Hypertext Markup Language (HTML) was first invented by British scientist Tim Berners Lee in 1989, it wasn't until 1993 that the phenomenon known as the "Web" fully impacted academic and technical users. By 1995, the World Wide Web revolution exploded, with commercial and consumer use swelling. Wider acceptance and myriad applications continued to emerge through the end of the decade. With its cross-platform environment, speed, ease of use, and round-the-clock global access (all for free or nearly free) the Web presented advantages for twentieth-century users that paralleled those of the movable-type printing press in the fifteenth century. According to NUA Internet surveys, as of August 2001, more than 513 million users worldwide were connected to the Internet. For libraries, Web technology has had a significant impact on customer demand. This has resulted in a need for patron instruction and has greatly transformed many internal operations, such as materials ordering, interlibrary loan, and document delivery. In addition, the rapid pace of changes brought about by Web publishing of information has necessitated a re-evaluation of print collections and the ongoing retraining of staff.

Still, the costs involved in constant upgrading of technology prevent many libraries from keeping pace. Acknowledging this problem, Microsoft founder Bill Gates has set up the Gates Library Foundation to award $200 million in cash, and an equal amount in Microsoft products, to help bring needy public library systems up to date technologically.

Resource Sharing

Since the 1960s, formal resource sharing among libraries and information centers has burgeoned as facilities of all types and sizes realize that there is strength in numbers and increased benefits to customers. Consortia have taken the form of same-type and multi-type library networks, with membership based on geographical proximity, on collection strengths, and on shared customer profiles.

An early example of a powerful library alliance is RLG (Research Libraries Group), a cooperative formed by Yale, Harvard, Columbia, and the New York Public Library in 1974. Today, RLG is an international network with more than 155 members, including universities and colleges, national libraries, archives, historical societies, museums, independent research collections, and public libraries.

Resource sharing in all its forms is the backbone of library services as it enables agencies to share personnel, to centralize cataloging and processing efforts, to lobby for improved purchasing power from vendors, and to provide patron access to a greater number of materials.

National Awareness of Libraries

The American Library Association first adopted its Library Bill of Rights in 1948 (see Appendix B) to establish guidelines for the rights of library users. Based on our nation's First Amendment to the Constitution, which guarantees the freedom of expression in speech, writing, reading, access to information, and so on, the Library Bill of Rights has been supplemented with interpretive statements several times to reflect new issues regarding the freedom to access information, censorship, and multimedia formats. Many libraries formally adopt this statement as part of their official policy.

U.S. libraries of all types benefited from legislation in the 1950s and 1960s that provided financial aid for collection development and facilities building. The Bicentennial Celebration of 1976, with its commemoration of the historical roots of our country, shined a new spotlight on libraries and archives, underscoring the need to preserve documentation of our national, regional, and local history.

The library boom years of the 1950s and 1960s contrast with the later observations made by the National Commission on Excellence in Education in their 1983 report *A Nation at Risk.* This study determined that the educational system in the United States was slipping in terms of quality and effectiveness and that publicly supported institutions such as library systems had fallen far behind as well.[21]

The American Library Association reports more than 129,000 libraries in the United States as of 2001. Although the funding levels can be counted on to vary widely among these diverse types of libraries, the new technological leaps and fresh challenges of the twenty-first century promise to keep libraries and information centers in the spotlight as they continue to provide information access to their clientele.

Study Questions

1. Describe some of the historical information needs that have driven the collecting of written materials.

2. Compare the Great Library at Alexandria to a modern library facility.

3. What was the impact of Gutenberg's technology on reading and printing at that time in Europe?

4. Describe the service philosophy of early colonial college libraries. How does this compare with your current college or university library's philosophy?

5. What were the major contributions of Melvil Dewey to the library profession? How did his accomplishments dovetail with other events in the field in the late 1800s?

6. What impact did Andrew Carnegie's program have on American communities? Are there similar privately funded grant programs in place for helping libraries and information centers today?

7. Describe the historical rivalry between the writing media of papyrus and animal skin. Can you draw any comparisons between the current competition between the printed book and the electronic dissemination of information?

Resources

Web Sites

-   Project Gutenberg
    http://promo.net/pg/index.html
    (Accessed November 16, 2001)
    A pioneer in the distribution of full-text, noncopyrighted classics of literature on the Internet. More than 3,000 electronic-text titles available for downloading.

-   *Jefferson's Legacy: A Brief History of the Library of Congress*
    http://lcweb.loc.gov/loc/legacy/toc.html
    (Accessed November 16, 2001)
    An illustrated Web version of the book by John Y. Cole (also available in print) discussing the early years of our national library and Jefferson's key role in the collection's development.

Videos

A Tour of the Library of Congress. (21 min.). Washington, DC: Library of Congress, 1986.
An overview of the founding and development of our national library.

Richest Man in the World: Andrew Carnegie. (120 min.). Produced and directed by Austin Hoyt. Boston: PBS/WGBH, 1997.
The American Experience series looks at the rags-to-riches story of controversial steel magnate Andrew Carnegie.

Print Resources

Harris, Michael H. *History of Libraries in the Western World.* 4th ed. Metuchen, NJ: Scarecrow, 1995.

Jones, Theodore. *Carnegie Libraries Across America: A Public Legacy.* New York: John Wiley, 1997.

Swerdlow, Joel. "The Power of Writing." *National Geographic* (August 1999): 110–32.

Van Slyck, Abigail A. *Free to All: Carnegie Libraries and American Culture, 1890–1920.* Chicago: University of Chicago Press, 1995.

Wiegand, Wayne A. *Irrepressible Reformer: A Biography of Melvil Dewey.* Chicago: American Library Association, 1996.

Notes

1. "Large Cache of Mesopotamian Tablets Found," *Los Angeles Times* (29 December 1987): A-2.

2. Jean Key Gates. *Guide to the Use of Libraries and Information Sources.* 7th ed. New York: McGraw-Hill, 1994, 5.

3. Lionel Casson. "Triumph from the Ancient World's First Think Tank," *Smithsonian* (June 1985): 158–68.

4. Will Durant. *Story of Civilization, Part III: Caesar and Christ.* New York: Simon & Schuster, 1944, 159.

5. G. Morley Sylvanus and George W. Brainerd. *The Ancient Maya.* 4th ed. Stanford, CA: Stanford University Press, 1983, 513.

6. Ibid.

7. John Y. Cole. *Jefferson's Legacy: A Brief History of the Library of Congress.* Washington, DC: Library of Congress, 1993, 12.

8. Ibid, 13.

9. Fremont Rider. *Melvil Dewey.* Chicago: American Library Association, 1944, 6.

10. Carl A. Hanson, ed. *Librarian at Large: Selected Writings of John Cotton Dana.* Washington, DC: Special Libraries Association, 1991.

11. Richard A. Peterson. "Phoebe: The Educational Charity of Phoebe Apperson Hearst," *California History* 63 (Fall 1985): 287.

12. Andrew Carnegie. "Wealth," *North American Review* 148 (June 1889): 653–64.

13.   Carnegie Corporation of New York—Andrew Carnegie. "Andrew Carnegie and his Philanthropies." Available: http://www.carnegie.org/philanth.htm (Accessed March 12, 1998).

14.   Elizabeth W. Stone. *American Library Development, 1600–1899*. New York: H. W. Wilson, 1977, 317, 326.

15.   Abigail A. Van Slyck. *Free to All: Carnegie Libraries and American Culture, 1890–1920*. Chicago: University of Chicago Press, 1995, 22.

16.   Nancy Smiler Levinson. "Takin' It to the Streets: The History of the Book Wagon," *Library Journal* (1 May 1991): 43–45.

17.   OCLC. "About OCLC." Available: http://www.oclc.org/ (Accessed January 8, 2002).

18.   Joy Wanden. OCLC staff, e-mail to author, 21 July 1998.

19.   ALA Reference Library. Telephone conversation with author, 10 March 1999.

20.   Barbara Lawrence. Senior Vice President, Peterson's, e-mail to author, 24 December 1997.

21.   United States National Commission on Excellence in Education. *A Nation at Risk: The Imperative for Educational Reform: A Report to the Nation and the Secretary of Education, United States Department of Education*. Washington, DC: The Commission, 1983.

Chapter 3

Types of Library Job Opportunities

This book presents an overview for those who are considering a career in libraries and library-like organizational settings. Before addressing specific career possibilities, one must have some common understanding of the varieties of organizational settings in which these career opportunities can be found.

It is clear as the twenty-first century begins that the entire landscape of libraries and information gathering is evolving with accelerating speed. Many question whether libraries will continue to exist as we knew them in the past century. However, the basic purpose of libraries to organize and disseminate information is needed now more than ever. No prognosticators have a crystal ball clear enough to convince us that they really know how this evolution will play out during the working life of those now beginning a career. Two observations, however, are very clear: Those who see themselves as the keepers of books will be shelved themselves, and those who demonstrate that they can help solve other people's information problems will always be in demand. This chapter is written to help the latter group build an understanding of the organizational environments in which they are likely to work.

What Is a Library?

What is a library? There are hundreds of different kinds of libraries and library-like organizations. In some ways, every library is different. In other ways, they are all the same. This chapter covers some of the differences. Subsequent chapters cover some of the similarities.

To the uninitiated all libraries are the same, just as all library workers are the same. They realize that some libraries are bigger than others and that library buildings look different from each other, but the differentiation ends there. Even fairly sophisticated library users generally do not understand the range of libraries that exist or that almost every library is different. Each library's clientele is different; therefore, its mission is different. Also, its collections are different; therefore, its services must differ.

What is it that makes an organization a library? Traditionally, libraries have been defined as organizations that acquire, organize, and disseminate information. This is certainly true, but it does not differentiate libraries from many other entities. For example, newspapers are among the many other kinds of organizations that meet each of these criteria. More will be said about the unique attributes of libraries in succeeding sections.

Each Library Is Different

In the twentieth century libraries were generally divided into four major categories:

- public libraries,

- school libraries,

- academic, and

- special libraries.

Each had a distinct mission and a specific group of customers to serve. There were many distinct subcategories within each of these four groups, and some libraries overlapped into more than one category. Often, the different types of libraries specialized to such an extent that students training for the field considered each to be almost a separate career track that, once embarked upon, was difficult to switch from. The balance of this chapter discusses how the different types of libraries have missions that were sometimes similar to—and sometimes distinctly different from—each other and how they are shaped by the clientele they serve.

The four types of libraries mentioned are only the primary kinds. In reality, many libraries are combinations or blends of more than one basic type. This is somewhat analogous to having variations of 16 or even 256 colors created from only three primary colors.

How Many Libraries Are in the United States?

By the close of the twentieth century, the ALA estimated that almost 130,000 libraries of all types were in the United States. These libraries range in size from small libraries with several hundred books, a single part-time staff member, and limited operating hours to the world's largest facility, the Library of Congress, with more than 120,000,000 items and thousands of employees. Table 3.1 breaks down libraries in the U.S. by type.

Table 3.1
Types of Libraries[1]

Public libraries		
Public library systems	8,943	
Public library branches	7,147	
Total public library sites		16,090
School libraries		
Public school libraries	77,218	
Private school libraries	20,951	
Total school libraries		98,169
Academic libraries		
Less than four-year colleges	1,293	
Four-year (or more) colleges	2,115	
Total academic libraries		3,408
Special libraries		
Armed forces libraries	341	
Other government libraries	1,411	
Other special libraries	9,993	
Total special libraries		11,745
Total libraries		129,392

Note: These statistics do not take into account the potentially vast number of libraries that are operated totally by volunteers for a few hours each week in churches and other not-for-profit organizations.

How Many People Work in Libraries?

According to the ALA it is not easy to attain an exact figure, but the number of people working in libraries may approach one half million. The library workforce includes librarians and other professionals, paraprofessionals, and clerical and technical personnel. Statistics are not consistently collected for each category of personnel in each type of library. Piecing it all together, the figures in Table 3.2 present a reasonable estimate of the paid library workforce at the close of the twentieth century:[2]

Table 3.2
How Many People Work in Libraries?

Types of Libraries	Librarians	Other Paid Staff	Total Staff
Public libraries	27,946	92,804	120,759
School libraries	72,160	92,483	164,643
Academic libraries	27,268	68,020	95,288
Special libraries	18,600	28,819	47,410
Total staff	145,974	282,126	428,100

The numbers in the table do not include the staff with library training and skills who work for library networks and regional cooperatives that supply services to individual libraries but do not directly provide services to individuals.

Vendors who develop and market products and services to libraries like to hire persons with library training, library experience, or both. The number of individuals who are employed in this capacity is not known. Often there is a revolving door through which individuals move to employment with vendors and back to employment in libraries. At other times, it is a one-way street. Consultants and freelance and temporary library staff comprise another arena of employment that is growing but that is very hard to measure.

Public Libraries

The public library is the one major type of library that serves every citizen at every stage of life. In the United States, public libraries seem to have taken seriously the admonition of the *Declaration of Independence* that our citizens should be able to pursue life, liberty, and happiness. Thus, in addition to helping individuals learn how to earn a living and lead their lives, recreational activities are also a legitimate function for the collections and services of public libraries. Historically, they have served as a resource for succeeding generations of immigrants to learn how to function as effective citizens—both economically and politically.

Public libraries serve a wider range of needs and objectives than most other libraries. They serve the leisure-reading needs of people from toddlers to senior citizens and the information needs of patrons from first-graders to scholars. The public library has even been termed the "people's university" because it can enable people to pursue their own search for knowledge in the library's treasure house of literary works and scientific and technical information. Because public libraries are so important in most everyone's life, more than 16,000 of them exist in communities both large and small throughout the United States.

Public libraries have the broadest mission because they have to be all things to all people. In some ways, their children's and young adults' departments supplement the local school libraries. Their reference departments and periodical and nonfiction collections supplement local academic libraries. Their business and adult services departments often provide services to local people, businesses too small to maintain their own libraries, and larger companies that need information services outside their primary economic focus. In addition, public libraries provide Internet access—often the only such access to this important source of information for those on the wrong side of the digital divide. As seen in chapter 8, this relatively new service often places public libraries at the forefront of political disputes as the public's right to know collides with the need to protect children.

The service areas of public libraries have been defined by a local geographic area, usually a city or county. The lines of this traditionally defined "home turf" are becoming blurred. Some states are introducing statewide borrower cards that can be used in any public library in the state. In other areas, consortia of libraries of all types have reciprocal agreements to honor each other's registered customers. These trends, combined with the ubiquitous nature of the World Wide Web, are redefining all library services, with public libraries often taking the lead.

Typically, public libraries are part of the municipal governmental agency responsible for their service area. Often public libraries are a department of the city or county government, with the library director reporting to the mayor, city manager, county executive, or similar authority. In other cases, the library is semi-autonomous, having a governing board appointed by the chief executive of the municipality. In this case, the chief librarian is responsible primarily to the library board and only secondarily responsible to the chief executive of the municipality. In rare cases, the public library is its own autonomous unit of municipal government, having its own elected governing board with independent taxing authority. In this case, the chief librarian is solely responsible to the elected library board.

The mission of the public library is to meet the needs of its particular community. It may carry out that mission through a single facility or through a sprawling system of libraries with scores of service locations. Even within the same city or county, different branches may require very different hours of operation, different collections of materials, and different patterns of service to meet the needs of their clients. For example, the socio–economic level, ethnicity, and average age of the clientele served by a particular facility dictates the solutions to the information needs of the community served by that facility. A community of young families would need different services than a community made up primarily of retirees. A community heavily saturated with recent immigrants would have different needs than a community in which most were native-born English speakers.

The urban or rural nature of the community and the predominant economic activity of the region also have major impacts. In congested urban areas, libraries must be conveniently located near public transportation. In the suburbs, ample parking is essential. Rural areas may require that libraries come to their patrons in the form of a bookmobile that makes regular rounds to reach the dispersed population. Finally, the level of technological penetration will suggest the speed with which services must be delivered over the World Wide Web.

Public Library Objectives

As community needs have changed over the years, American public library objectives have changed to keep pace. Through much of the nineteenth century, education (adult education in particular) was the foremost objective of the public library. Late in that century and early in the twentieth century, recreational reading and reference were added. The recreational reading was initially added to create new readers who could be converted to more serious endeavors. However, leisure reading gradually became a legitimate end in itself. The social consciousness of the 1960s accelerated efforts of public libraries to help poor and uneducated people fit into a highly scientific and technical society; a trend that is currently receiving new emphasis.

As the new century dawns, public libraries are mobilizing again to meet new community needs. The World Wide Web exploded into our society during the last few years of the 1990s. It has fundamentally changed the way that Americans view information. This has caused librarians to re-examine whether the library is a place or a function. Should information be served to customers any time and any place they want it? If so, what role does the library have in selecting and organizing the electronic information thus distributed? How can the public library provide access for those who do not have independent access to the information available on the World Wide Web? These questions pose great challenges to the future of libraries and to future librarians. Whether libraries overcome these challenges will determine the relevance of libraries to society in the future.

The biggest challenge will be developing and delivering Web-based services while continuing to maintain current in-building services to those who are better served in that mode. It is not a choice between cyber or paper. It is both at the same time and that is expensive in resources, staff, and time.

Public Library Standards

The major direction for today's public libraries was set when the ALA published its post-war *Standards for Public Libraries* in 1943. These standards emphasize that a public library should provide free library service to the residents of a particular community. This direction was expanded in 1966 with the publication of the *Minimum Standards for Public Library Systems,* which included the concept that "service to all" is the reason that a library exists. This enhanced concept meant that libraries were looking beyond their typical library patron—the married, middle-class, educated, adult female who represented only a minority of the population. They were looking toward the unserved one-third of the population who had never used a library and to the millions of Americans who had no access to free public library service because they lived in rural communities or because of their race.[3]

The emphasis in these standards for library systems was on the quality of library service provided rather than on the quantity of library materials. The standards required the public library to develop written selection policies and choose materials that are accurate, include opposing views, and to appeal to all members of the community. Materials should be purchased and discarded on a planned basis. Services and programs should be developed to satisfy the needs of all individuals and groups. Standards for services to many of these groups, such as children, young adults, and people who are blind or have physical disabilities, were developed and published in separate standards by the responsible divisions of the ALA.

Although library systems are based on qualitative standards, librarians had long recognized the public relations value of stating these standards in quantitative terms. They found that government and community leaders could relate to standards that stated, for example, a certain amount of "money per capita should be spent to support library services." Thus, the 1966 standards also included quantitative standards for such areas as services, materials, and staffing. These standards recommended that the local community library be open at least six days a week and that bookmobile services be provided to areas without libraries. Staff should include one-third professional and two-thirds support staff. Minimum numbers of staff were identified based on the population served. The number and types of materials to be provided were also identified by population served, and community library collections were backed up by a larger collection at the library headquarters.

These quantitative standards were not meant to be definitive but were intended to be guidelines that libraries should strive to meet. Although some libraries quickly and easily surpassed the standards, many libraries took 5 to 10 years to reach them, and others have yet to achieve them.

As librarians were striving to meet these quantitative standards, they also began to recognize that each library had its own unique characteristics that sometimes did not fit into any standard formula. The Public Library Association (PLA) assisted librarians in this approach by publishing *A Planning Process for Public Libraries* in 1980.[4] This process stressed that an analysis of an individual library and its community, by community members, library board trustees, and library staff members, could be used to help identify library needs and set directions for library services.

Although many librarians welcomed this emphasis on local community needs, they still felt a need to maintain some quantitative standards against which they could evaluate their library's current level of services and materials. They recognized that many community leaders and governmental authorities were impressed by statistics such as the number of people who used the library and its materials and services. To help meet this need, the PLA published another document, *Output Measures for Public Libraries: A Manual for Standardized Procedures,* in 1987.[5] It gave specific instructions for measuring library uses such as the number of library visits or reference questions per capita. Use of the collection was measured in circulations per capita and the turnover rate (i.e., the number of total items in the collection divided by the items checked out). Even the availability of library materials was measured to determine how many material requests were filled and how long it took to fill them. These output measures could be used in conjunction with more traditional input measures (such as the number of items added to a collection) to quantify a library's services. By comparing their own results with those from similar libraries, they could assess their library's effectiveness. Many states provide aid to encourage libraries to improve their findings in these measurements.

Public Library Services

Once libraries had selected the roles of service they would strive to fulfill, they developed differing material collections, programs, and services within these roles to satisfy their individual communities' needs. Perhaps the greatest differences were in the variety of library collections developed to fulfill specific roles. For example, to fulfill the popular materials library role based on the makeup of their communities, some libraries developed ample collections of popular materials, others developed ample collections for children and young adults, and still others developed ample collections of media and computers. In fulfilling the formal education support center role, many libraries provided public access computers, others provided multiple or reserve copies of materials needed by schoolchildren, and still others supplied supplementary materials to their local schools for classroom use.

In addition, libraries also expanded their collections to include a wide variety of materials. The traditional print materials of books, magazines, and newspapers were expanded to include large-print books and magazines, college catalogs, pamphlets, business reports, and updating reference or financial services such as *Facts on File* and *Value Line.* Audiovisual materials became included in the mainstream of library services and were made available to patrons as readily as were print materials. Outdated audiovisual materials, such as films and records, were often replaced in the collection by audiocassette tapes, CDs, videotapes, DVDs, computers, and computer databases. Sometimes libraries even produce their own radio and TV programs or run their own cable TV channels to reach all segments of their populations.

Age-Specific Services

In addition to developing diverse collections to satisfy different roles of service, libraries established a variety of programs and services to meet the differing needs of various populations. For example, most public libraries provide collections, programming, and staff for children's services. Collections in these library departments usually include picture books, audiotapes and videotapes, multimedia, puppets, developmental toys, games, and animals (both live and stuffed). These materials are sometimes housed in a separate preschool room, where children can climb on playscape equipment or sit quietly looking at books. They can listen to stories read aloud by their parents, watch mock puppet shows, or take part in a learning or craft activity without distracting other library patrons. Preschool story hours and puppet shows are presented to children at the library and at preschools, day-care centers, and play groups. Parenting materials and child development programs also are sometimes provided.

Libraries provide programs and services for school-age children, too. In many of these libraries, circulation of all children's materials can be as much as one-third to one-half of the library's total circulation. To encourage such use, some libraries extend their former summer reading clubs to year-round programs. They combine them with contests, such as Battle of the Books, which offer prizes and awards. Regular monthly programs often feature puppet shows, magic shows, animal acts, or visiting performers.

Another group of library patrons who use the library frequently after school is teenagers from age 12 to age 17. Libraries provide programming for these young adults, which includes informational programs such as baby-sitting clinics, child development classes, and college entrance examination preparatory classes. Libraries also provide paperback collections containing multiple copies of books on topics of particular interest to young adults. Some libraries hire young adult librarians and establish young adult advisory councils or peer homework support groups.

Reference Services

Most public libraries emphasize reference service as one of their major roles. To support this service, libraries develop collections containing general reference encyclopedias, directories, dictionaries, yearbooks, handbooks, atlases, and indexes. Depending on their communities' needs and interests, libraries might also develop specialized subject reference collections. These could be business and financial collections, genealogical and local history collections, or special interest collections, such as art history or gardening and landscaping. In addition to books, many collections contain such media as weekly or daily updating services, periodicals on microform, and online and local government archives. To help their patrons use these materials more effectively, libraries provide individual or group instruction about use of the library and its collections.

Libraries also provide reference staff to help patrons locate information. Such reference help includes remote ready-reference service (via telephone or e-mail), on-site assistance in using the library's reference tools, database searching, and securing additional information through interlibrary loan. The range of services depends on the library's size and resources. Large public libraries have banks of telephones to answer many questions at one time using their special-subject collections. Small libraries use computer and telephone links to headquarters or system libraries to locate answers to patrons' questions that cannot be answered using the local resources. The newest mode of reference service is e-reference, where patrons e-mail queries or complete a request on the library's Web page. Library staff then respond with the answer to the question electronically. Almost half of all library patrons use some form of these reference services.[6]

Libraries develop large collections of current fiction, including multiple copies of bestsellers and genre books, such as mysteries and biographies. They also promote these materials with individual and group book lists, library displays, and merchandising techniques such as face-out display shelving similar to that found in bookstores. In addition to books, other popular library collections include feature videotapes, popular as well as classical CD and DVD recordings, art prints, and sculptures. Programs for adults range from book discussions and informational lectures to how-to programs, such as cooking or photography classes, to travel-film or feature-film programs. Most libraries provide programs and services for persons with special needs, such as senior citizens. Libraries also include materials and services for individuals with physical disabilities, and features such as captioned videotapes for the hearing impaired, talking books (recordings of books read aloud to the blind), Braille materials, large-print materials, and computer terminals that display text in large fonts.

Outreach Services

Many libraries further serve the independent learning needs of their adult customers. Some librarians serve as examination proctors for distance-learning courses or make their meeting rooms available for private or group study. In cooperation with other educational institutions and community agencies, the library helps individual patrons study for credit courses or take high school equivalency tests, such as the General Education Degree (GED). Sometimes adult education classes are conducted at the library, or video courses or computer software are made available to library patrons. Also in support of adult independent learning, libraries attempt to reach beyond their traditional middle-class educated patrons to their underserved populations. In keeping with the push for national literacy, which gained momentum in the 1980s and 90s, libraries participate in adult literacy programs by providing adult basic education materials and study rooms for literacy students and their volunteer tutors. Some libraries provide foreign-language collections for their foreign-speaking populations and host classes in English as a second language. When the economic climate of their communities dictates it, some libraries will establish job placement centers to help unemployed patrons.

In trying to meet the needs of their underserved populations, libraries also design outreach services for persons who cannot get to a main or branch library. Bookmobiles travel rural highways and city streets to bring popular materials to all ages. In inner-city areas, bookmobiles are painted in bright, attractive designs and stocked with easy reading material, paperbacks, and magazines to help attract nonreaders. "Mediamobiles," as shown in Figure 3.1, tour inner-city areas bringing library programs to children and young adults on their own street corner.

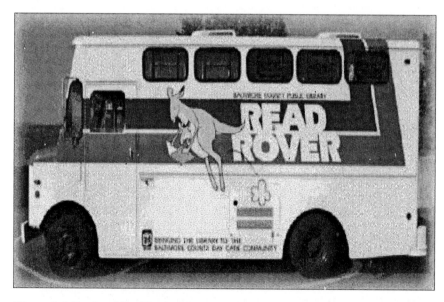

Figure 3.1. Bookmobiles like the Read Rover, from Baltimore County Public Library in Maryland, deliver essential library services to citizens of all ages. Reprinted by permission of Baltimore County Public Library.

As libraries reach out to serve these underserved patrons, many establish storefront branches or place materials collections in urban housing developments and local ethnic or senior citizen centers. Prefabricated kiosk-type libraries are erected in such diverse communities as a small rural hamlet or a sophisticated urban shopping mall to provide quick and easy access to library materials. Local community members staff these facilities, and foreign-language-speaking librarians develop collections and services that meet the needs of the community's various ethnic populations. In addition, libraries work with other agencies to provide voter registration, notary publics, income tax forms, tax assistance for seniors and people with low income, and health-testing programs. Libraries make their meeting rooms available so that community and government organizations can present public information programs or so that cultural groups can present lectures, concerts, and art shows.

Libraries provide community information centers to help residents find agencies that meet a variety of needs. In this role, libraries gather information about community organizations, businesses, and governmental agencies and make the information available to the public. This information often is shared with other agencies, published in directories, or made available through computer databases. Libraries work with social service, health, educational, business, governmental, and economic agencies and organizations to locate and provide information to help people resolve health, housing, family and legal problems. As referral agents, librarians present available alternatives to the patron.

Public Library Management

Although many consider the public library to be an institution basic to civilization, public library collections and services are always affected by economic conditions. National and local economic recessions impact library services, as do the local community's political and social situations. As an agency that serves all persons from cradle to grave, public libraries sometimes try to be all things to all people. Public library staff have attempted to provide equal service to patrons of all age and interest groups in their communities. They consider the ups and downs of library budgets, the availability of electronic technology, and the capabilities of networking with other libraries as they develop library programs and services to satisfy the needs of all their patrons.

Of primary importance to public libraries in the development of their programs and services is their vulnerability to economic changes in their own communities. With their almost total reliance on public property taxes, public library revenues are controlled by the allocation of tax revenue. In some states and cities, the public library's ability to increase tax revenue is limited by legal or political considerations. In others, libraries have to appeal to the voters to get approval for increasing their tax limits, and these elections are not always successful. To minimize their dependence on these sources, libraries have begun to explore additional sources of income and to develop creative and innovative sources to finance their services and programs.

Public libraries in growing communities have begun collecting developer impact fees from real estate developers to help finance library services to owners of new residences. Libraries have joined the Public Library Foundation or similar investment pools to increase the interest paid on their library funds. Many libraries form a nonprofit Friends of the Library support group (see Figure 3.2). Such an organization will conduct used-book sales, library auctions, or sell library-related merchandise to raise additional funds. A few libraries even allow profit-making ventures, such as restaurants or friends-of-the-library-operated retail shops, within the library building. Such activities serve to raise the library's visibility in the community, as well as garner some supplemental financial support.

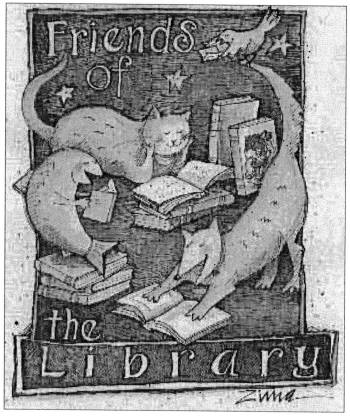

Figure 3.2. Friends' groups help to support a library through promotion, fund raising, and by increasing the level of community involvement. Reprinted by permission of Paula Zima.

Overdue fees, charged by a majority of public libraries, have been increased, and many libraries charge higher or additional processing fees for lost items. To help ease their economic plight, some libraries have initiated fees for formerly free services, such as reserves and interlibrary loans. Others also charge fees for expensive services, such as database searches, or the loan of expensive materials, such as videotapes, best sellers, and equipment. These latter fees cause considerable debate within the library profession. Opponents of such fees claim that the income raised from them is not a sufficient reason to deny access to library materials and services by patrons who cannot afford them. In the final analysis, the revenues raised from all of these various methods account for only a small portion of the average public library's budget. Furthermore, libraries must be careful not to get involved with revenue schemes that can divert more staff time and energy from the direct provision of services than can be replaced in terms of additional revenue.

Cooperative library networks have had a positive effect on the ability of libraries to stretch their budgets and to share their resources. By sharing the costs of automation technology, even small libraries can afford to join bibliographic cooperatives with circulation, cataloging, and interlibrary loan capabilities. Regional and statewide resource networks allow them to share their materials and services with other libraries as materials are sent from library to library by van delivery and mail systems. Increasingly, these delivery systems are supplemented by facsimile and online computer transmissions. In addition to exchanging materials, libraries exchange their patrons, too.

Reciprocal borrowing agreements among libraries enable patrons to visit and check out materials at other libraries throughout a regional system or state. Another benefit to cooperative agreements is that patrons can use a computer, either in the library or in their homes, to see which libraries have the materials they want and whether the materials are available. All types of libraries participate in many such cooperative networks. Therefore, public libraries are able to provide the desired service to all, and, at the same time, expand the resources to which their primary clients have access.

In providing library service to all of their patrons, library administrators and their staffs take great care to ensure that everyone is treated alike—whether the patron is a city council member, a library board trustee, or a young child. They generally adopt the ALA *Library Bill of Rights* (see Appendix B) and the American Film and Video Association's *Freedom to Read and View* statements and institute policies and procedures to protect the freedom of intellectual inquiry for their patrons. Such policies include free access to the library's collections by children and also provide the protection of patron records from public inquiry.

Staffing

As libraries develop new roles and goals of service, their staffing needs change. Computer literacy to varying degrees has become essential in almost every position. Children's staff have been expanded to include specialists in preschool and young adult services who are knowledgeable about the psychological and educational growth and development of their patrons. A library's ability to fill these changing staff positions, however, is often difficult. The supply and demand of such specialties is not always well balanced. In recent years, specialists in children's library services often have been in short supply.

These library staffing needs vary greatly depending upon the size of a library and its location. A public library staff ranges from a one- or two-person branch to a main library with 50 to 100 people. Medium-to-large libraries usually have a large range of library positions at all levels filled with appropriately trained personnel. They might have many specialized librarians responsible for administration, reference and readers' advisory services, collection development, and programming. Paraprofessional library technicians and clerical staff perform supportive tasks in such areas as children's services, bookmobiles, outreach, and technical services.

Smaller libraries might have only one or two librarians to handle reference and children's services. In very small libraries, or branches and on bookmobiles, the staff members tend to be generalists who share all the jobs from checking out materials to helping a person find a book. In these very small libraries, there may not be a great differentiation between library positions, and the person in charge may be a technician with or without formal library education.

As libraries grow in size and complexity, their staff members tend to become more specialized in their responsibilities, and the staff members' job classifications become more distinct. Many of these staff members have advanced education, although they might not have masters' degrees in library science. Their education and training is often in specialties other than library science. Graphic artists, TV technicians, computer programmers, and specialists in information science or public relations are just a few of the varied types of personnel found in public libraries. Also, in these larger library systems, there is a very definite pattern of specialization among library personnel.

It is not unusual for library employees to work many years in one particular area of either public or technical services. For example, in the circulation department, one clerk may be responsible for reserves, one for overdue collections, one for stacks maintenance, and others for checking materials in and out. These clerks may be supervised by a library technician or by a librarian, and they also may be supported by library pages or shelvers.

To organize these varied staff members most effectively, public library administrators need to examine and evaluate their personnel policies and procedures. Library administrators recognize that they should take the personal needs of their staff members into account as they design these policies. Nowhere is this need more evident than in scheduling staff for the public service desks.

It is not unusual for a public library to be open from 9:00 A.M. to 9:00 P.M. Monday through Friday, 9:00 A.M. to 5:00 P.M. on Saturday, and 1:00 P.M. to 5:00 P.M. on Sunday. Library administrators and supervisors find it challenging to schedule the 60- to 80-hour weeks that require one and one-half to two separate staffs working 40 hours each. In addition to making sure the library is well staffed, supervisors try to consider their staff members' personal preferences for the hours they work.

Many recent developments in public libraries have centered on the revolutionary impact of the World Wide Web on information exchange. Two of these events, e-rate legislation and the involvement of the Gates Foundation, have been highly visible factors in helping extend access to the World Wide Web to almost every public library in the country. This almost universal implementation of this transforming technology led to one of the dominant public debates of recent times—to filter or not to filter public access Internet terminals. That issue is discussed later in chapter 8.

The E-Rate

E-rate, or education rate discounts on telecommunications charges, was established as part of the balancing act when the Telecommunications Act of 1996 deregulated many of the services of telecommunications carriers. According to the ALA, more than 30,000 schools and libraries soon completed the application process to benefit from the fund set up to ensure universal access to the World Wide Web.[7] E-rate was funded by some of the windfall profits realized by telecommunications companies as a result of partial deregulation of their operations set forth in the Telecommunications Act.

E-rate is certainly no panacea, but it is another revenue stream that can make a critical difference in funding because the deepest discounts go to the most needy schools and libraries. In 1996 only one in seven public library systems was able to offer public access to the Web, with the primary obstacle to providing Internet access being the ongoing cost of telecommunications charges.[8]

> A sampling of the 30,000 e-rate applications shows 33 percent for telecommunications services, 4.4 percent for Internet access, and 63 percent for inside wiring. The latter is not surprising given the number of classrooms that lack Internet access. More than 50 percent of discount requests for internal connections come from the neediest schools and libraries eligible for 80–90 percent discounts. . . . FCC [Federal Communications Commission] rules prohibit discounts from being spent on workstations, applications software, training, or other purposes.[9]

E-rate has made a valuable contribution to our society because the public library is often the Internet option of last resort for those who do not have access at home or at work.

Gates Foundation

The Gates Library Foundation provided a nice counterbalance to e-rate. Although the amount of money provided did not approach the $2 billion generated by e-rate, the foundation did provide a source of funds to pay for the items that e-rate would not provide. During the first round of funding, the foundation worked with approximately 1,000 libraries, with a special emphasis on those serving low-income communities. Grants were used to provide new computers for library patrons and for staff technical training and support. First-year grants ranged from $4,000 for a small rural library requiring only one computer to $30,000 or more for larger library buildings that received 10 or more computers. Like e-rate, the foundation targeted libraries in the most needy states and communities, using U.S. Census statistics and a study conducted by the ALA on public libraries and poverty to establish eligibility guidelines.[10]

Public Library Use

Are public libraries used now and will they be needed in the future? A May 1998 Gallup Poll revealed the following findings:

- 64% of all respondents reported using the public library at least once in the past year

- of those respondents who reported using the public library in person in the last year,

  - 81% said they had taken out books

  - 65% had consulted a librarian

  - 61% used reference materials

  - 50% read newspapers or magazines

  - 32% took out CDs or videos

  - 11% connected to the Internet

  - 15% heard a speaker, saw a movie or attended a class

▸ 35% of the respondents had children, and 65% of those respondents said that they brought their children to the library

▸ 90% of the total respondents believe that libraries will exist in the future

▸ 2 out of 5 (40%) said that they consider the library to be one of the most important tax supported services[11]

In a study of more than 55,000 households, published in 1997 by the National Center for Education Statistics, the following results were discovered:

- 65% of the households reported that individuals in the household had used the library in the past year, and 44% reported that individuals in the household had used it in the month prior to the interview

- 61% of households with children under the age of 18 reported using the public library in the past month

- only 35% of households without children under the age of 18 reported using the public library in the past month

- in the month prior to the survey

  ▸ 36% of all households reported borrowing from or dropping off a book to the public library

  ▸ 18% reported visiting the library for some other purpose such as a lecture or story hour

  ▸ 14% reported calling to renew a book or to get information

  ▸ 4% reported using a home computer to link to the public library[12]

These studies suggest that public libraries, at the turn of the century, were seen by most citizens as being useful community resources.

Whether public libraries will continue to succeed in meeting patron needs is subject to conjecture. Visions of the public library in the year 2025 range from the library as a fully automated and robotized institution to one that completely disappears. Some library futurists see the library as a place where wondrous and exotic adventures can be experienced, whereas others see it replaced by home access to information and entertainment.[13] However, whether the public library as we knew it in the last century will survive until 2025 will depend greatly on the effort, imagination, and perseverance of everyone connected with it, from the library board and director to the newest library clerk.

School Library Media Centers

A school library is an integral part of a school that educates students in kindergarten through the twelfth grade. They may be either private or public and are frequently called library media centers or school media centers. These libraries, as well as academic libraries, are responsible for supporting the curriculum of the institutions to which they belong. Improving basic literacy is a key function of the library media center. In addition, school libraries also share with academic libraries the responsibility for promoting information literacy. It is important for library staff members in schools and academic libraries to teach students the process of how to find the information they need, rather than to find the information for them. This process is essential for students if they are to become lifelong learners and function effectively as citizens in the economic and political arenas.

In many of today's schools, a well-run library media center may very well be the most active room in the entire school. Individual children go there to choose books, use computers, view videotapes, or listen to audio materials. Entire classes go to learn how to use the media center or to locate information for their reports. Groups of students may come for help in making transparencies or producing videotapes for class projects. Professional librarians or media specialists, library media technicians, and clerks assist these students. These active media centers have shown how important they can be in a modern educational system. Yet it is amazing that school library media centers have taken so long to become a basic part of the educational institutions of this country.

The Beginnings

Not until the 1950s did most secondary schools have libraries, and even in the 1970s many elementary school libraries were just getting started. What took the educational system so long to recognize that libraries are necessary components of the educational process? The answer to this question lies in the schools' educational goals and methods. In the early centuries of our country's history, school consisted primarily of students memorizing information presented by a teacher. There were few textbooks, and students were not encouraged to become intellectually curious. In the nineteenth century and the early part of the twentieth century, emphasis was on subject content, which was mainly learned from textbooks. In the 1920s and 1930s, the emphasis shifted to the learner, and finally, in the 1940s, the emphasis was placed on life adjustment and the education of all youth for their future roles.[14]

However, the space race of the 1950s and 1960s placed new emphasis on subject mastery so that U.S. education would be equal to education in the Soviet Union. To achieve this end, the 1960s emphasized the education of individual students according to their needs and abilities to prepare them for participation in American society. Unfortunately, economics often prevented schools and libraries from meeting these commendable goals. The situation became so grave that the U.S. National Commission on Excellence in Education published a report, *A Nation at Risk,* in 1983 that identified the United States as just that. This report determined that the United States had let its formal educational system deteriorate to a very dangerous level.[15] In response to this report, librarians drafted *Alliance for Excellence,* a statement that identified the important steps school libraries should take to reverse this deterioration process.[16]

School Library Standards

At the turn of the twentieth century, accreditation associations provided the major impetus for the development of centralized secondary or high school libraries. The purpose of these associations was to rate high schools so that colleges could compare graduates of one high school with graduates of another. Because libraries were included in the criteria listed by the associations, schools that wanted to become accredited had to develop libraries that met the standards of the accrediting associations.

In the 1920s, accrediting associations and the ALA began to develop standards for school libraries. However, they did not become widely adopted. Instead, the major type of library service that schools provided, particularly below the high school level, consisted of traveling library collections from state agencies. In many cases, public libraries provided school collections to the classrooms and provided public librarians who visited the schools. Sometimes the public library was actually part of the school system or housed branches in the school buildings. These services seemed to be satisfactory for those school systems that still considered learning to be largely classroom oriented.

As educators in the 1940s began to recognize that students should be involved in the discovery of learning based on study and inquiry, library services and materials were needed to support the expanded curriculum. To help identify needed library services and materials, the ALA published standards for school library service in 1944 titled *School Libraries for Today and Tomorrow.*[17] The ALA also identified qualitative and quantitative standards for library resources and services that should be provided by a professional staff in a centralized library. Although these standards were applied in some high schools, very few elementary school libraries were established, and, on the whole, the concept of library services envisioned by the standards was seldom implemented.

To encourage library development, in 1956 the ALA published a policy statement identifying the important role the school library should play in the school's total instructional process. For the first time, the library was envisioned as a central school library that included all types of learning materials available to both students and teachers. The concepts of this statement were translated into new standards, *Standards for School Library Programs,* in 1960.[18] The adoption of these standards was greatly facilitated by the country's interest in the educational system after the Russian satellite *Sputnik* was launched in 1957. In addition, the National Defense Education Act (NDEA) of 1958 provided funds for schools to buy print and nonprint materials and equipment. Sometimes states also used these funds to hire school library supervisors at the state level to help local libraries purchase these materials.

The standards helped usher in a new era for library services. Educators began to recognize that libraries should be an integral part of the educational curriculum. Central libraries containing all types of learning materials began to be developed in elementary, junior, and senior high schools. Librarians were recognized as teachers whose subject specialty enabled them to help students and teachers use such materials as books, audiotapes, records, films, filmstrips, transparencies, and programmed instruction. These materials were used in both the classroom and the library to help students learn. The concept of a school library changed to that of instructional materials center (IMC), where many learning activities took place simultaneously.

In the IMC, students and teachers could listen to or view the library's media, or they could produce their own. Students and teachers also could work in the library on group projects, hold meetings in its conference rooms, or study independently in the quiet areas. Library technical and clerical staff were hired so that they could provide instruction in the use of the library and its resources or to help students learn independently. Librarians were able to perform such professional tasks as offering in-service training to teachers in the use of audiovisual materials and equipment. They became active members of curriculum committees and teaching teams. In many school districts the modern school library finally arrived in the 1960s.

With IMCs well on their way to becoming a part of many local school systems, new standards were proposed in 1969 by the American Association of School Librarians (AASL) and the Association of Educational Communications and Technology (AECT). These *Standards for School Media Centers* carried the IMC concept one step further.[19] They proposed that schools develop media programs and services that integrate all types of media into the curriculum based on their contributions to the educational program of the school, rather than on their formats. The standards also proposed replacing the terms *library, librarian, audiovisual center,* and *audiovisual specialist* with the new terms *media center* and *media specialist* to better identify the integration of all forms of media.

From Library to Library Media Center

The concept of a media center caused great consternation in the educational and library worlds in the 1960s and 70s. Many school systems enthusiastically endorsed this concept and combined their library, audiovisual, video, and graphics operations and programs into one media department. Titles for such new departments varied from media center and library media center to learning resource center, instructional media center, instructional resource center, or resource center. However, no matter what their titles were, they all attempted to provide the media services recommended in the standards. Other librarians and audio-visual specialists had difficulty adjusting to this new concept, which required them to alter their thinking and their focus. Often, they, as well as many educators, believed that the standards were utopian rather than practicable. To add to this confusion, the economic crisis of the 1970s practically wiped out the federal monies that had been used to develop library services. To provide direction in this chaotic time, the AASL and AECT published new standards in 1975.

The 1975 standards, *Media Programs, District and School*, expanded the concept of media programs beyond the individual school to include services and facilities that could be provided at the district level.[20] The standards were based on the principle that media were a central part of the learning process and that if schools were to meet students' needs, they must provide quality media programs. These programs were seen to be a combination of district-wide and building-level services that would be tailored to fit the educational goals and objectives of each individual school system. Although quantitative standards were included, the emphasis was on the qualitative aspect of the programs.

This emphasis was extended in 1988 with AASL's and AECT's publication of *Information Power: Guidelines for School Library Media Programs*. These standards responded to issues that had been raised in the U.S. National Commission on Excellence in Education's report, *A Nation at Risk*, and answered in librarians' *Alliance for Excellence* statement.[21] In particular, *Alliance for Excellence* identified important steps that school library supporters should take to develop quality library services and resources for every school library. For example, the statement said that libraries should incorporate their services and resource collections into their schools' curricula. They should provide access to, and instruction in the use of, information resources both within and outside the library. Each library should be well funded and staffed by well-educated and well-paid library media specialists. These library media professionals actively indoctrinate teachers and administrators in the appropriate role and activities of the school library.

Information Power provided the guidelines and directives to help library media personnel carry out these recommended steps. This publication described the library media program's vital role in helping students gain the information skills necessary to function in a learning society. The document's primary focus was to help the building-level library media specialist develop a team partnership with administrators and teachers to identify and establish the best instructional programs.

The guidelines reinforced the role of the library media specialist as that of an information specialist, teacher, and instructional consultant working with teachers to fulfill curriculum needs. Access to information outside the library would be provided via interlibrary loans, multi-library networks, and electronic technologies. A strong emphasis on intellectual freedom and intellectual access to diverse viewpoints was also encouraged. Finally, extensive guidelines were presented for the development of library media facilities designed specifically to serve individual school and curriculum needs. They are reprinted in figure 3.3.

1. Offers a sequential program of library skills instruction.
2. Coordinates library skills instruction with classroom instruction.
3. Informally instructs students in the use of various types of materials and equipment.
4. Conducts in-service education for teachers in the effective evaluation, selection, and use of media.
5. Assists curriculum committee in selecting appropriate materials and media program activities for resource units and curriculum guides.
6. Helps individual teachers to coordinate media program activities and resources with subject areas, units, and textbooks.
7. Helps teachers to develop, select, implement, and evaluate learning activities requiring various types of media.
8. Provides teachers with information about new educational and media developments.
9. Provides reference assistance to teachers.
10. Assists students in locating information and resources valuable to their educational needs and to the growth of their personal interests and ability.
11. Helps students and teachers find and use relevant information sources outside the school.
12. Provides interlibrary loan services to students.
13. Provides interlibrary loan services to teachers.
14. Provides reading/listening/viewing guidance to students.
15. Helps parents realize the importance of assisting their children to understand the benefits of reading, listening, and viewing for pleasure as well as for gaining information.
16. Coordinates in-school production of materials required for instructional use and other activities.
17. Provides technical assistance to students in the production of materials.
18. Provides technical assistance to teachers in the production of materials.
19. Coordinates textbook selection, ordering, and distribution program in school.
20. Coordinates school-operated radio station.
21. Coordinates video production activities in school.
22. Coordinates cable or other TV transmission and utilization activities in school.

From Information Power: Guidelines for School Library Media Programs. *Reprinted by permission of AASL, Appendix A, p. 1160.* © *1988 by ALA.*

Figure 3.3. School library media services.

Implementation of these guidelines was affected by both the educational and economic situations. The majority of teachers continued to rely on lecturing that did not need strong library media support. In addition, many administrators and teachers did not expect much involvement by library media specialists in the school's educational process. In such an educational climate, some school library media specialists felt uncomfortable adopting these new roles and becoming agents of change. The economic climate was also not conducive to the development of such comprehensive school library media programs. Although *A Nation at Risk* had recognized the need for a strong educational program, local communities were often reluctant to finance such programs. To encourage these latter communities to implement strong school library media programs, most states had adopted statewide school library media standards by 1990. Many of these states required local schools to meet these guidelines if they wanted to receive state or federal monies. Strong regional accreditation associations also encouraged the development of strong library media programs through their accreditation standards and local self-study requirements.

School Library Media Programs

Although state and national guidelines have had some impact on the development of school library media programs, such development also has been strongly influenced by the philosophies, objectives, and economics of the individual school systems served. In many school systems, the library media programs not only stopped growing during the late 1980s and 90s but also began to stagnate or shrink. In other school systems with excellent educational programs, outstanding library media programs were developed. These superior library media programs are no accident, however. The more successful and effective programs are based on stated philosophies and objectives carefully designed by everyone concerned. Library media center staff, administrators, teachers, students, and parents have worked together, sometimes in advisory committees, to develop library media programs and activities to meet the needs of individual students.

Many of the resources provided in these library media centers now include much more than the traditional print and film resources of the 1970s. Many books, magazines, newspapers, pamphlets, and catalogs are also available in foreign languages or in formats that students with disabilities can use. Nonprint forms include not only the more common audiovisual formats such as art prints, realia, microforms, and videotapes but also materials such as compact and laser discs and, more recently, DVDs. Technological advancements also have enabled library media centers to provide access to information in new ways. Many library media centers provide computers for the students' own use as well as for computer-assisted instruction, access to extensive resources via CD-ROM, and computer-based catalogs. Library media centers provide dial-up access or online access to local, regional, and national union library catalogs and bibliographic and full-text databases. Some centers provide cable television, interactive video, and satellite and online distance learning programs.

To make these library media resources more readily available to students and teachers within the schools, library media centers adopt flexible scheduling to accommodate both classes and individualized instruction. They expand their programs to include access to resources outside the school. Library media centers have joined with other schools and other types of libraries in networks and consortia to share their resources through interlibrary loan networks; access to special collections, such as film collections; and facsimile transmission of materials, such as magazine articles. Access to other collections is extended through direct loans to schools, student access to other libraries, and cooperative collection development.

In addition, businesses and corporations have become involved in local "adopt-a-school" programs to help schools and library media centers expand their programs. Some national companies such as Apple and IBM offer educational discounts and programs. Other corporations make news broadcasts on channels such as CNN (Cable News Network) and Channel One available to schools without cost. Through these and other cooperative activities, library media specialists find that they can stretch their budgets. At the same time, this increased access to additional resources and information expands the library media program's impact on the educational process.

This impact is further heightened by library media specialists, who take on the roles of teacher, information specialist, and instructional consultant. As teachers and instructional consultants, library media specialists not only teach library skills but also work with teachers to integrate these skills into curriculum projects. Many of these specialists not only develop computer laboratories, but they also teach students, teachers, administrators, and parents how to use these resources. Specialists work with students and teachers to develop such resources as independent learning programs or packages on specialized subjects using all types of media. Games and kits are developed and produced by students and teachers to encourage students to think.

As information specialists, library media specialists also work with teachers to emphasize literature and the enjoyment of reading. Programs such as reading incentive programs, reading clubs, and contests are developed with teachers, administrators, parents, and other libraries to encourage and reward students for increasing their reading. To further encourage participation in these programs and to disseminate information about the total library media program, media specialists also publicize their programs through newsletters and public relations campaigns.

In addition to these expanded resources and programs, the library media center itself also is changing. Many school systems with more than one school have established library media programs at the district level to assist the building-level library media center staff. In such systems, district library media centers often provide centralized services such as ordering, cataloging, and processing; graphic production and duplication; television or radio production; and the distribution of expensive media collections, such as films, kits, and live animal exhibits. In the 1980s and 90s, these services were automated and expanded to include the centralization of other library operations, such as circulation, media bookings, and bibliographic and administrative support. The district library media staff also helps building-level library media personnel develop programs to meet the educational goals of their individual schools.

The organization of building-level library media centers depends upon the educational programs of the schools they serve. Some library media centers are centralized in one geographic area, whereas others have a central library media center supported by satellite subject resource centers. These satellite centers may be adjacent to the central facility or adjacent to classes in their subject areas in other parts of the building. Some schools adopt an "open concept" of learning that produces media centers without walls. Others develop library media centers that include small rooms for study groups as well as classrooms large enough for coordinated library-subject instruction. However, it is not the pattern of organization alone but the program's ability to become fully integrated into the school's curriculum that determines how effective such a program is.

School Library Media Personnel

The development of quality library media programs depends on the development of qualified library media staff to direct and operate these programs. Most states require that teacher-certified personnel must be in charge whenever children are present. Thus, teacher-certified library media specialists staff the majority of library media centers. These specialists usually have either an M.L.S. degree or a master's of educational media degree, and many work under district media coordinators. Some media staff also include other professionals with varied backgrounds and experiences. At the building level, media specialists often work outside the media center as integral members of the educational staff.

In fact, the success of the library media program in each school often depends on the specialist's ability to become accepted by the other teachers as an important member of the educational team. For specialists to be able to fulfill this role beyond the walls of the library, they need well-trained paraprofessionals and clerical staff who are capable of operating the library hour by hour or even day by day. Librarians plan services and coordinate programs with their staff and with teachers and administrators. When such a team is in place, students learn.

However, the commitment to adhere to professional standards for certification varies considerably from state to state. For example, although 77 percent of the public school head librarians in the United States are state certified, the percentage of public school head librarians who are certified by their states as librarian media specialists varies from a low of 25 percent in California to a high of 90 percent or more in Alabama, Arkansas, Georgia, Kansas, Kentucky,

Missouri, Nebraska, North Carolina, South Carolina, South Dakota, Tennessee, Virginia, and Wisconsin.[22]

Funding levels for hiring librarians for school libraries also varies widely from community to community and from state to state:

> In 1995, public schools nationwide employed an average of only two librarians for every 100 teachers. Wyoming (2.03), Alaska (1.99), and Colorado (1.98) were the most typical states in this regard. Arkansas and Montana topped the list at approximately three-and-a half (3.60 and 3.45, respectively) librarians per 100 teachers. California ranked lowest in this statistic, with less than one librarian for every 100 teachers (0.39 per 100).[23]

Readers are advised to check the situation in their own localities.

As library media specialists become more successful in their educational role, they turn the day-to-day operations of the library media center over to their support staff. Encouraged by national and state guidelines, many schools develop full-time media center staff based on a ratio of one specialist to one technician and one clerk. At the building level, this means that library media technicians often supervise clerks, students, and volunteers in checking materials in and out. Library media technicians also supervise building resource centers that are separate from the main library media center. In some smaller schools, library media technicians operate building-level media centers under the direction of a system-wide media specialist.

In larger school systems, staff in the building-level library media centers are often backed by district library media staff who provide further professional or technical expertise. Specialists and technicians in such specialized areas as graphics, television, cable, audiovisual production, and computer technology can be found in district library media centers. These staff members produce resource materials to be used in classrooms and building-level media centers. District-wide processing centers provide centralized support staff to order and process materials for the individual media centers. Centralized booking services for films, videotapes, and computerized learning are usually staffed by clerks, technicians, or both, as are many of the centralized automation services.

Although many of the technical duties in these library media centers require specialized skills (e.g., computer literacy), formal library training has not always been a prerequisite for library media clerical and technical personnel. In some cases, this was because of the economic recession of the 1980s, which saw the decline of library media technician training programs. In other cases, this was because of the constant availability in earlier years of a large pool of untrained but talented workers. These workers were usually homemakers willing to volunteer or work at very low wages so they could have work hours and vacations that coincided with their families' vacations. However, the economic need for people to earn more than the minimum wage has almost eliminated this pool of workers. Thus, if school library media centers are going to meet their growing need for library media support staff with more specialized skills, they will have to change their hiring patterns. They will have to seek out and pay well-trained technical and clerical staff to fulfill their schools' missions.

School Library Media Centers Help Students Achieve

Emphasis on accountability in education is receiving increasing attention, and it seems that this trend will continue in the new millennium. At least at a rhetorical level, it appears to have been embraced by the administration of President George W. Bush. Generally, the method used to establish this accountability is to link performance on standardized tests with rewards and/or penalties for the schools. A growing body of research supports the long-held intuitive belief that good library media centers have a positive impact on student performance on such tests.

Apparently, there is no substitute for professionally prepared librarians backed by well-trained LTAs and clerks. And the level of professional preparation really does matter. Three decades ago, Lucille Wert demonstrated that school librarians holding an M.L.S. offered more services and spent less time in housekeeping tasks than did those with similar experience and responsibilities who had undergraduate minors in library science and teaching credentials.[24] Within the past few years, these services and staff qualifications have been linked statistically with significantly higher student performance:

> Students in schools with appropriate and sufficient library collections and qualified library personnel tend to perform better on standardized tests, especially in reading, according to studies of school library programs in Alaska, Colorado, and Pennsylvania. Making the school library an integral learning center and encouraging teachers and librarians to collaborate on lesson plans and classroom assignments could help raise student achievement, the report suggests.[25]

When library media center "predictors are maximized (e.g., staffing, expenditures, and information resources and technology), CSAP reading scores tend to run 18 percent higher in fourth grade and 10 to 15 percent higher in seventh."[26] These predictors of academic achievement cannot be explained away by school differences, including:

- school district expenditures per pupil

- teacher/pupil ratio
- the average years of experience of classroom teachers, and
- their average salaries; or
- community differences, including:
  - adult educational attainment
  - children in poverty
  - racial/ethnic demographics.[27]

These results would appear to provide powerful ammunition to secure increased resources for school library media centers; however, that outcome is yet to be achieved in the political arena.

Academic Libraries

Academic libraries are found in public and private post-secondary institutions of higher education—that is, colleges and universities. Although logic might lead one to consider high school libraries to be academic libraries, they do not fit within this definition. The mission of an academic library is to support the faculty, students, and staff of the college or university and in so doing to help achieve the mission of the parent institution within which the library is located. This mission varies considerably from institution to institution.

For example, the community college has the mission to teach lower-division undergraduate students (i.e., students in their first two years of college). The curriculum generally includes academic programs to prepare students to transfer to upper-division programs at four-year colleges as well as vocational training programs to prepare students directly for the workforce. As junior colleges have evolved into colleges of the community and for the community, their missions have expanded to include support of lifelong learning and support of community economic development. Thus, the mission of the community college library also has expanded from that of just classroom support to include service to the community users enrolled in noncredit courses and other tailor-made training courses. Distance learning courses are expanding and challenging libraries to keep pace with the information needs of geographically scattered students.

The library of a four-year institution, including those with graduate degree programs, will have a much different focus than a two-year college library. The funding levels, scope of collections, and often highly technical materials will contrast greatly with a community college facility. A large university will maintain many separate departmental libraries (e.g., biological sciences, music, art, business) and may also have distinctive library facilities serving undergraduates and graduates. At times these branch libraries will resemble special libraries (discussed in the next section) as much as they do traditional academic libraries.

An important development that had it roots in the 1970s but did not fully blossom until the 1990s is that of academic libraries changing from storehouses of books to learning and research centers, providing access to information in all of its varied forms. Previously, the volume count had defined prestige. By the turn of the twenty-first century, access to rather than ownership of information resources had become the criterion against which academic libraries were being measured. With this change came a change in library services and the roles of staff within academic libraries.

Types of Academic Libraries

The library world, as mentioned previously, defines an academic library as a library in an institution providing education beyond the high school level. This level of education is called post-secondary or higher education. By 1990 there were more than 4,600 libraries at this level in the United States. They are found in four-year colleges and universities, community colleges, junior colleges, and technical institutions. The number and levels of degrees granted by an academic institution greatly impact its library development.

Within higher education circles, institutions are categorized using the Carnegie Classification, which has evolved over the past three decades. The 2000 version of this system has the following major categories:

- Doctoral/research universities
- Master's colleges and universities
- Baccalaureate colleges
- Associate's colleges
- Specialized institutions:
  - ‣ Theological seminaries and other specialized faith-related institutions
  - ‣ Medical schools and medical centers
  - ‣ Other separate health profession schools
  - ‣ Schools of engineering and technology
  - ‣ Schools of business and management
  - ‣ Schools of art, music, and design
  - ‣ Schools of law
  - ‣ Teachers' colleges
  - ‣ Other specialized institutions
  - ‣ Tribal colleges and universities[28]

These classifications attempt to describe the breadth and depth of programs. Some institutions seem to straddle two or more classifications. In fact, doctoral/research universities are likely to include many of the other categories within their structure. However, the purpose of including this taxonomy here is not to discuss such fine distinctions but to highlight the different philosophies of library service that may be appropriate within the range of categories.

Although community service is paid lip service to within the mission statements of all levels and categories of higher education, this role generally does relatively little to shape the basic collections and services of academic libraries. What really defines the different approaches taken by academic libraries is the extent to which their parent institution emphasizes the creation of new knowledge.

All colleges and universities are engaged in disseminating knowledge to their students. However, some of them have an expectation that new knowledge will be created and added to the knowledge base of humankind. The extent to which an institution focuses on this mission will affect the library in two distinct ways. Supporting cutting-edge researchers in a discipline calls for very different collections and services than does supporting novice learners in that same discipline. Researchers at the forward edge of their specialty need to know everything possible about their specialty, including what has happened in the last five minutes. This requires very specialized sources of information for not just the discipline but also for the narrow sub-discipline within which the scholar is working.

Therefore, library collections of millions of volumes are not uncommon. Information sources are generally specialized refereed journals, and even these do not publish new results fast enough to be of great use to those dedicated to enhancing the knowledge base of their fields. Scholars do not want to waste their time duplicating work that, unknown to them, has just been completed by another researcher somewhere in the world.

Lower-division undergraduates, on the other hand, are just assimilating an overview of their discipline and some of its basic vocabulary and concepts. They need much more basic information. One of the myths of academic librarianship is that if you have a collection rich enough to support researchers, you will have more than enough resources to satisfy the needs of the undergraduates studying that same discipline. This is not the case. Undergraduates are not generally prepared to understand and benefit from the highly technical vocabulary and specialized context of discourse at the leading edge of their discipline. At this stage in their learning experience, a much smaller but tailored collection, measured in tens of thousands, may be most appropriate for lower-division undergraduates; for upper-division undergraduates a library collection of a few hundred thousand appropriate volumes may suffice. Support for the curriculum being taught in the classroom is the measure of a good library at this level.

Faculty roles, and, therefore, librarian roles differ within these institutions as well. Within the community colleges, faculty assignments are weighted almost exclusively toward classrooms and laboratories. Evaluation of instructors is centered on how well they help students learn—as are rewards, such as promotion and tenure. In research universities, faculty are expected to bring exciting new nuggets from their research to class to enhance the learning environment. Evaluation is focused on progress in research and publication.

If librarians have faculty status, then these same expectations carry over to them as well. In an undergraduate college that is focused almost exclusively on teaching and learning, librarians have educational backgrounds comparable to that of classroom faculty. The role each plays in helping students learn is also similar. In this environment, it is appropriate for librarians to share the same status and meet the same performance expectations.

The college library staff is generally much smaller than that of a university library. College libraries are likely to be staffed by 5 to 10 professionals who are supported by clerical and student personnel. University libraries require many more, often highly specialized, staff members to acquire, process, and disseminate the information contained in much larger collections, which can range from several hundred thousand volumes to millions of volumes. These larger libraries may be staffed by as few as 25 and as many as several hundred professional, associate, technical, and clerical personnel who are supported by sometimes hundreds of student helpers. Also, university libraries generally have large collections in almost every subject area, whereas college libraries tend to concentrate on the general arts and sciences with a strong emphasis on humanities, social sciences, and the physical and biological sciences.

Development of College and University Libraries

The majority of academic libraries generally began as mere adjuncts to the classroom, housed in small rooms and administered by part-time faculty members. Further library development was accelerated by the rapid expansion of the world's known information. As late as the 1920s even the largest university libraries were no bigger than those of a medium-sized college of today. As published knowledge began to expand rapidly, academic libraries expanded their collections accordingly. During the mid-twentieth century the collections of research university libraries doubled every 17 to 20 years. The large influx of students after World War II, largely funded by veterans' benefits, also placed a demand on libraries to provide materials in great quantities.

A typical academic library of the 1950s would have contained only print materials (books, serials, and pamphlets) housed in an architectural monument named after some benefactor. Universities often kept most of their collections in closed stack areas to which only graduate students and faculty members were admitted. Undergraduates had to ask for books at a circulation desk and wait for the materials to be paged or delivered to them. Many universities attempted to help the first- and second-year students adjust to the wealth of library materials by providing separate undergraduate libraries.

The primary objective was to contribute to the goals and philosophy of the academic institutions the libraries served. Because the academic institutions were still largely faculty, graduate student, and research oriented, library objectives also leaned in that direction, rather than focusing directly on the students' need for support of classroom learning.

The sudden increase of published information made it clear that no library could meet all of the needs of their faculty and students. This encouraged cooperation with other libraries so that they could mutually strengthen library resources available to all. Still, the interlibrary loan process mainly targeted faculty and graduate students. Undergraduate students rarely had access to materials their college or university did not own. Undergraduates were also hampered by not knowing how to find materials the library did own because library instruction was often limited to a single orientation tour for freshmen during their first week on campus.

Learning Resource Center Programs and Services

As their parent institutions changed, academic libraries also changed to support the new educational programs. Many libraries began to experiment and to expand their library collections beyond the traditional print materials. The media explosion that impacted the elementary and secondary schools expanded to include higher education. Some libraries began to incorporate all types of media into their collections and programs, including audiotapes; videotapes; microforms; transparencies; films of all forms, shapes, and sizes; programmed learning; and computer-assisted instruction. The academic library had become student-oriented.

The growth and development of these new types of libraries and library services in the 1960s encouraged the development of new academic library standards over the past three decades of the twentieth century. Whereas previous academic standards had emphasized traditional library materials and services, the new standards emphasized quality learning resources programs and student access to all media within the library. The Association of College and Research Libraries (ACRL) adopted standards for all types of academic libraries. The most recent versions of these are "Standards for Community, Junior, and Technical College Learning Resource Programs" (1994);[29] "Standards for College Libraries" (2000)[30]; and "Standards for University Libraries" (1989).[31] However, rather than setting the pace for library services as the school standards had done, these academic standards seemed to follow rather than lead the development of innovative library services.

No matter what form the academic library took in the 1970s and 80s, one student-centered philosophy developed. This shift was to change the entire character of academic library service. Previously, the focus, particularly in university libraries, had been on serving the needs of faculty and advanced graduate students. As the needs of undergraduate students gained more importance, it became more obvious that this group needed professional assistance to identify and interpret the information resources that were most appropriate to meet their needs. As a result, the information contained in the books and other materials gradually became an increasing focus for public services staffs. Amassing large collections in anticipation of what someone might need 20 years from now was no longer enough in and of itself. The books, though still important, were no longer the end in themselves—they increasingly became the means to the end of conveying information. However, this new focus on information would take on new meaning with the advances in technology that were then on the horizon.

Other library services and procedures were often changed to match students' needs. Many new university library buildings housed their major book collections in open stacks that were made accessible to undergraduates for the first time. The interiors of these buildings also changed. Group study rooms that allowed for conversation and collaboration also began to appear. Library hours became extended and more flexible with some libraries staying open until midnight, and some even staying open 24 hours a day. Professional staff were often available for student assistance whenever the library was open, including during traditional holiday or semester breaks. The academic library had removed some of the physical barriers that had restricted student access to its collection.

Academic Library Technology

Academic libraries also took advantage of the emergence of relatively reliable and affordable computer technology to develop automated systems for library operations. Some of these libraries were so successful in this development that they sold their products commercially under labels such as UTLAS (University of Toronto), BRS (Bibliographic Retrieval Services, State University of New York), and NOTIS (Northwestern University). As technology became more sophisticated, computer systems grew from single-purpose systems for internal operations (e.g., circulation or cataloging) to integrated library systems. Integrated library systems, such as Illinois's Library Computer System (ILCS), included not only circulation and cataloging but also online public access catalogs (OPACs). Students and faculty from a cooperating academic institution could use the database as union catalog to borrow materials through "direct borrowing" (i.e., in person) or by requesting that an interlibrary loan be delivered to their home campus library. Some systems included serials control systems (e.g., Serials of Illinois Libraries [SILO]), online search systems (e.g., BRS), and materials acquisitions systems that were also used for collection analysis and development.

In addition to providing automated services for the library, academic libraries took the lead in intra-campus and inter-campus networking. In some cases, institution-wide computer centers and programs were added to the academic library's service roles. Computer labs were made available in libraries for students' homework use, and some schools, such as Carnegie-Mellon, made computers available in students' dormitory rooms. OPACs were made accessible to students and faculty in their dormitories, offices, or homes. Libraries promoted inter-campus networking with link-ups for teleconferencing and two-way audio and video telecourses via satellite or TV and, more recently, online on the World Wide Web.

Libraries marketed their services to community business and economic leaders. Services such as business library cards, journal photocopying services, document delivery, computer search services such as DIALOG, and professional librarian consulting services were made available for a fee or in exchange for business donations. Many institutions made their resources available for a fee to any citizen either in the library or outside the library. An example of such comprehensive services is found at the University of Southern Florida, where the library and information services department is responsible for the library, the computer center, all information flow on campus, and the use of campus information resources by the business community. However, these quasi for-profit ventures were not uniformly successful.

Academic libraries also took the lead in developing resource-sharing networks with other libraries. These libraries recognized many years previously that they must share their resources, both bibliographically and physically. This sharing originally began on an informal basis, with academic libraries in the same geographic area sharing materials or allowing reciprocal borrowing among their patrons. In the 1970s library budgets failed to keep up with the publication explosion that produced more materials than a single library could buy. These informal arrangements became formal agreements for interlibrary cooperation. This cooperation took many forms and provided many varied services. Some academic institutions joined consortia to formally share their educational resources and prevent costly duplication of subject specialties. Another type of cooperative endeavor is illustrated by the Center for Research Libraries, which provides cooperative storage facilities of little-used materials for its members.

This expanding wealth of access options placed renewed emphasis on the need to teach students how to make efficient use of them. In addition to giving orientation tours of the library, librarians developed computer and media programs that explained parts of the library or individual library resource tools. They also taught credit and noncredit bibliographic instruction courses. This was not a new activity. Some progressive institutions, such as Iowa State University, offered library instruction throughout the twentieth century. However, these programs have received new emphasis. In some cases these courses were competency based, and students were required to pass them to become upperclassmen or to graduate. Libraries also established programs to help nontraditional students overcome their reluctance to use the library as a learning tool. Some libraries developed ongoing programs to help retain these students and worked with high school enhancement programs or programs for underachieving students.

Academic librarians have long had the urge to promote library use to undergraduates. However, such direct marketing efforts are rarely successful. Students have so many demands on their time that most can direct their attention to only what is absolutely necessary to preserve their academic status. Indirect efforts aimed at the faculty have a much better chance of success. Almost any course in a college or university can be taught so that students can earn an "A" without ever having to darken the door of a library. On the other hand, those same courses can be structured in such a manner that the students must be in the library every week to have a chance to survive the course with a passing grade.

Academic Institutions in the Twenty-First Century

At the beginning of the twenty-first century libraries are faced with the dilemma of keeping up with the new electronic forms of information. Electronic products offer opportunities to provide library services in ways that were not previously possible—information delivered anytime to any place. However, these services cannot be offered without funding for the infrastructure and staff needed to support these innovations. At the same time, it is not often possible to stop providing services in the traditional manner. There is little evidence that the rest of the academic world is ready to move uniformly to embrace these new services. Textbooks, lectures, and assignments from library reserved-book collections continue to be at the heart of most college teaching by faculty who themselves are not always comfortable in libraries.[32] It is understandable then that a study by the Carnegie Foundation of 5,000 undergraduate students showed that 65 percent of them used a library for only four hours or less per week, whereas one-quarter of the students did not use the library at all.[33] A more discouraging commentary for libraries was that most of these students used the library only as a place for quiet study.

The Carnegie Foundation has provided some momentum for change, suggesting that the quality of colleges should be measured by the resources they offer for learning on the campus and the extent to which their students become independent, self-directed learners.[34] As higher education slowly makes changes in this direction, libraries have opportunities to become more integrated into the total learning experience.

This may erode the concept of the library as a physical "place." As mentioned previously, more information services can now be provided remotely. These include

- electronic reserves

- e-books

- full-text (and even better, full-image) periodical articles

- remote media booking services

- online information competency tutorials

- online public access catalogs (OPACs)

- other online indexes and databases

- online reference assistance

- online interlibrary loan requests

So far, studies have been mixed as to whether these enhancements in service reduce or increase the likelihood that students and faculty will visit their campus library. One group of results suggests that it is no longer necessary to come to the "bricks and mortar" library to get needed information and services any longer. Other studies suggest that users are more likely to come to the library if they can check online in advance and determine that there is information of relevance waiting for them at the library.

Academic Library Management

Generally speaking, the library director is a dean of learning resources who reports to an academic vice president. The library dean is not only the administrator of a large department and budget but also is active in the council of deans and the total university administration. This expanded administrative role often strengthens and solidifies the library's place in the entire academic institution.

Increasingly, librarians are freed from supervising in-house library operations so that they can serve on faculty and institution committees and work with their faculty colleagues. Supervision of in-house library activities is delegated to technical support staff because libraries discovered that technicians can operate most library functions on a day-to-day basis once service parameters are established and policies are set. These developments give impetus to librarians' quest for faculty status, tenure, and pay equity. Their success in achieving such demands depends on their success in becoming an integral part of their academic institutions.

The reality that funding for publicly supported academic institutions is based on political considerations is not lost on academic librarians. Many of them serve on state higher education advisory committees. They join forces with librarians from other types of libraries to lobby for recognition and funding from local, state, and national library and higher education governmental agencies. However, as important as funding is, Richard DeGennaro reminds us that "the greatest challenge facing academic libraries in the next decade is not funding or technology, but leadership and administrative ability."[35] Library leaders must be committed to making their libraries more productive, innovative, and entrepreneurial to fulfill their major roles of developing information-literate students, integrating libraries into the academic curricula, and providing access by students and faculty to all the information they need without regard for its location or format.

Special Libraries and Information Centers

Special libraries include corporate, medical, law, religious, governmental, prison, not-for-profit organization libraries, and many other highly specialized collections. A few very different examples include the small Hearst Castle Staff library, the Smithsonian Institution's research library, and the voluminous LDS (Mormon) library of family history in Utah. Often, the term *special library* is used as a catch-all term to mean any library that is not a public, school, or academic library. A common thread, though, is that collections and services are very narrowly focused to support the activities of the parent organization.

The lines between special libraries and other types of libraries are not precise. Often, the subject-specific departmental libraries within large university library systems or within large public libraries function more like special libraries than they do like general academic or public libraries. The professional orientation of the staff may be more toward the subject matter than to the type of library in which the particular departmental library is located. For example, music librarians often have their primary allegiance to the Music Library Association (MLA) rather than to the broad-based ALA.

Even within a specialized subdivision of special libraries, there is unlimited variation in the types of libraries and the opportunities for employment. Although the following discussion uses law libraries to illustrate the point, similar illustrations could be given within almost any other sector of special libraries.

One of the authors formerly taught in a library technician-training program in the Los Angeles area. In the introductory course, a panel of law librarians was invited to address the students. The panel was composed of the following:

- a librarian from a very large law firm in downtown Los Angeles

- a librarian from the Los Angeles County Law Library

- a librarian from the University of Southern California School of Law library

- a librarian from the Ninth District Court of Appeals library

- a librarian who had left traditional library employment and organized a personnel agency that specializes in placing temporary and permanent employees in law libraries

All of these librarians work within the context of law librarianship. However, the commonality ends there.

The librarian of a large firm and the court librarian serve no one other than those within their own organization. For the firm this is a competitive issue: They are in business to make money and their information resources are one of their most valuable commodities. They do not want competitors to know what they are researching, let alone make it easy for those competitors to do similar research. In the case of the court library, confidentiality and privacy, more than competitiveness, are the driving forces. The entire clientele of the library comprise the judges and their immediate staffs. The judges need to be able to complete their research without being exposed to the prying eyes of others or the interruptions of chance encounters with parties to the litigation they are adjudicating.

At the opposite extreme, the Los Angeles County Law Library functions almost as a public library. Its collections make it the largest law library west of the Mississippi River. Although L. A. County's primary clientele are judges, lawyers, and their staffs, the general public, conducting personal legal research, constitutes more than 30 percent of the customers.

Dress codes are another area in which the law libraries differ greatly. The general rule of thumb seems to be that staff dress just slightly more conservatively than the typical clientele. One large law firm took the dress code one step further. It required all non-lawyers to wear a uniform. The firm was so large that not everyone knew the other employees who worked there. The lawyers felt the need to be able to walk into a room and immediately know who were members of their team. Therefore, the company bought staff members blue blazers and gray skirts or slacks to wear on the job. Many of this firm's clients were bankers and others active in the financial community who dress very conservatively.

Employees at other law libraries in Los Angeles dress less formally. Firms that specialize in entertainment law encourage their staff to dress more casually to blend in better with the customary attire of most of their clientele. And then there are the law school libraries where the primary clientele are college students and faculty. Again, the rule of thumb is to dress just slightly more conservatively than the customers.

With all this diversity, is there a unifying theme or common core that ties all of these libraries together? The term *special library* is used as an umbrella term to describe many different types of libraries. There have been many attempts to define what special libraries really are. What could a large scientific library with thousands of volumes and many paid staff members have in common with a small local historical museum library with 1,000 books and a photographic collection cared for by volunteer staff members? What characteristics of these two libraries would enable one term to be used to define both?

Of the characteristics that are most common to these libraries, the primary one is that their collections include materials relating to specialized subject areas. Second, these libraries gather their collections and design their services to directly support and further the objectives of a parent organization, rather than to support a curriculum as school and academic libraries do. Finally, these libraries are primarily concerned with actively seeking out and providing information that the parent organization's clients or patrons need rather than just acquiring and preserving the information in a collection. In other words, special libraries provide special and even individualized services for their patrons. These three characteristics are key elements of any special library or information center.

There are almost 12,000 different libraries that fit this definition of a special library.[36] Usually, they are libraries devoted to special subject areas, such as music and art libraries; libraries devoted to special forms, such as map libraries and archives; or libraries devoted to special clientele, such as medical patient libraries and prison libraries. Special libraries can also be identified by their parent organizations or institutions, such as bank or insurance libraries, church libraries, and federal libraries. However, these designations are far from comprehensive. If there is an organization, corporation, institution, or group of people with a special need for library and information services, then a special library has probably been developed to serve them.

Although most librarians are attracted to faddish terms, special librarians seem especially susceptible. Perhaps this is because of their need to constantly market their services as being at the cutting edge. For example, special libraries are often referred to as information centers. At this writing, the term *knowledge management* is being associated with some special libraries. Each term communicates a slightly different image of the services of the library and its relevance to the parent organization.

The growth and development of special libraries has varied widely. Yet for all of their variety in funding, type, subject, and clientele, special libraries and information centers continue to have more similarities than differences. Their financing, governance, resources, and services are more strongly affected by their importance to the well being of their parent organization than in any other type of library. Therefore, their fortunes can change quickly, as the fortunes of their parent organizations either flourish or falter.

Research Libraries

Research libraries are some of our most important special libraries. Because they have been developed to support the research needs of the world's scholars, they have traditionally been allied with academic libraries. Most are actually a part of a large university, but many can be found outside academe. The New York Public Library has its own, mostly privately funded, research library as its central library. (The branches are tax-funded public libraries.) Most research libraries were originally established and endowed by wealthy benefactors. Limited funds have forced most research libraries to limit and refine their subject interests, but, through careful purchases, many libraries have been able to develop definitive collections in narrow subject areas.

Independent research libraries are unique because they do not belong to any other institution and exist for their own sake. Generally, they have been established by wealthy benefactors, are governed by their own self-perpetuating boards of directors, and manage their own facilities and endowment funds. In some cases, the focus of the library may be based on the private collection of the library's benefactor, such as the Folger Shakespeare Library, or it may be chosen to coordinate with other research libraries. For example, the subjects of the Newbery Library (humanities) and the John Crerar Library (physical and natural sciences) in Chicago were chosen to complement each other and those of the Chicago Public Library (social sciences). Sometimes these libraries may lose their independent status, as the John Crerar Library did when it was absorbed into the University of Chicago in 1984. Although these libraries have been called independent research libraries, they have become important—and often unique—links in the network of national information resources.

Federal Libraries

Federal government libraries are another important link in our national information resources. They include such libraries as national health, agriculture, technical, and institutional libraries, as well as academic (e.g., the Air Force Academy), school (e.g., on federal reservations), and quasi-public (e.g., military base) libraries. However, all federal libraries are still considered to be special libraries because they serve the goals of their parent institutions and their users are usually members of these institutions. There are more than 2,500 federal libraries serving the various departments and agencies of the U.S. government. About 40 percent of these libraries are scientific and technical (including health and medical) libraries that serve the special objectives of agencies to which they belong. Almost as many serve as quasi-public libraries for persons at military installations, veterans' hospitals, and federal prisons. About 20 percent of all federal libraries serve the educational needs of personnel in U.S. armed forces, the military academies, and military–dependent schools overseas.

The importance of federal libraries to our national information resources is seen in the extensive research and subject collections found within them. The most comprehensive federal collections are contained in the three national libraries: the Library of Congress (LC), the National Library of Medicine (NLM), and the National Agriculture Library (NAL). These three libraries not only provide extensive research collections in all forms of media but also represent one-third of the total federal collections, one-half of all federal library expenditures, and two-fifths of all the personnel in federal libraries. The LC alone has a staff of almost 5,000 employees.

> The enormous size and variety of its collections make
> the Library of Congress the largest library in the
> world. Comprised of approximately 115 million items
> in virtually all formats, languages, and subjects, these
> collections are the single most comprehensive accumula-
> tion of human expression ever assembled. True to the
> Jeffersonian ideal, the collections are broad in scope,
> including research materials in more than 450 languages,
> over 35 scripts, and in many media.[37]

These national libraries provide library services to the nation and serve as national information resource centers. The NLM and the NAL have developed subject collections in medicine and agriculture and their allied fields; the LC covers all the other subjects.

Serving as a national library is still an unofficial function of the LC, although it has been steered in this direction by two important events. The first was the U.S. Congress's purchase of Thomas Jefferson's collection, which contained materials on a great variety of subjects rather than just legisla- tive materials. Over the years, librarians of Congress continued to strengthen these subjects. The second event was the passage of the Copyright Law in 1870 that required that two copies of every copyrighted work be submitted to the LC. This national library function was further enhanced in the early 1900s, when the library began to sell its classification schedules and catalog cards. The *National Union Catalog* (NUC) and the *Union List of Serials* (ULS) also enabled libraries to share the LC's collection as well as the collections of the largest libraries in the United States. Finally, the LC became the national resource for materials for people who are blind or physically disabled.

In spite of these services to the nation, the primary purpose of the LC is still to serve as a legislative library for Congress. Librarians of Congress have judiciously nourished this relationship, and their skillful public relations have helped gain unparalleled financial support for the library and its programs. This financial support has enabled the LC and the other national libraries to provide leadership in the development of library automation programs of inter- national significance. For example, the LC-developed format for exchanging computerized cataloging information, MAchine Readable Cataloging (MARC), has, with minor variations, become the standard worldwide.

By the early 1990s, the actual LC catalog became available online to other libraries. Recent initiatives have digitized rarely held materials that are in danger of disappearing because of the deterioration of the paper on which they are printed. One of the most ambitious of these projects, *American Memory,* is a gateway to rich primary source materials relating to the history and culture of the United States. The site offers more than 5 million items from more than 90 historical collections."[38]

The LC was not the only national library that made its collection readily available to the world. The NLM developed *MEDLARS*, an online service, which made 25 medical literature databases accessible to its 30,000 users by the early 1990s. The NLM's computerized cataloging information in the biomedical area was made available to medical libraries on *CATLINE*. Citations and indexes to articles were made available through *Index Medicus* or online through *MEDLINE* for the field of biomedicine. Because many of *MEDLARS*'s users were individuals, the NLM also provided *Grateful Med* software so that health professionals could have access to more than 13 million references and abstracts via their personal computers. *PubMed*, a service of the National Library of Medicine, provides access to more than 11 million citations from *MEDLINE* and additional life science journals. *PubMed* includes links to many sites providing full-text articles and other related resources."[39] In addition, the NLM provides document delivery to medical libraries and health professionals and establishes regional medical libraries throughout the country to serve as resource centers between the user and the NLM.

The NAL also took its place as a national leader in providing library and information services to the agricultural community. As early as 1970, the NAL made its computerized database *AGRICOLA* (AGRICultural On Line Access) available to other libraries. The NAL was an active member of *AGLINET*, a voluntary association of 27 agricultural libraries. It was also active in *USAIN* (U.S. Agriculture Information Network), a national forum to discuss agricultural information issues. Because the success of any agricultural effort often depends on worldwide climatic conditions, the NAL also became an important part of the international agricultural information network. This worldwide network developed interconnecting resource centers that provide electronic access to data, documents, and computer files throughout the world. This network was made available so that both the scientist and the layperson could understand its information. As with the medical community, access to this international agricultural network was also made available via computer link-ups to users, such as farmers, at the local level.

Corporate Libraries and Information Centers

The private world of business and industry has kept pace with the government in developing libraries and information centers to support research needs. Almost all businesses and industries, including banks, insurance companies, utilities, advertising agencies, newspapers, chemical companies, and aerospace corporations, have their own libraries. Though these companies' products may vary considerably, their libraries and information centers are similar in that their collections and services are completely correlated with the objectives of their parent organizations. Figure 3.4 depicts a corporate library from the 1950s.

Figure 3.4. The 1957 movie **Desk Set,** *starring Katharine Hepburn and Spencer Tracy, takes place in a "modern corporate library." Notice the state of the art computer in the background. Reprinted by permission, private collection.*

Because large corporations are now so multifaceted, completely different libraries are often found within the same organization. For example, Kaiser Permanente, a large health care organization, has medical libraries at each of its hospitals. However, at its administrative center it has a business library that focuses on management issues. The Art Institute of Chicago maintains at least three separate libraries: (1) a research library used by staff and other qualified researchers to authenticate and establish the provenance (chain of ownership) of items of art; (2) an educational center for the museum's children's programming that includes resources for schoolteachers of art; and (3) a library (including a media center) for the School of the Art Institute.

Businesses such as law firms, communications media, insurance companies, advertising agencies, and high-tech and marketing firms are so dependent on the quick retrieval of information that they provide well-funded collections and trained staff in their libraries. For example, law firms subscribe to expensive legal databases, such as *Lexis* or *WestLaw*, that make current court decisions instantaneously available upon release, rather than weeks later in printed form.

Other types of businesses, particularly smaller businesses, might consider information services as peripheral to their profit goal and cut their libraries' staffing, materials, and funding when profits begin to sag. Thus, a library's or an information center's success in convincing upper management that it is contributing to the parent corporation's bottom line is essential to guaranteeing its continued existence.

The need to successfully contribute to the corporation's profit by providing information is so vital that corporate libraries have become information centers rather than bona fide libraries. Although there is no precise defining difference between the two, the information center tends to be more involved in the flow of internally generated information, which may not be intended to see the light of day outside the organization. Information specialists and other employees who have subject and library expertise and a solid grounding in the corporation's objectives and organization will staff these information centers.

Using their expertise, information specialists have developed collections that include resources in all types and forms. This information may be contained in externally published materials, such as books, microforms, serials, patents, and conference reports, or in internally generated materials, such as research and technical reports, corporate and product indexes, correspondence, and market surveys. However, it is not the format of the information but its currency that is of primary importance in special libraries and information centers. In fact, the most important service any information center provides may be rapid access to journal articles and research data through extensive serial collections or electronic databases.

To facilitate easy access to relevant data, information centers usually collect and index everything written or published, both externally and internally, about the corporation, its products, and its competitors. Because their collections are used by every division in the corporation, information centers also include information about the corporation's clients or customers, competitors, business indicators, economic factors, and business administration. In cataloging these materials, information centers have often devised simplified classification and subject-heading systems because many documents do not have the necessary information for standard cataloging.

Information centers also provide in-depth indexing for information of interest buried within relevant book chapters, periodical articles, and specific subjects, rather than just providing traditional bibliographic descriptions of books or periodicals as a whole. Access to these materials has been further enhanced by recent technological advancements. These advancements enable information centers to make digital images of their materials available to any member of the corporation anywhere in the world.

The economic model on which the special library is based is very different than that of other libraries. Its customers are on the company payroll, unlike the school and academic library (and to some extent the public library), where student or patron research time is not a cost to the institution. Therefore, it is costing the company, no matter if researchers do their own information gathering or if that task is performed for them by information center staff. Generally, it is more cost-effective for information center staff to perform this activity because they are more skilled and may also be paid less per hour than other specialized employees of the organization. As a result, the staff members in special libraries will go much further than those of other libraries not only to locate bibliographic citations in a particular area but also to obtain the documents, read and analyze them, and write a report for the requesting department. In some corporations, information specialists join with department teams to work as researchers on corporate projects. Such active participation in a company's programs has helped prove the library's worth to many corporate executives.

The information specialist may also save corporate personnel valuable time and, at the same time, improve the competitive position of the organization by providing individualized and specialized services such as current alert services. Such services search current literature according to profiles tailored to an individual's or group's specific needs. It can be one of the most productive services for keeping researchers abreast of new research developments in their fields as the information is published. Information specialists usually interview the patron to determine what specific type of search or information is desired. The specialist then identifies subject descriptors or subject headings to create a profile for that person. This profile is run against new information sources as the company acquires them, and the researcher is notified of any relevant matches that occur.

Most corporate information centers circulate books, route serials, publish and distribute bibliographies and acquisitions lists, provide abstracting and translating services, compile files of news clippings, maintain electronic bulletin boards, publish information bulletins, and provide copies of relevant articles or patents. Through these many services, the corporate information center attempts to improve the corporation's efficiency and profits by taking an active part in its day-to-day operations.

Other Special Libraries

Some of the more common examples of other special libraries are museum libraries, association libraries, and organization libraries. Within each of these areas, there are numerous variations based on the subject areas or organizations or institutions that a library serves. For example, about 3,000 libraries are located in historical museums, art museums, science museums, and other museum-type establishments such as zoos, arboretums, historic houses, and national parks. All of these libraries vary in size and are funded by both private and public agencies. Although a few of them have large collections and well-trained staff, most have small collections (1,000 to 5,000 items) that may be staffed by volunteers who may or may not have library training. Museum-type libraries are primarily open during regular business hours to serve the staff and researchers at their institutions as well as qualified off-site scholars and researchers.

Other kinds of institutions served by special libraries include associations and agencies. Professional associations such as ALA, the American Dental Association, and the American Medical Association are just a few of the associations that provide libraries for their executive staff and their members. State and local government agencies provide libraries to serve their staff, although these are not nearly as extensive as the federal libraries. Law libraries are located in practically every county in the United States.

Access to archival materials is also made available by many governments, institutions, and organizations through limited reference service, photo duplication, and lending policies. Such library-like services are encouraged by the Society of American Archivists (SAA), which provides a voluntary certification program for archivists. As with the other types of special libraries, all of these libraries serve the major objectives of their parent organizations and institutions by providing both in-depth research and current information to their members as quickly and efficiently as possible.

One type of institution, the hospital or health care center, is unique because it often has two types of special libraries or one library that provides two distinct types of services. The first type is the patient library, which provides recreational and leisure reading for patients. These libraries usually have very flexible circulation routines, and services may be provided by volunteer staff rather than by paid technical or professional staff. The second type serves the research needs of the medical and other professional staff. On rare occasions, library staff in this latter type of library have been credited with making a difference between life and death. The typical example is that of a surgical team opening up a patient and discovering something totally unexpected. At that point, time and accuracy are certainly of the essence if additional technical information is required.

Among the other institutional libraries are prison libraries, which serve their incarcerated populations. The goals of prison libraries have varied throughout the years as the philosophy of prison reform has changed. The first prison library collections contained moral and religious works to help prisoners see the error of their ways. Next, prison collections became important in supporting the educational system in the prison, and, finally, the library became a part of the prison's rehabilitative function. By the 1990s, literacy programs had become a major activity in many prison libraries. The biggest growth in prison libraries, though, has been in the area of legal information. Since the 1970s, federal courts have required that prisons provide adequate legal information that inmates can consult for drafting legal papers and briefs. As a result of this requirement, prisons have developed their own law libraries.

Many subject specialty libraries are connected with universities and colleges. They can be as numerous and as varied as the university departments themselves. To support these diverse libraries, special library associations have developed. These include associations for art, architecture, agriculture, astronomy, documentation, film archives, geography and maps, law, medicine, music, social science, sound archives, and theater. In addition, there are religious library associations such as the theological, Jewish, Catholic, and Lutheran library associations.

Special Library and Information Management

The management and staffing of special libraries and information centers are more varied and distinct than that found in other types of libraries. Often, the administrator responsible for the library or information center is not a librarian but a director or officer of a major department or division. In business and industrial libraries, the directors of research and development or the vice presidents of marketing may be given responsibility for administering the library or information center. These administrators usually hire library and information staff who support their own conceptions of library services. Thus, if a research and development (R&D) director considers library services important, then that person will provide a sufficient number of well-trained staff members to support the R&D function. Such a library might have a staff of information professionals supported by technicians and clerks. If another R&D director considers the materials more important than the services, then the library staff might consist of only clerical workers. If either director were replaced, the services in that library or information center might be changed once again to fit the new director's viewpoint.

Personnel working in special libraries and information centers usually have more varied backgrounds than do staff in other types of libraries. Ideally, personnel should have both library and subject expertise. The special librarian or information specialist may have a degree in a subject specialty as well as in library science, and the staff may also include subject and language specialists. In fact, this subject expertise may be so important to companies and businesses that they may prefer a technician with subject specialization to a professional with a master's degree in library or information science. Large libraries often include professional librarians or information scientists backed up by subject specialists, technicians, programmers, and clerks.

In reality, however, sometimes the only staff member in a special library may be a secretary who has been put in charge of a collection of books and magazines. In other special libraries, someone who is a librarian or information specialist in name only may supervise several clerks and technicians. This manager may have a degree in the subject specialty of the parent corporation or institution but may not have much knowledge of library or information science. In other cases, a technician may be offered a high wage to perform professional responsibilities for which he or she may not be fully prepared. At the opposite end of the spectrum, professional librarians or information specialists are often offered technician-level wages. Sometimes library services are outsourced (i.e., provided on a contract basis by an outside agency or vendor). Some organizations hire a professional library consultant to set up a library that is then turned over to lower-paid personnel who are charged with carrying out daily operations.

Because the major purpose of the parent corporation is to make a profit, the major purpose of the corporate library is to collect, organize, and put to use the knowledge in its collections for the greatest efficiency of the corporation. It is this characteristic that distinguishes corporate business and industrial libraries from other special libraries. The profit-making motive may be one of the most influential factors in the makeup of a business or industrial library. In private sector corporations, libraries sometimes are operated as profit centers, rather than being treated as general overhead, and, therefore, a cost center.

Psychologically, this changes the entire equation. Such libraries must demonstrate their worth annually to the company by generating a profit similar to how other divisions of the organization are expected to make a profit. This is a foreign concept throughout much of the library business. Charge for library services? Although, intellectually, most library workers believe in the value of information, few of us expect to put this belief to the test daily in the marketplace.

The way this works in some firms is that the time of the librarian/researcher is billed out for the hours he or she works on a client's project. This billable time is inflated to cover all of the overhead costs associated with the research—collections, facilities, technology, supplies, subscriptions, support staff, and so forth. Therefore, billing rates in excess of $100 per hour are necessary to cover the costs of the services provided to the client. Often, these costs are billed directly to the client, along with the chargeable time of other professionals in the firm, such as lawyers, accountants, scientists, engineers, and consultants.

This constant financial need has forced special libraries and information centers to be entrepreneurial. More special libraries have charged back their services to the corporate department end user, such as the engineering or marketing departments. In addition, by the 1990s, some firms, such as law and engineering firms, began "passing through," or billing the costs of such library and information services to the end-user client. Also, many special libraries and information centers began to provide fee-based services and consulting to external corporate or individual users who were not members of their own organization. Fees were charged for services such as online searches, reference service, and document delivery.

The fees often enabled a library or information center to provide additional services for its primary clients that it might not otherwise be able to afford. In contrast with public and academic libraries that have to face freedom-of-access concerns when charging similar fees, the special library or information center has to ensure that the benefits of providing such fee-based services do not reduce any services to its primary clientele.

Sometimes, rather than working in a special library, a librarian or information specialist may prefer to use these problem-solving skills to become an information broker. An information broker is an independent or freelance librarian or firm who will search out and provide information on a profit-making basis. The information broker provides services ranging from searches of computerized databases to translations to market surveys. An information broker's clients may include corporations and individuals who do not have access to information centers. Or, the clients may be libraries or information centers that need specific information outside the realm of their collections. The information brokers' ability to specialize and produce results in a short span of time has made them invaluable resources for libraries and information centers.

Summary

Although those in the library business categorize all libraries into four groups, (i.e., public, school, academic, and special), many libraries of the almost 130,000 libraries have properties of more than one of these types. Approximately half a million library staff members each attempt to serve the unique needs of the community or the organization of which they are a part.

Public libraries serve all citizens at every stage of life, whether they live in a large city or in the most remote rural area. Public libraries have developed collections, programs, and services to help them fulfill their principle of service to all. Each library examines its community to identify and provide programs and services that are coordinated with other community agencies and services. In this process, each library's success in meeting its own community's needs will always be significantly affected by prevailing economic and political conditions at the local, state, and national levels.

School libraries play an important role in helping students learn. To emphasize that all forms of media are used to help students learn both inside the classroom and beyond, many school libraries have changed their names from libraries to instructional materials centers or media centers. Similarly, school librarians and audiovisual specialists have taken the titles of media specialists and are supported by media technicians and clerks. As librarians become more involved in curriculum development and are assisted in daily operations by well-trained support staff, evidence is growing that good school libraries make a significant difference in student achievement levels.

Academic libraries have grown and evolved over the years to meet the changing educational objectives of their parent institutions. Along with school libraries, they have put increasing emphasis on building information literacy by teaching students how to find and evaluate information. Collections have been expanded to include all media, and library services have become more student-oriented. Computer technology has expanded library resources and services and has placed additional strain on budgets. Academic libraries have joined networks with other libraries to acquire, preserve, and share their resources.

Special libraries and information centers provide services in a narrowly defined subject area or in a specialized format for a homogeneous clientele. They are more varied and distinct than any other type of library. Special libraries often have extensive information collections as well as extensive staff and services to support the research needs of their parent organizations. Staff members go further than in other types of libraries to anticipate, locate, and even synthesize the information needed by other members of the organization.

All libraries exist to meet the objectives of their parent institutions or their communities. Their fortunes mirror the economic health of those institutions and communities. The libraries that thrive are those that convince the leaders of their institutions and communities that they actively facilitate achieving the goal of the larger body.

Library Visits

Document your visits to at least four libraries. They should be libraries of the type you think you might like to work in some day. At a minimum, collect the information needed to answer the following questions:

1. What are the complete name, address, telephone number, and Web site address (uniform resource locator or URL) of the library?

2. How easy is it to find the library?

3. How easy is it to find parking nearby?

4. How readily available is public transportation?

5. How is the primary clientele to be served defined? What special information needs do they have?

6. Is the library open to the public? If so, on what basis?

7. How many clients are eligible for service?

8. How many clients are served?

9. What is the budget of the library?

10. To which governing body or to which official does the head of the library report?

11. What special services are offered to clientele?

12. What hours is the library open?

13. Describe the nature, size, and scope of collection.

14. What is the nature and size of the staff?

15. What staff did you observe? What impression did you get of the staff? Were they businesslike, courteous, sloppy, friendly?

16. What technology is used?

17. What is the size and adequacy of the physical facilities?

18. Describe the adequacy and attractiveness of staff work areas.

19. When you first enter the library, stop and look around. Is it obvious without consulting the staff where the following are located:

    the circulation/reserve desk?

    the reference/information desk?

    the library catalog?

    the periodical indexes?

    the Internet terminals?

    the periodicals?

    the restrooms?

    the copiers?

    the elevators and stairs (if the library has more than one level)?

    the pay telephones?

    the water fountain?

20. What kind, number, and variety of seating is there for library users?

21. What most impressed you about this library?

22. What most concerned you about this library?

23. Would you feel comfortable using this library in the future?

24. Do you think you would like to work here? Itemize both to plusses and minuses.

Study Questions

Public Libraries

1. Identify the roles of library service that a public library might select.

2. Identify some of the major services libraries provide to fulfill these roles.

3. State the underlying philosophy of library service for public libraries as presented in the PLA planning documents.

4. Identify the levels of input and output measures recommended by the state library agency for the state in which you live.

5. Visit a public library you have not visited before. Compare the objectives. Are services of this library aligned with those discussed

in the text? Also, compare the library's input and output measures in question number 4 with the staff, collections, and so forth.

School Libraries

1. Identify the major objectives of school library media center programs.

2. Briefly describe school library media development from the classroom library to school library to library media center.

3. Discuss the differences in philosophy between the 1966 and 1974 national school library standards.

4. Compare your own state's standards with the guidelines of *Information Power.*

5. Identify the kinds of media that can be found in a school library media center.

6. Describe some services and programs provided in successful library media programs.

7. Identify duties of the different levels of staff in the modern library media center.

8. Visit a school library media center and compare its objectives, staff, collection, and services with those described in this chapter.

Academic Libraries

1. Define an academic library and describe some of the major types of academic libraries.

2. What are the main objectives of an academic library?

3. Describe the changes in academic libraries from library to learning resource center.

4. What are some of the major services academic libraries provide?

5. What are some of the changes brought about in staff development by the installation of automated library services?

6. List some examples of cooperative academic library resource-sharing and networking programs.

7. Visit a local academic institution and compare it with the objectives and services discussed in this chapter and the standards identified for that type of library.

8. Visit two types of academic institutions, such as a community college and a four-year college or university, to compare and contrast their libraries.

Special Libraries

1. Identify the major objectives of special libraries and information centers.

2. Describe the relationship of a special library or information center to its parent institution.

3. Describe the scope and services of the three U.S. national libraries.

4. Describe the kinds of materials usually included in corporate libraries and information center collections.

5. List 10 examples of special libraries or information centers.

6. Visit one or two special libraries or information centers and compare their objectives, services, and collections to those discussed in this chapter.

Resources

Public Libraries

Future of the Public Library. Conference proceedings of OCLC Online Computer Library Center, Dublin, OH, March 20–22, 1988.

Giacoma, Pete. *The Fee or Free Decision: Legal, Economic, Political and Ethical Perspectives for Public Libraries.* New York: Neal-Schuman, 1989.

Ihrig, Alice B. *Decision-Making for Public Libraries.* Hamden, CT: Shoe String, 1989.

Mayo, Diane. *Wired for the Future: Developing Your Library Technology Plan.* Chicago: American Library Association, 1999.

McClure, Charles R., et al. *Planning and Role-Setting for Public Libraries. A Manual of Options and Procedures.* Chicago: American Library Association, 1987.

Nelson, Sandra S. *The New Planning for Results: A Streamlined Approach.* Chicago: American Library Association, 2001.

Nelson, Sandra S., Ellen Altman, and Diane Mayo. *Managing for Results: Effective Resource Allocation for Public Libraries.* Chicago: American Library Association, 2000.

Palmour, Vernon E. *A Planning Process for Public Libraries.* Chicago: American Library Association, 1980.

Public Library Association. *Minimum Standards for Public Library Systems, 1966.* Chicago: American Library Association, 1967.

Public Library Mission Statement and Its Imperatives for Service. Chicago: American Library Association, 1979.

Sager, Donald J. *Managing the Public Library.* 2d ed. Boston: G. K. Hall, 1989.

Shuman, Bruce A. *Beyond the Library of the Future: More Alternative Futures for the Public Library.* Englewood, CO: Libraries Unlimited, 1997.

Van Horn, Nancy, et al. *Output Measures for Public Libraries: A Manual for Standardized Procedures.* 2d ed. Chicago: American Library Association, 1987.

Webb, T. D. *Public Library Organization and Structure.* Jefferson, NC: McFarland, 1989.

School Libraries

AASL. *Realization: The Final Report of the Knapp School Libraries Project.* Edited by Peggy Sullivan. Chicago: American Library Association, 1968.

AASL/AECT. *Standards for School Media Centers.* Chicago: American Library Association, 1969.

———. *Media Programs: District and School.* Chicago: American Library Association, 1975.

———. *Information Power: Guidelines for School Library Media Programs.* Chicago: American Library Association, 1988.

ALA Yearbook: A Review of Library Events. Chicago: American Library Association, 1976–2001.

Haycock, Ken, ed. *Foundations for Effective School Library Media Programs.* Englewood, CO: Libraries Unlimited, 1999.

Kulleseid, Eleanor R. *Beyond Survival to Power: For School Library Media Professionals.* Hamden, CT: Library Professional Publications, 1985.

Lance, Keith Curry, Marcia J. Rodney, and Christine Hamilton-Pennell. *How School Librarians Help Kids Achieve Standards: The Second Colorado Study.* San Jose, CA: Hi Willow Research & Publishing, 2000.

Liesener, James W. "Information Power: A Broader Perspective." In *School Library Media Annual, 1989.* Englewood, CO: Libraries Unlimited, 1989.

Loertscher, David V. "Dave's List of Professional Materials for School Library Media Specialists Jan. 97+." Available: http://www.lmcsource.com/davepro.html (Accessed December 6, 2001).

Loertscher, David V., May Lein Ho, and Melvin M. Bowie. "Exemplary Elementary Schools and Their Library Media Centers: A Research Report." *School Library Media Quarterly* 15 (Spring 1987): 147–53.

Parsons, Larry A., comp. *A Funny Thing Happened on the Way to the School Library: A Treasury of Anecdotes, Quotes, and Other Happenings*. Englewood, CO: Libraries Unlimited, 1990.

Prostano, Emanuel T., and Joyce S. Prostano. *The school library media center.* 5th ed. Englewood, CO: Libraries Unlimited, 1999.

"School Libraries in the '90s." *Illinois Libraries* 72 (7): 1990.

School Library Media Annual. Littleton, CO: Libraries Unlimited, 1983–2001.

Standards for School Library Programs. Chicago: American Library Association, 1960.

Woolls, Blanche. *The School Library Media Manager.* 2d ed. Englewood, CO: Libraries Unlimited, 1999.

Academic Libraries

Association of College and Research Libraries. "The Mission of a University Undergraduate Library: Model Statement." *C&RL News* (October 1987): 542–44.

———. "Standards for University Libraries: Evaluation of Performance." *C&RL News* (September 1989): 679–91.

———. *Standards for Community, Junior, and Technical College Learning Resource Programs, 1994.* Available: http://www.ala.org/acrl/guides/jrcoll.html (Accessed December 6, 2001).

———. *Guidelines for Media Resources in Academic Libraries.* Available: http://www.ala.org/acrl/guides/medresg.html (Accessed December 6, 2001).

———. *Standards for College Libraries 2000 Edition.* Available: http://www.ala.org/acrl/guides/college.html (Accessed December 6, 2001).

Breivik, Patricia Senn, and E. Gordon Gee. *Information Literacy: Revolution in the Library.* New York: American Council on Education, 1989.

Breivik, Patricia Senn, and Robert Wedgeworth. *Libraries and the Search for Academic Excellence.* Metuchen, NJ: Scarecrow, 1988.

Budd, John. *The Academic Library: Its Context, Its Purpose, and Its Operation.* Englewood, CO: Libraries Unlimited, 1998.

Lynch, Beverly P., ed. *The Academic Library in Transition: Planning for the 90's.* New York: Neal-Schuman, 1989.

McCabe, Gerard B., and Ruth J. Person, eds. *Academic Libraries: Their Rationale and Role in American Higher Education.* Westport, CT: Greenwood Press, 1995.

Spyers-Duran, Peter, and Thomas W. Mann, Jr., eds. *Issues in Academic Librarianship: Views and Case Studies for the 1980s and 1990s.* Westport, CT: Greenwood Press, 1985.

Van House, Nancy A., Beth Weil, and Charles R. McClure. *Measuring Academic Library Performance: A Practical Approach.* Chicago: American Library Association, 1990.

Veaner, Allen B. *Academic Librarianship in a Transformational Age: Programs, Politics and Personnel.* Boston: G. K. Hall, 1990.

Special Libraries

American Library Association. *The ALA Yearbook of Library and Information Services: A Review of Library Events.* Chicago: American Library Association, 1976–2001.

Bierbaum, Esther Green. *Museum Librarianship.* 2d ed. Jefferson, NC: McFarland, 2000.

Bulletin of the Medical Library Association. Chicago: Medical Library Association, 1911–2001.

Journal of the Medical Library Association. Chicago: Medical Library Association, 2002.

Larsen, John C., ed. *Museum Librarianship.* Hamden, CT: Shoe String, 1985.

Larsgaard, Mary Lynette. *Map Librarianship: An Introduction.* 3d ed. Englewood, CO: Libraries Unlimited, 1998.

Medical Library Association. *The Medical Library Association Guide to Managing Health Care Libraries.* Edited by Ruth Holst, Sharon A. Phillips, and Karen McNally Bensing. Chicago: 2000.

Porter, Cathy A., et al. *Special Libraries: A Guide for Management.* 4th ed. Washington, DC: Special Libraries Association, 1997.

Russell, Keith W., and Maria G. Piza, eds. "Agricultural Libraries and Information." *Library Trends* 38, no. 3 (1990): 327–38.

Special Libraries. Washington, DC: Special Libraries Association, 1910–2001.

Strauss, Lucille J., et al. *Scientific and Technical Libraries: Their Organization and Administration.* 3d ed. Melbourne, FL: Krieger, 1991.

White, Herbert S. *Managing the Special Library: Strategies for Success Within the Larger Organization.* Boston: G. K. Hall, 1984.

Notes

1. "How Many Libraries Are There in the United States?" *LARC Fact Sheet* Number 1, January 2001. Available: http://www.ala.org/library/fact1.html (Accessed March 26, 2001).

2. "How Many People Work in Libraries?" *LARC Fact Sheet* Number 2, October 2000. Available: http://www.ala.org/library/fact2.html (Accessed March 26, 2001).

3. Public Library Association. *Minimum Standards for Public Library Systems, 1966.* Chicago: American Library Association, 1967.

4. Vernon E. Palmour, Marcia C. Bellassai, and Nancy V. DeWath. *A Planning Process for Public Libraries.* Chicago: American Library Association, 1980.

5. Nancy A. Van House, et al. *Output Measures for Public Libraries: A Manual of Standardized Procedures.* 2d ed. Chicago: American Library Association, 1987.

6. Glenn R. Wittig. "Some Characteristics of Mississippi Adult Library Users," *Public Libraries* 30, no. 1 (1991): 30.

7. "The E-Rate." *ALA Fact Sheet,* November 1998. Available: http://www.ala.org /pio/factsheets/erate.html (Accessed March 30, 2001).

8. Ibid.

9. Ibid.

10. "Gates Library Foundation Releases Grant Guidelines." ALA Press Release, October 28, 1997. Available: http://www.ala.org/news/gatesgrants.html (Accessed March 30, 2001).

11. "Public Library Use." *LARC Fact Sheet* Number 6. Available: http://www.ala.org /library/fact6.html (Accessed March 26, 2001).

12. Ibid.

13. Bruce A. Shuman. *The Library of the Future: Alternative Scenarios for the Information Profession.* Englewood, CO: Libraries Unlimited, 1989, 116.

14. Jean Key Gates. *Introduction to Librarianship.* New York: McGraw-Hill, 1968, 220–21.

15.   United States National Commission on Excellence in Education. *A Nation at Risk: The Imperative for Educational Reform: A Report to the Nation and the Secretary of Education, United States Department of Education.* Washington, DC: The Commission, 1983.

16.   *Alliance for Excellence: Librarians Respond to a Nation at Risk: Recommendations and Strategies from Libraries and the Learning Society.* Washington, DC: U.S. Department of Education, Office of Educational Research and Improvement, Center for Libraries and Education Improvement, 1984.

17.   American Library Association. Committee on Post-War Planning. *School Libraries for Today and Tomorrow: A Statement of Standards Prepared by the Committee on Postwar Planning of the American Library Association, Division of Libraries for Children and Young People and its School Libraries Section.* Chicago: American Library Association, 1944.

18.   American Association of School Librarians. *Standards for School Library Programs.* Chicago: American Library Association, 1960.

19.   Joint Committee of the American Association of School Librarians and the Department of Audiovisual Instruction of the National Education Association. *Standards for School and Media Programs.* Chicago: American Library Association, 1969.

20.   American Association of School Librarians. *Media Programs: District and School.* Chicago: American Library Association, 1975.

21.   American Association of School Librarians and Association for Educational Communications and Technology. *Information Power: Guidelines for School Library Media Programs.* Chicago: American Library Association, 1988.

22.   Bradford William Chaney. *School Library Media Centers, 1993-94.* Washington, DC: U.S. Dept. of Education, Office of Educational Research and Improvement, 1998, A-130.

23.   "Librarians, Teachers & Librarian/Teacher Ratio in U.S. Public Schools: State Variations & Trends, 1989–95. *Fast Facts: Recent Statistics for the Library Research Service.* (April 8, 1999, ED3/110.10/No. 159). Available: http://www.lrs.org/documents /fastfacts/159lmctrends.pdf (Accessed December 6, 2001).

24.   Lucille Mathena Wert. *Library Education and the High School Library Services.* Ann Arbor, MI: University Microfilms, 1970.

25.   Kathleen Kennedy Manzo. "Study Shows Rise in Test Scores Tied to School Library Resources," *Education Week on the Web,* 22 March 2000. Available: http://www .educationweek.org/ew/ewstory.cfm?slug=28libe.h19 (Accessed April 1, 2001).

26.   Keith Curry Lance, et al. *How School Librarians Help Kids Achieve Standards: The Second Colorado Study.* Denver: Colorado Department of Education, 2000, 5.

27.   Ibid.

28.   "The Carnegie Classification of Institutions of Higher Education." *The Carnegie Foundation for the Advancement of Teaching,* 2000. Available: http://www .carnegiefoundation.org/Classification/index.htm (Accessed April 5, 2001).

29.   Association of College and Research Libraries. "Standards for Community, Junior, and Technical College Learning Resource Programs," July 1994. Available: http://www.ala.org/acrl/guides/jrcoll.html (Accessed December 6, 2001).

30.   Ibid. "Standards for College Libraries 2000 Edition," January 2000. Available: http://www.ala.org/acrl/guides/college.html (Accessed December 6, 2001).

31.   Ibid. "Standards for University Libraries: Evaluation of Performance," February 1989. Available: http://www.ala.org/acrl/guides/univer.html (Accessed December 6, 2001).

32.   Patricia Senn Breivik and Robert Wedgeworth. *Libraries and the Search for Academic Excellence*. Metuchen, NJ: Scarecrow, 1988, 29–32.

33.   Ibid. 7–8.

34.   Ibid. 13–24.

35.   Richard DeGennaro. Foreword to Allen B. Veaner, *Academic Librarianship in a Transformational Age: Programs, Politics and Personnel*. Boston: G. K. Hall, 1990, xiii.

36.   American Library Association. "How Many Libraries Are There in the United States?" *LARC Fact Sheet* Number 1, January 2001. Available: http://www.ala.org/library/fact1.html (Accessed December 6, 2001).

37.   Library of Congress. "About the Collections." Available: http://www.loc.gov/rr/collects.html (Accessed December 6, 2001).

38.   Ibid. "American Memory: Historical Collections for the National Digital Library." Available: http://memory.loc.gov (Accessed December 6, 2001).

39.   National Library of Medicine. *PubMed*. Available: http://www.ncbi.nlm.nih.gov/PubMed/ (Accessed December 6, 2001).

Chapter 4

Library Collections

When it comes to assessing the quality and resources of a library or information center, one of the major aspects to consider is the facility's collection of materials. Today, that no longer means just what a library physically owns, but, increasingly, what they provide access to, regardless of the format. Collections now consist of hard-copy books, magazines, newspapers, videos, CDs, CD-ROMs, and DVDs, along with free and subscription-based documents, periodicals, images, and multimedia that are available electronically to patrons of that library. New formats of information packaging are emerging regularly to add to the list.

Yet, regardless of the delivery format, library collections are acquired, cataloged, processed, and supplied to customers based on well thought-out collection development policies, user profiles, and organizational principles. This often comes as a surprise to patrons. Unlike the highly visible services of the Reference and Circulation departments, the selection, purchasing, cataloging, and processing of items does not usually involve the public directly but rather takes place behind the scenes. Typically, the division where these activities take place is called the Technical Services Department.

It is probably fair to say that the development of library collections is one of the least understood aspects of library work to outsiders. When one of the authors worked in an urban public library, a patron was quite upset when she discovered that a particular new title was not in the collection. "Why don't you have it?" she complained. "I thought publishers sent libraries free samples of all the new books." False!

User Needs

Every library has its own distinct set of user needs that influence the development of its collection. As the staff endeavors to make a collection as responsive as possible to those information needs, they turn to direct patron input (e.g., surveys, suggestion boxes, requests), demographics of their client base, staff observations, and usage patterns. Publishing trends, new product releases, and current events are also factors to be considered as the library's staff attempt to meet ongoing needs and anticipate future demands.

Advisory committees or library boards may also contribute their input to collections. Of course, the library or information center's budgetary resources will also greatly impact overall purchasing decisions.

The end result is that no individual library or information center collection is alike. And their primary users wouldn't want them to be. For example, academic library collections will typically reflect the curriculum offered. Thus, a polytechnic university with large science, engineering, and architecture departments can be expected to have significant library holdings in those areas, as well as a broad-based collection supporting lower division, general education classes. A local public library will offer a wide range of popular materials on business topics, recreational reading, consumer information, regional history, and local government issues suited to its users' demographics. An art museum research library can be expected to collect overview information on art history and material on the museum's specific art holdings, periods, and artists, as well as data on interpretation, preservation, and curatorial techniques.

A Glut of Information

For years we have been hearing of the information explosion that surrounds us, and there is no sign of it letting up anytime soon. And although computer technology has made great inroads (especially in the library field) in the storage and retrieval of massive quantities of information, there does not seem to be any reduction in the volume of data, but, rather, the contrary. An often cited statistic from early 2000 estimated the size of the Web in 1999 to be 1.5 billion Web pages with a growth rate that doubles every year.[1] As of late 2001, the google.com search engine site claimed to search more than 2 billion pages with each query it received.[2] Any way you try to measure it, the exponential growth of the WWW only adds to the information glut that already engulfs us.

As for books, "the United States remains the number one book producing nation in the English-speaking world," according to the yearly industry analysis provided in the *Bowker Annual*, and the current trend supports only a small decline in the overall output of titles.[3] It does seem rather overwhelming. How will a researcher ever find the Web site, book, article, or item of data that he or she needs? How will an information specialist know which quality products to add to his or her information center?

Selection Tools

Although there are no comprehensive magic lists, librarians rely on industry tools, along with direct user input and their own professional judgment, to make selection and purchasing decisions. These selection tools include reviewing media, core collection lists or bibliographies, and industry listservs.

Review Media

Critical or evaluative reviews of books, as well as those of magazines, videos, CD-ROMs, DVDs, and audio CDs, are published by many sources for the retail trade and for the library business. Such reviews help library professionals decide on relevance and quality before making a purchase. Because it would be impossible to preview, read, or listen to each individual item under consideration, perusing reputable review media is a time-saver. Bear in mind that there are many items in print and multimedia that are never reviewed. Whether a favorable review, poor review, or no review, the decision is still up to the library's selector.

Listed below are some of the established reviewing sources for books and other media.

Major reviewing media for adult titles

Booklist

Choice

Kirkus Reviews

Library Journal

New York Times Book Review

Publishers Weekly

Science Books & Films

Major reviewing media for children's titles

Hornbook

School Library Journal

Besides being well respected, these publications devote the bulk of their space to reviews, each covering thousands of releases annually. Many other specialized and nontraditional periodicals with critical reviews exist as well, although the numbers of reviews included will be much smaller. For most titles listed, the current trend is for the reviews to be available in the print periodical version, available by paid subscription. Free Web companions offer news releases but not the reviews. For some weekly newspapers, such as the *New York Times*, Web access to a searchable archive of its book reviews is free for a limited time period. No doubt policies and access will continue to change as electronic distribution and subscription models evolve. In addition, many online booksellers post in-house editorial comments, clips from critical reviews, and reader opinions free of charge on their Web sites.

Core Collection Lists

Vendors, library trade associations, and publishers produce core collection lists or bibliographies. They serve as a starting point for establishing an opening-day collection or for updating an existing one. Such lists may or may not be annotated or contain reviews. However, inclusion in such a list is usually an implied recommendation. The following are just a few representative core lists—there are many more available. Full citations are listed in the resources section near the end of this chapter.

Periodicals

   Magazines for Libraries

Reference collections

   Recommended Reference Books for Small and Medium-Sized Libraries and Media Centers

   Guide to Reference Materials for School Library Media Centers

Children's collections

   Best Books for Children: Preschool Through Grade 6

   Best Books for Young Adult Readers

   Best Books for Young Teen Readers

Medical libraries

   Selected List of Books and Journals for the Small Medical Library

Academic libraries

   Choice's Outstanding Academic Books, 1992–1997

Industry Listservs

Listservs or electronic discussion groups that focus on a particular type of library or information center can be helpful because they often include reviews by group members as a regular feature of their postings. These are best used as an augmentation to perusing the major reviewing media because the quantity of items covered is very limited on listservs. Listserv reviews can be a good source for discovering publications by small publishers, specialty items, or items written by colleagues in the field.

Who Selects?

Responsibility for the selection process will vary considerably depending on the size of a library or information center and the number of professional librarians on staff. Large university and research libraries with collections numbering in the millions of items will have many subject specialists, resource coordinators, or bibliographers who are expert in their field. Each librarian specialist has responsibility for the selection of materials within their area of expertise; for example, French language and literature, environmental sciences, architecture and city planning, American literature, and so forth.

For smaller libraries, areas of responsibility are usually delineated among staffers. In a medium-sized public library, selection assignments might be divided up as follows: children's materials, young adult materials, current fiction, general reference, business reference, medical reference, local history, art and architecture, and so on. Sometimes staff assignments are based on classification system divisions (e.g., 000s, 100s, and so on for collections using the Dewey Decimal scheme). Branch librarians may have direct responsibility for building their own collections, or they may work with a centralized system-wide selection team.

For the solo librarian or technician operating a small special library independently, selection is just one of the many tasks to be juggled.

Collection Development Policies

Most well-run libraries and information centers have a written statement that articulates their vision and their policies for developing their collection. Two terms in frequent use for this statement are *materials selection policy* and *collection development policy*. Although sometimes used interchangeably, they are different. University of Oregon Acquisitions Librarian, Richard Brumley, puts it succinctly:

A materials selection policy is much more limited: [It discusses] what criteria are used in purchasing (or accepting gift) books, journals, CDs, videos, etc., for a library. A collection development policy is much broader: in addition to criteria for selecting materials, it will include such things as collection assessment, weeding criteria, preservation and conservation, balance of monographs to serials, switching formats (print to CD to Web), liaison to academic departments, serials cancellation projects, etc. One is more apt to use the term *collection development policy* in academic libraries or large research libraries, while the term *materials selection policy* has a greater public library connotation.[4]

Written Selection Policies

Why do we need material selection or collection development policies in our libraries and media and information centers? Having a written selection policy has many advantages, including the following:

It formalizes a plan for selecting materials. By drafting a document, library staff are forced to plan ahead and to think critically about their selection procedure. What are the library's collection goals? What does the library intend to acquire? By making the policy statement formal, the staff is guided in making selection decisions and discouraged from making frivolous purchases. A written policy is taken more seriously than an informal, verbal one. It also gives the agency a starting point for continuous review and revision. As with any effective policy, periodic updating is needed.

It provides a chance to draft a new mission statement for the library or revisit an existing one. In the past, many library agencies placed most of their efforts into the routines of day-to-day operations, such as assisting patrons, stocking and restocking materials, essentially keeping the "store" open. Long-term planning efforts were minimal or overlooked. A written document forces staff to identify or draft a mission statement, which is a vital first step in the planning process. Whether beginning the design for a new facility or updating a policy for an existing library, a mission statement provides a focal point for ensuing discussion and reflection. To begin with, review of the parent agency's mission statement will be necessary. From that, the drafting of the library's own mission statement evolves. This can be a thought-provoking exercise that leads staff to discuss the purpose of the organization, its clientele, its objectives, and other visionary and organizational concepts.

It prioritizes areas for purchase. As discussed previously, both materials selection and collection development policies describe priority areas for purchase as well as delineate limitations or types of material not collected. For example, public libraries may indicate that they do not collect comic books, textbooks, or workbooks, considering these consumable items best purchased by patrons for their individual use. Smaller college libraries may indicate that they purchase materials related only to class offerings. A corporate information center may decline to purchase fiction or popular bestsellers, focusing instead on technical, work-related materials.

It establishes responsibility. A written policy usually spells out which staff positions are charged with selection and also who has the final responsibility for what is on the library's shelves, network, or Web site. For schools and other publicly accessible libraries, it should also delineate who has the authority to approve or deny removal of a challenged title.

It becomes official policy. A formal policy statement may need to be reviewed by a governing board or council. This process allows for input and review from other employees or the library's constituents. In the best case, this process helps build support and understanding of the library's role at all levels.

It protects library and staff in cases of complaint or controversy. When a complaint arises and a citizen, parent, or patron questions the appropriateness of an item in the collection, a written policy gives the library or information center credibility. With an approved plan in hand, staff can respond that the purchase meets the selection criteria, is an award-winning book or resource, has received positive reviews, is age appropriate, and so on. A thorough policy should set out specific requirements for the process of challenging an item for removal from the collection.

Criteria for Selection

As part of their written collection development policy, many libraries will delineate specific criteria that they look for when considering materials for purchase. These criteria should also be applied to donations that are accepted for the collection as well as to items culled during discarding. Some commonly used criteria include the following:

1. *Topic:* Is this a subject area that the library collection focuses on?

2. *Reading level:* Is the level appropriate for the library's clientele?

3. *Currency:* Is the information up-to-date and timely?

4. *Demand:* Is much demand anticipated for the topic or for the author; is it tied in with other media?

5. *Cost:* How does the price compare with other similar items? *Bowker Annual Almanac* tracks average pricing in many categories.

6. *Author's credentials:* Does the author seem to be credible and knowledgeable on the topic?

7. *Publisher or producer's reputation:* Is the publisher a small, specialty, or vanity press or a major publishing house; what other titles have they produced?

8. *Features:* Does it have "extras": for example, an index, bibliographies, special appendices, a CD-ROM, companion Web site, and so forth?

9. *Resource sharing:* Will other local libraries purchase it?

10. *Available in other media:* Which version is the most appropriate: print, multimedia, electronic?

Censorship

No treatment of libraries and information centers in the United States would be complete without a discussion of censorship and the concept of the freedom to read. Guaranteed by the First Amendment of the Constitution, the right to free speech and expression has been broadly supported by library trade associations, the publishing industry, retail bookstores, and by many individual librarians. For staff this has meant discouraging censorship, advocating patrons' freedom to read or view materials, stocking a diversity of information from different viewpoints in a library collection, refraining from limiting library materials because of personal beliefs, and remaining neutral when providing access to information.

The ALA devised its *Library Bill of Rights* (see Appendix B) in 1948 to interpret library services in light of the First Amendment. Within ALA, its high-profile Office for Intellectual Freedom is charged with educating librarians and the public about the importance of freedom of expression. Their Web site is an excellent source of information on the office's activities and on the promotion of free access to libraries and library materials. Other groups also advocate an individual's right to view or read; for example, the American Film and Video Association's "Freedom to View" statement supports the access rights of minors and adults to multimedia materials. Such statements share the belief that it is the right of each individual to make his or her own decision regarding what to read or view. In the case of minors, these policies explicitly state that it is the responsibility of a parent to supervise and monitor children's choices. Many library agencies and information centers have incorporated these concepts into their own policies.

In practice, academic and research libraries and corporate information centers are more realistically able to support full access and to take an uncompromising anti-censorship stance because their clientele is adult. Those in public and school libraries regulate access to controversial materials and have long been creative in their strategies: from locking bookcases, to requiring parental permission slips for access, to avoiding the purchase of controversial books or videos. In some schools, sensitive materials may be housed as special reading and require a counselor's or teacher's referral for access.

What Is Censorship?

What, then, is censorship? A broad definition is *the practice of suppressing or deleting material considered to be objectionable.* As it most often applies to public or school libraries, censorship is the act of removing titles from the library collection. Typically, books are challenged because they have been selected as required school reading for a certain class or grade level. Parents or other interested parties will often protest the choice as objectionable and seek to have it removed from the reading list, and, perhaps, also from the library.

Classics, dictionaries, contemporary novels, nonfiction works, picture books (the familiar as well as the lesser known) all show up on the list of titles banned, removed, or challenged. John Steinbeck's *Of Mice and Men;* Maya Angelou's autobiographical, *I Know Why the Caged Bird Sings;* many of Judy Blume's teen novels; the *American Heritage Dictionary;* and Mark Twain's *Adventures of Huckleberry Finn* are perennial targets for removal. See *Banned in the USA* by Herbert Foerstel listed in the resources section for a detailed treatment of this heated topic.

Challenging books generates a hotbed of controversy and media coverage for public and school libraries, with much debate ensuing on both sides of the issue. Ironically, challenging books also stirs up much interest and curiosity about the item in question, which frequently results in increased readership of a controversial title. In the challenge process, library staff are called upon to justify their criteria for having purchased the title, and this often translates into submitting their selection policy to public scrutiny. Most savvy library and school administrators will have in place a detailed process to be followed in consideration of the withdrawal of a title. Based on a Supreme Court ruling, the formula for determining obscenity is to measure an item against the community standards of each specific locality. In other words, each local area sets its own standard for considering items objectionable or appropriate based on the collective opinion of the citizens of the community. This can be a rather imprecise measure for settling a challenge case.

Another twist on censorship that doesn't draw media attention but is all too familiar to library staff is the stealthy actions of individual patrons to censor materials they deem offensive. Some library customers take it upon themselves to remove these materials by ripping out the offending pages, mutilating pictures, or stealing the items in question.

Censorship Versus Selection

Naturally, the question arises: How does the selection philosophy and process that takes place in libraries differ from censorship? As discussed previously in this chapter, the selection process is based ideally on articulated criteria for purchasing the highest quality and most appropriate material for a given collection and is not used as a means to ban information.

Librarians and information managers have a professional responsibility to be inclusive, not exclusive, in their collection development and to refrain from withholding topics because of their own personal stance on an issue. At the other end of the acquisitions continuum, weeding also should not be seen as a means for removing controversial items. Ideally, libraries and information centers, as nonpartisan suppliers of information, should support in their holdings a wide range of ideas and viewpoints for their customers to access, leaving the customers to draw their own conclusions.

Selection policies might include prioritized categories for purchase or, conversely, areas that are omitted in the collection process. Although some might argue that this is censorship, the intent is to prioritize purchases based on established local needs because few libraries can afford to buy everything.

What About the Internet?

But now, the Internet comes along. This is a new medium for librarians to apply and test the freedom of access philosophy. And the quandary is that the old laws don't apply. The concept of selecting quality materials based on local criteria doesn't apply because the Web is not acquired piecemeal. It's an all or nothing acquisition. Official government sites, online retail stores, personal home pages and more abound, all with text, colorful images, photographs, sound, and video. It just happens that this same environment works equally well for distributing pornographic material as it does for federal tax forms. So although the Internet vastly expands the research sources available to patrons, it also introduces new problems.

The Internet knows no geographical boundaries per se, so the old rule of relying on community standards to determine what is offensive cannot be applied here. The federal government has been unable to successfully place limits on pornographic content on the Internet through the so-called decency act and other similarly intentioned bills.

Librarians are coping by implementing policies that discourage viewing of pornographic material, such as placing terminals in full view of staff, installing privacy shields on computer monitors, requiring parental signatures on consent forms, and posting acceptable use policies. School libraries often make use of filtering software to restrict access to predetermined pornographic sites and also to block searches using offensive keywords. Many public libraries fall back on their support of the freedom to read and view policies, warning all adult patrons that it is up to them to screen and monitor their children's use of the Internet just as they would with videos, CDs, books, and other materials.

As library staff would be the first to admit, this is straddling a difficult line—promoting access to information while dealing with concerns about pornographic viewing in a public place. But there is something very different about a patron peering at a full-color screen of pornographic images in plain view of children and others, as opposed to a solitary reader perusing an art book of nude figures while tucked away in a corner cubicle. The freedom to read and view has become an even more complex issue, with no easy answers.

Weeding

Mention weeding to most library staff and they will either groan or reply virtuously that they never have enough time to get to it. Although it is everyone's least favorite task, weeding or de-selecting is an essential aspect of maintaining a relevant, appealing, and timely collection of materials.

Weeding is defined as the evaluation of existing library holdings for possible replacement, repair, updating, or discarding. It is often carried out in conjunction with an inventory project, a move into new quarters, bar coding installation, or conversion to an automated system.

It's doubtful that any other library can rival the mission statement of the Library of Congress, which is "to sustain and preserve a universal collection of knowledge and creativity for future generations."[5] Nonetheless, even that venerable institution with more than 120 million items does not collect everything. Although many large research, academic, and special libraries do maintain serious, scholarly, historical collections of great breadth, all collections still need periodic, and often regular, weeding. Thoughtful de-selecting of obsolete, damaged, superseded, or otherwise inappropriate materials complements the care given to the selection of new materials at the beginning of the collection development process.

Another driving force behind the need to cull collections is shelving or storage limits. Floor and stack space are often at a premium; thus, it's not efficient to clutter costly space with unneeded materials. One of many advantages promised with the digital revolution in publishing is the potential savings in storage or display space of online editions.

The decision to transfer to a Web-based document, a CD-ROM, or other electronic version of a print title needs to be evaluated by each library or information center. The answer may differ depending upon clients' preferences and use, the facility's space needs, and cost considerations. A colleague's recent quandary over the possible discarding of the standard reference source nick-named the *Thom Cat* exemplifies the typical decisions facing librarians as they renew, purchase, or weed familiar sources each year. A multi-volume source very familiar to many public, academic, and corporate libraries, the *Thomas Register of American Manufacturers,* has been published since 1906. The 33 oversized, green volumes offer a comprehensive directory of firms that manufacture anything from thermostats to buttons to toner cartridges. The alphabetical listing reads just like the telephone book's Yellow Pages, and two other companion listings include trademark information and excerpts from actual vendor catalogs of selected manufacturing companies. The retail price for a hardcopy set in 1998 was about $240, whereas access to the Web version was absolutely free. In terms of space, it takes an entire bay of shelving to house this heavy, outsized set.

Our colleague was pressed to consider discarding the print set and to instead rely solely on the Web version because her library had run out of space in their reference stacks. After weighing the options, soliciting input, and carefully reviewing the contents of each version, she reached her decision. For the time being, she decided to keep the print version because of its superior ease of use. Many patrons use the source to generate a list of vendors with telephone numbers and addresses. The online version—though attractive and well maintained—did not offer this ease of use and also had eliminated some of the cross-references found in the print set. When it comes time to purchase next year's *Thomas Register,* the decision will have to be reconsidered.

As with selection, the issues to consider in weeding are many. Cost, currency, physical or electronic storage space, ease of use, and customer preference are frequently critical considerations.

Changing Formats of Information

As we enter the new century, librarians and information specialists can be sure of one thing: the continued repackaging of information, often at a rapid and overwhelming pace. Other current trends include the continuing merger of large national and international publishers, an emphasis on convert-ing print reference titles to Web-based products, and reliance on the Web for subscriptions to full-text periodical databases. Electronic publishing of text-books and original book-length works is now in its infancy, but it promises to become a serious venture.

As publishing formats continue to morph, a problem faced by many libraries attempting to maintain in-depth research or historical back files is the inevitable gap between leasing temporary access and permanent owner-ship. "Renting" electronic access means that libraries no longer possess their own copies of books, periodicals, or other works. Rather, they are at the mercy of publishers who may or may not change their access policies or may begin charging additional fees for access to archives. For serious research and larger libraries, this uncertainty often means maintaining dual subscriptions—both print and electronic—to ensure access to the complete run of a periodical or reference title. Thus, collecting a comprehensive collection can be expensive.

Once touted as the cost-saving answer to the problem of mushrooming materials costs for libraries, electronic publishing does provide significant added value with the many conveniences and enhancements over print equivalents. But electronic reference products and services rarely provide cost savings over print versions. And the unspoken reality is that traditional allocations for book budgets keep shrinking as the funds are used to pay for electronic editions.

In an era of changing information formats that is at once both exciting and confusing, perhaps the touchstone for collection managers is to adhere to the old adage of "knowing the collection"—both hardcopy and virtual collections—while continuing to seek out the customers' changing needs.

Study Questions

1. Find a copy of the mission statement for your college library. Where did you find it published (e.g., Web site, college catalog, other)? Do you agree with the mission as stated? Why or why not?

2. Study the collection development policy for a library of your choice. Is it up-to-date? Does it specify guidelines for weeding as well as collecting new materials? Discuss the similarities and differences between these two processes. Does it include the process for handling challenges or requests for removal of materials?

3. Some libraries are posting their collection development policy on their Web sites. What are the pros and cons of publishing such a policy on the Web?

4. What is Banned Books Week? Who sponsors it and what is its purpose?

5. Are you aware of any recent attempt to challenge a book at your local public library? Describe the circumstances and the outcome.

Resources

Articles

Brandon, Alfred N., and Dorothy R. Hill. "Selected List of Books and Journals for the Small Medical Library." *Bulletin of the Medical Library Association* 85 (April 1997): 111+.

Miller, Greg. "Libraries Work to Address X-Rated Excursions Online." *Los Angeles Times* (15 January 1999).

Urschel, Donna. "The Desire to Acquire: Detailing the Library's Selective Acquisition Process." *LC Information Bulletin* (September 1997): 292–95.

Books

Bartlett, Rebecca Ann, ed. *Choice's Outstanding Academic Books, 1992–1997.* Chicago: American Library Association, 1998.

Calvert, Stephen J. *Best Books for Young Adult Readers.* New York: R. R. Bowker, 1997.

Foerstel, Herbert N. *Banned in the U.S.A.: A Reference Guide to Book Censorship in Schools and Public Libraries.* Westport, CT: Greenwood Press, 1994.

Gillespie, John T., ed. *Best Books for Children.* 7th ed. Westport, CT: Bowker-Greenwood, 2001.

Gillespie, John T., ed. *Best Books for Young Teen Readers: Grades 7–10.* New York: R. R. Bowker, 2000.

Katz, Bill, and Linda Sternberg Katz. *Magazines for Libraries: For the General Reader and School, Junior College, College, University, and Public Libraries.* 10th ed. New York: R. R. Bowker, 2000.

Safford, Barbara Ripp. *Guide to Reference Materials for School Library Media Centers.* 5th ed. Englewood, CO: Teacher Ideas Press, 1998.

Wynar, Bohdan, ed. *Recommended Reference Books for Small and Medium-Sized Libraries and Media Centers.* 21st ed. Englewood, CO: Libraries Unlimited, 2001.

Web Sites

- Library Resource Guide
  http://www.libraryresource.com
  (Accessed November 16, 2001)
     A paid advertising site operated by publisher R. R. Bowker. This Web site contains alphabetical and categorical listings for many supply companies, publishers, and industry vendors.

- *New York Times Book Review*
  http://www.nytimes.com/books/
  (Accessed November 20, 2001)
     Searchable, online, free full-text archive of the respected *New York Times Book Review* from 1996 to date.

- Office of Intellectual Freedom
  http://www.ala.org/alaorg/oif/
  (Accessed November 16, 2001)
      From ALA's Office of Intellectual Freedom. An extensive resource of updates, policies, and interpretations on the freedom to view and read as it affects libraries, librarians, and patrons.

Notes

1. David Lake. "The Web: Growing by 2 Million Pages a Day," *The Industry Standard. IDG Publications*, February 28, 2000. Available: http://www.thestandard.com/article /0,1902,12329,00.html (Accessed December 6, 2001).

2. *Google*. Available: http://www.google.com/ (Accessed December 17, 2001).

3. Dave Bogart, ed. *The Bowker Annual: Library and Book Trade Almanac,* 46th ed. New Providence, NJ: R. R. Bowker, 2001, 485.

4. Richard Brumley. E-mail to author, January 27, 1999.

5. Library of Congress. "Mission and Strategic Priorities of the Library of Congress, FY 1997–2004." *Mission and Strategic Priorities of the Library of Congress.* (Last updated January 20, 1996.) Available: http://www.lcweb.loc.gov/ndl/mission.html (Accessed April 26, 1999).

Chapter 5

Preparing Materials for Use

The careful selection of library items as described in the preceding chapter is just the first of multiple stages in the preparation of materials for use by customers. Further steps include acquisition, cataloging, classification, and physical processing of each requested item. Although every library develops its own routine for handling these operations, there are many shared activities and functions common to both the largest and smallest of collections.

Acquisition

Selection is the systematic process of choosing materials relevant to a library or information center, whereas acquisition is the nuts and bolts of procuring items and paying the publishing companies that produce the items. As with selection, acquisition is usually under the umbrella of Technical Services in a library and takes place out of the public's eye.

According to *Bowker Annual: Library and Book Trade Almanac*, in 1999 more than 119,000 book titles were produced in the United States alone.[1] These were the products of nearly 3,500 American book publishers.[2] The relationship of buyer and seller closely binds libraries and publishers together.

There are many types and sizes of publishers, with many now offering multimedia and electronic works in addition to the more traditional print titles. Most libraries and information centers select books and other publications from a multitude of publishers to fill their collection needs. Publishers vary by specialty, too. They include large corporate publishers owned by powerful media outlets; university presses, which produce more scholarly and esoteric titles of limited appeal; regional publishers specializing in a geographic area; children's publishing houses; and small or alternative presses, which produce limited print runs on a variety of material, including poetry, literature, health, religion, and other topics.

Reference book publishers closely target the library market and may include library professionals as editorial consultants to develop relevant and timely products. Trade publishers direct their products at a particular professional or industry group. Seasoned librarians develop name recognition of and an appreciation for many specific publishers as they purchase their materials over the years. This is helpful in the selection process because the reputation of the publisher can influence a decision on whether to buy an item.

As in the rest of the corporate world, mergers are occurring in the publishing industry, both nationally and internationally. This trend tends to make library professionals and others worry about the resulting tight control of what gets published and the quandary of having too few outlets to allow for varied voices and points of view. Additionally, the consolidation of multiple media under one roof; for example, print, TV, and online, as exemplified by the America Online and Time Warner merger, further narrows the information sources to which the public is exposed.

To gain an overview of the North American publishing industry, browse the annual reference work *Literary Market Place* (LMP). A comprehensive directory of the publishing industry, LMP is essential for locating and identifying information about publishers and ancillary services, such as jobbers, binders, and so forth, and includes a classified index to publishing houses by specialties.

Some publishing companies depend exclusively on regional sales personnel to market and sell their products. The sales representatives regularly call on libraries in their territory to promote and vend their title list. Many other publishers work either directly with libraries and retail outlets or through middlemen known as *jobbers* to sell their products.

The Services of a Jobber

The method most commonly used by libraries, media, and information centers for acquiring materials is the use of a jobber or wholesaler. These are industry middlemen who supply books, videos, CDs, DVDs, and other materials to retail stores and libraries from hundreds of individual publishers. Familiar industry names include Brodart, Baker and Taylor, Mook and Blanchard, Academic Books, Midwest, Blackwell, and many more. For library science students and novices to the library world, conferences and industry trade shows also provide good opportunities to visit jobbers' booths and find out about their many specialized services.

Jobbers pass on to libraries a discount from the publisher on the suggested retail or list price of an item. Typically, discounts range from a low of 5 percent to a high of 40 percent. Other services offered by wholesalers include customized processing and cataloging of materials, special heavy-duty bindings, MARC records on tape, catalog card sets, bar codes, and opening-day collections.

Although the majority of library purchases are handled through jobbers for convenience, efficiency, and cost savings, some small presses and specialty producers may require that an order be placed directly with them, thus bypassing jobbers. For libraries purchasing thousands of titles each year, relying on jobbers for the bulk of acquisitions is a necessity. Because direct orders are more time-consuming for the library staff to handle and track, these are typically kept to a minimum.

Most libraries work with a number of different wholesalers to acquire the variety of materials their collection demands. Just as there are general and specialty publishing firms, there are jobbers that handle mainstream current releases of print and nonprint titles and those that deal exclusively with medical or legal titles or only with periodical subscriptions. Thus, most libraries will have accounts with multiple wholesalers to procure all the materials they need. And even with various jobbers to choose from, there are occasions when a library or information center makes purchases from their community or online bookseller because of immediate need, exclusive distribution, or other considerations.

Order Plans

Many jobbers and individual publishers offer an acquisitions service known as an approval plan. When subscribing to an approval plan, the library submits a detailed profile of its selection criteria to the jobber, who then automatically ships materials matching the profile to the library. Items are still subject to approval by the acquisitions librarian or other designated staff. After review, undesirable items are then returned. The objectives are to save staff time in the selection and ordering processes for certain predictable subject areas, to be able to select with the book in hand, and to expedite the receipt of materials. Generally, approval plans work best for very large libraries, which are likely to purchase the majority of titles released by designated publishers anyway. If much more than 5 percent of the titles received on approval are being returned, then the library' profile needs to be adjusted.

Standing orders or continuation plans are another time-saver for libraries and good business for publishers or wholesalers. With a standing order contract, a library indicates that it will automatically purchase each new edition of a title; there is no need to be on the watch for an upcoming edition. Upon release, the publication is immediately supplied and the library is billed. Standing order status is most likely to be applied to standard reference works and sets, where a library is confident it wants each new edition of a must-have title.

Another service offered by some companies is the rental of books, as opposed to outright purchase. For example, the McNaughton Books service by Brodart, which allows libraries to lease a certain quantity of new releases, is a popular choice among public and university library facilities. The staff preselects titles from a monthly catalog of forthcoming titles. This provides a steady infusion of new titles that can either be returned when their popularity has waned or, if needed, purchased to add to the permanent library collection.

This service provides an effective solution for meeting the rush of interest that often accompanies the release of highly promoted titles and popular best-sellers. Multiple copies of such a title can be rented at a savings, and, because the service provides the books as shelf-ready, staff processing time is saved as well. Rental plans can then improve customer satisfaction while saving the staff time and money. Some libraries pass on the cost of such a program to patrons, charging daily rental fees for these books; others choose to absorb the cost and circulate them free of charge.

Many jobbers and vendors employ professional librarians on their staff to enhance their customer service and provide innovative ideas for products. As a job seeker, you may want to explore employment opportunities among the many industry wholesalers, product vendors, and supply companies.

Although a company sometimes may function both as a wholesaler of materials and a seller of library-specific supplies, there are many firms that vend only the unique equipment, furnishings, shelving, housing, security devices, and other supplies targeted for the library industry.

Leasing

Many business, financial, and marketing publications, such as telephone company crisscross directories and corporate directories, have long been available to library collections; not through outright purchase, but through a lease agreement. This keeps older, used copies from being retained or resold, thus allowing the publishers tighter control over the use of their valuable data and the final published product.

Licensing

As libraries' reliance on electronic sources of information, or e-collections, grows, so does negotiating the licensing agreement with the publisher, a standard part of the acquisitions process. Commonplace with personal computer software, then with CD-ROM products, and now with Web-delivered sources, licensing is a growing area of library responsibility. The procurement of online sources is most often handled directly with the company that produces the database, periodical index, full-text books, or other information product; jobbers or periodical subscription agents, so commonly used with book and hardcopy periodical purchasing, have not yet entered into this market. In some cases, where library consortia such as academic library systems have negotiated group purchase deals, an intermediary agency may serve as a bursar or third party in implementing the leases. This third-party arrangement gives libraries more leverage in bargaining with large corporations.

As in the leasing arrangements mentioned above, a license gives the library or information center access only; they do not purchase the product outright to have, to hold, to keep, to weed, and so on. Licenses are arranged for specific periods of time—typically on an annual basis, but also in multiple-year agreements. Access to the e-collection, once the license period is over, will vary, depending on the terms of the agreement. In some cases, if the contract is not renewed or paid, access to the e-collection vanishes overnight, with nothing to show for the library's past investments. Thus, the licensing concept is a very significant one for libraries, with access rather than ownership as a core issue.

Publishers use licensing as a legal means of controlling the use of their products. Thus, licensing agreements are legal contracts that bear scrutiny by the acquiring party, in this case, the library (licensee). Generally, the seller (or licensor) prepares the contract with the terms of the agreement. In many cases, individual libraries do not have a level negotiating position in dealing with large content providers. In this situation, libraries run the risk of giving up certain rights that they and their patrons would have enjoyed if the rights had been defined by copyright laws that allow for fair use, particularly in educational settings. Care should be taken to make sure that the library understands what it is being asked to agree to when it negotiates a license.

Fees are usually determined by the approximate number of users allowed access; for example, the number of employees in a corporation, the size of a school's student body, the current enrollment of a university, or the population served by a public library. A site license may include access for multiple offices, branches, or campuses affiliated with the main library agency, or the agreement may require additional site licenses to provide access to these other physical locations. In some agreements, a password allows users remote access from off-site, such as from home or from another location. In other cases, access is restricted to on-site computers only, based on a range of authenticated IP (Internet Protocol) addresses, which uniquely identify the computers in the licensee's library.

Although providing value-added service and an ever-increasing number of convenient options, typical licensed electronic products, such as indexing and abstracting services and full-text databases of journals, are not cheaper than their print equivalents. In fact, they often cost substantially more. In some cases, the publisher imposes restrictions or conditions along with the electronic access, such as requiring the licensee to maintain simultaneous print subscriptions to their products, although this practice appears to be waning.

Consortia Efforts

As statewide and regional library consortia in the United States mature, a high priority for them is seeking site licenses to make selected electronic resources available to their entire membership. These consortia may include libraries of similar size and type, such as an academic library group, or may be a regional, multi-type of network with everything from prison libraries to school media centers to museum research facilities and more. An example of the latter is the newly formed Library of California, which has received start-up funding from the state's legislature and is actively pursuing universal online database subscriptions for the state's 8,000 libraries. In Britain and other European countries, national site licensing is being piloted for all the university and polytechnic libraries of an entire country. This means that all current students and all faculty members have access to certain products in electronic form.[3] For such library groups or consortia, negotiated contract rates for library regions, university systems, or other memberships can often provide significant price breaks.

Library Concerns

Besides the expense of electronic subscriptions and the slippery issue of perpetual access, there are other drawbacks to e-collections. Especially noticeable with periodical databases is that, to appeal to the widest possible range of potential library clients, publishers often mix scholarly and popular titles into one product. The result can be an unfocused mishmash—something that wouldn't have resulted with customized, individual print subscriptions. And the library cannot narrowly refine their collection within an e-journal product as they could with individual hardcopy subscriptions; it is a package deal.

Some vendors are now talking about allowing individual libraries to tailor the list of titles they want to include in the index along with the full-text offered to patrons. It remains to be seen if this trial option will be judged as commercially viable. It is much more labor intensive, both for the vendor and for the library. It is easier to try to make one size fit all. However, from the researcher's point of view, it might be best to have an index to all electronic and print holdings for which full text is immediately available—whether online or on-site. Why tantalize customers with citations if the documents are not readily available?

Other concerns include licensing restrictions on what librarians consider standard library services and practices, such as providing interlibrary loans for periodical articles from an electronic resource. Also, there is no guarantee that the particular titles found in an e-collection today will, in fact, be there tomorrow. The arrangements between the actual periodical publishers and the producers of the e-product are subject to change and revision, resulting in the addition and deletion of titles without notice to subscribers.

Some good guidelines and active discussions of the issues surrounding e-collections can be found by visiting the Web sites of the leading trade associations and by joining listservs focusing on licensing issues. The licensing of electronic resources is very much an evolving area where the old rules don't apply. Library staff responsible for acquiring these resources and for negotiating licenses will want to keep up-to-date on the issues and should be encouraged to actively lobby with publishers to make their collection needs known.

Finally, never accept publishers' definition of what *copyright* or *fair use* means. This is one of the few issues on which publishers and librarians have divergent viewpoints and conflicting interests. Many publishers use a license agreement as an attempt to get librarians to give up rights inherent under the fair use clause of the copyright law. On the other hand, many publishers are very generous in granting libraries, particularly those in educational institutions, rights to use their materials in ways that may well go beyond what copyright laws mandate.

Electronic Ordering Systems

Compared to the neighborhood book dealer, the chain store at the mall, or the burgeoning online entertainment centers, the local library has always been plagued with an abysmally slow turnaround time in making hardcopy materials available for patrons. Many of the services offered by jobbers now focus on speeding up delivery and outsourcing the processing and cataloging tasks. The end result should mean faster provision of materials to library customers.

The advent of Web-based order placement has delivered on the promise of speed at that starting point in the acquisitions process. Established customers can quickly place an order by accessing the Internet, and, with the click of a mouse, instantly submit their order to the jobber. The old, tedious task of generating paper order cards, then filing and tracking them, has been left behind with Web-based ordering. Figure 5.1 shows an acquisitions ledger from the 1940s.

To take full advantage of this new way of doing business, the library staff may be required to use a bank credit card for payment. This is the only way that many e-businesses are set up to operate. Parent institutions may need to be educated about the advantages of allowing library staff to commit funds in this manner, which appears to bypass some of the fiscal safeguards that are typical in the workplace. As an added incentive to customers using Web-based ordering, some vendors may offer discounts when a credit card is used because this method frees them from complicated billing procedures.

In addition to the advantages of paperless orders and swift submission of those orders, Web-based acquisition consolidates what were once several separate, time-consuming clerical tasks. Most bibliographic verification can now be accomplished through browsing publishers' or retailers' Web sites. By toggling back and forth between a bibliographic utility, the library's circulation system, and the jobber's Web site, order requests can be checked quickly against current holdings, then the verified order submitted. Accounting records are generated easily, and the MARC record for the on-order item can be added immediately to the library catalog, giving patrons a status report on the title.

The standardization of Web technology is an improvement over earlier, automated ordering systems which relied on software and hardware that was specific to each vendor. With a Web interface, the process is familiar, easy, and doesn't require disks or CDs. The speed, ease of use, and consolidation of tasks that have resulted from Web-based ordering frees up staff time for learning new technologies, computer maintenance and troubleshooting, special projects, and other tasks.

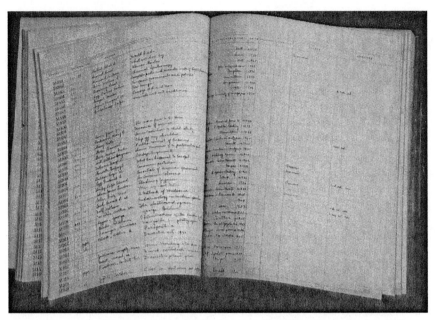

Figure 5.1. Before the era of automated library operations began in the 1960s, acquisitions and circulation data were often logged by hand into large ledgers. This Acquisitions Accession Book is from Pasadena Junior College, circa 1940. Reprinted by permission of Pasadena City College Library.

Out-of-Print Materials

Books, videos, individual periodical issues, and other materials in demand by researchers and needed as replacement copies for library collections often may be out of print. This means that the publisher is no longer producing the item, and no new copies are available for order. Out-of-print status may be temporary or permanent. Either way, a library may then contact a search service or out-of-print dealer to attempt to procure a copy. Out-of-print dealers abound online now, and, of course, there are the traditional "brick-and-mortar" dealers as well. Surcharges added by dealers vary considerably.

Cataloging and Classification

As new items arrive in the Technical Services area, they are unpacked, checked against packing slips, and examined for defects. If there are no problems, then they are ready for the cataloging staff to handle. The purpose of cataloging materials is twofold: (1) to provide a shelf address or location for each book, CD, video, or other item, and (2) to provide specific information for the library holdings database. After Technical Services staff assign classification numbers (more commonly referred to as call numbers), determine subject headings, and provide descriptive information on an item, all is entered into the library's database, known as an OPAC (online public access catalog). This database of information provides a master inventory of holdings and allows patrons to search the automated catalog, whether on site or off site. It answers the following questions, among others: "What books or resources does the library carry on my topic?" "Does the library have a specific book or resource?" "Where is it located?" "Is it available now?"

The two most common classification systems in use are LC and Dewey Decimal. LC evolved from the original organizing scheme that Thomas Jefferson used for his own book collection before selling it to the new national library. An alpha–numeric system, it is in use mostly in larger libraries, such as academic and research facilities. Melvil Dewey's decimal-based scheme was introduced in 1876 and remains the standard among public and school libraries. An example of a more specialized classification is the Superintendent of Documents (SuDocs) system, used for large government document collections. SuDocs divides a collection into subgroups of documents based on the agency that issued or produced the item.

The automation of library bibliographic records began with the invention of the MARC record. MARC records are a standard way of recording and sharing information about a bibliographic item. By using three types of content designators—tags, subfield codes, and indicators—the information is stored electronically and can be retrieved and interpreted by any other computer in the world that is programmed to read MARC records. For example, anyone reading a MARC record can assume that information found in the 245 field is information about the title and author, listed exactly in the form as it is shown on the title page of the book. Variant title information, such as the spine title, would be in the 246 field. The records can contain all the information displayed in OPACs as well as additional information about the item that is useful to librarians. It is beyond the purpose of this text to fully explain the intricacies of the actual MARC coding. See the resources section at the end of this chapter for a citation to a tutorial for those seeking a deeper level of understanding.

Once a library has cataloged a book or another real or virtual bibliographic item and has coded the resulting cataloging data into MARC format, that data can be passed on to other libraries and read by their cataloging software without human intervention. This allows libraries to acquire cataloging data from the Library of Congress and other libraries with respected cataloging standards without repeating the labor-intensive effort of original cataloging. The receiving library has to verify only that the MARC record actually describes the item in hand and not some other edition or variant.

MARC format was originally developed by the Library of Congress in the 1960s but quickly evolved into the international standard for exchanging bibliographic data. For example, the Diet Library in Tokyo serves many of the functions of the national library of Japan. Japanese books are cataloged there and coded into MARC format. The resulting MARC records can be used by libraries the world over who want to have Japanese vernacular records for the Japanese books in their collections.

Descriptive Versus Subject Cataloging

There are two types of cataloging that take place for each item. *Descriptive cataloging* delineates the physical characteristics of a book, video, data file, or other material. Depending on the format, this could include data such as size and physical dimensions, number of pages, length of running time, accompanying leaflets or CD-ROMs, and so forth. *Subject cataloging* focuses on identifying the primary subject or subjects of the item and then assigning the best subject headings and classification number to reflect this. The result should be that researchers searching an OPAC by keyword, author, title, subject or other access point are able to locate an item of potential interest based on the carefully assigned headings and call numbers.

At one time, most cataloging was done on a one-by-one basis, with each individual item scrutinized and cataloged from scratch. This was a labor-intensive activity performed by each library that was acquiring the book or other resource and resulted in massive duplication of effort. With the invention of many time-saving solutions, such as the catalog card distribution program at the Library of Congress, the ability to purchase digital cataloging data from jobbers, and today's cooperative catalogs and worldwide bibliographic utilities, there has been a sizeable reduction in the amount of original cataloging required by library staff. Instead, copy cataloging has become commonplace for a large majority of items.

By searching a large, reliable database of completed MARC records, such as those on OCLC (Online Computer Library Center), a library cataloging technician can locate the data for a specific item, then download or copy that information to use in local records. The customary placement of Cataloging-in-Publication (CIP) data in new releases, a joint effort since 1971 by Library of Congress and publishers to standardize cataloging data, is another helpful tool to expedite cataloging. Check the verso page (i.e., the reverse side of the title page, which will be a left-hand page) to find CIP data in many books.

Cooperative databases, such as the substantial OCLC holdings referred to previously, are built from records submitted by the Library of Congress and supplemented by member libraries, museums, and other research agencies. As of 2000, OCLC's record count exceeded 40 million,[4] and the database grows by more than 2 million records annually.[5] Even video and nonprint titles are increasingly represented on this database. Thus, the need for labor-intensive, original cataloging still exists, but on a decreasing basis.

A significant amount of original cataloging does take place in larger academic and research libraries with collections that include government documents, manuscript and archive materials, foreign language titles, scholarly serials, and scientific proceedings. In these facilities, there are often many language specialists among the Technical Services staff whose responsibility it is to catalog all items in their area (e.g., Romance languages, Slavic languages, Asian languages).

Along with the decrease in the need for original cataloging, the automation of most libraries' card files has also meant the elimination of much of the previous tedious, repetitive updating and filing of cards in the physical catalog drawers and in the accompanying shelf list. Cataloging operations changed dramatically over the last 25 years of the twentieth century. The authors have observed that most libraries now provide original cataloging for less than 10 percent of their acquisitions, and many smaller libraries can find acceptable cataloging copy for all but one or two percent of new items. Rather than reinventing the wheel at each library around the world, the cataloging process has become much more streamlined.

Processing

The last step in the chain of events before stocking the shelves for customer use is to physically process each item. Although many aspects of Technical Services are highly automated, the processing that must take place before an item is shelf-ready remains a low-tech operation. Stamping materials with library ownership stamps, adhering call number labels and label protectors, installing magnetic security tapes, and other tasks are necessary to protect materials from theft and to make them accessible on the shelves.

Larger libraries have separate acquisitions and cataloging divisions within the Technical Services department where head librarians oversee each operation as well as the library technicians, clerks, student assistants, and volunteers. For those with a preference for limited public contact, many find their niche in the predictable workflow of acquisitions and cataloging. They also take much satisfaction in the ongoing stocking of the library and the knowledge that they are providing patrons with the materials they need.

Physical processing requires an exacting attention to detail and an ability to follow through on lengthy, complex tasks where accuracy is critical. In larger research libraries, a knowledge of foreign languages is often required, as is an understanding of the subdivisions of fields of knowledge. In these facilities, the processing of monographs may be an entirely separate operation from the processing of serials and periodicals, with different departments maintained to acquire, catalog, and physically prepare each category for researchers' use. In the largest Technical Services departments, workflow may be assigned based on the language or subject of the material being processed. In contrast, one person does it all in the smallest of branches or information centers—from the most menial to the more intellectually challenging tasks.

Special Materials

Certain types of information formats that libraries collect don't conform to the standard acquisitions, cataloging, and processing model described previously. In fact, within research, university, and larger public libraries, it is typical to find separate departments organized around formats such as periodicals, manuscripts, rare books, institutional archives, local history, microforms, and government documents. Each of these materials has unique housing, display, and access needs that warrant the organization of its own discrete department.

Periodical Collections

Any discussion of periodical collections must take into account the definitions of the terms *periodical* and *serial*. Based on the authors' experiences and conversations with colleagues, there is considerable ambiguity as to the precise meanings of the terms. Added to that, there are many localized variations of use in the workplace; variations that are often dependent on the size of the library's collection.

Arlene Taylor uses the following definitions in her classic textbook *Wynar's Introduction to Cataloging and Classification.*[6]

> *Serial:* A publication issued in successive parts at regular or irregular intervals and intended to continue indefinitely. Included are periodicals, newspapers, proceedings, reports, memoirs, annuals, and numbered monographic series.

> *Periodical:* A publication with a distinctive title, which appears in successive numbers or parts at stated or regular intervals and which is intended to continue indefinitely. Usually each issue contains articles by several contributors. Newspapers and memoirs, proceedings, journals, etc., of corporate bodies primarily related to their internal affairs are not included in this definition.

As is apparent from the definitions, serial is a much broader term than is the narrower category of periodical. And in very large research and academic libraries with sizeable holdings of scientific proceedings, annuals, and so on, the distinction will have great significance. For purposes of general discussion, this book will use the more common term *periodical.*

Periodicals account for a critical part of any library, media, or information center's research collection. In many disciplines, particularly scientific and technical, they form the primary and almost exclusive means of communicating new knowledge. Published with predictable frequency, which may be weekly, monthly, quarterly, or at other intervals, periodicals provide a continual flow of fresh information into the library collection.

Periodical publications differ in concept and coverage from books. Also known as monographs, these books are single works, although they may come out in multiple parts or volumes, are not intended to continue indefinitely, and tend to treat a topic in more depth than an article. The term *monograph* also has a more narrow, technical meaning, but in this work the term will be used in its generic sense. Each periodical issue is numbered consecutively with sequential volume and issue numbers to differentiate between each unique part and to reflect their publishing order.

Frequent fluctuations in the publishing of periodicals, such as title changes, title splits, mergers, acquisitions, cessations, and other events, require special cataloging expertise to properly compile and revise holdings records for them.

Categories of Periodicals

Based on their targeted audience and technical level, periodicals are typically divided into several categories. *Magazines* tend to be written for the layperson, use vocabulary easily understood by the average reader, and are glossy, full-color publications replete with advertisements and photographs. Think of the familiar publications found on newsstands and in doctors' waiting rooms—those are magazines.

In contrast, *journals* are written for a particular academic or professional audience. Scholars and professors in the field are the major contributors. Articles and studies may be reviewed or juried by an editorial board of highly respected peers before being accepted for publication into a particular journal. Journals assume a specialized vocabulary and knowledge of their readers, often at a highly technical level. Expect journal articles to be signed; that is, the author or authors are given an obvious byline with their professional credentials noted. At the end of the journal article, there is usually an extensive bibliography, list of works cited, or other documentation for further reference.

In terms of physical appearance, journals are not as eye-catching as magazines because they do not try to appeal to the general public. Often, they have few ads and few illustrations. Graphs or charts that are included often require some technical knowledge on the part of the reader.

Trade periodicals fall in between the two previous categories. These tend to be written for a specific professional or industry group, such as nurses, librarians, electricians, network managers, and so forth. Their content is narrowly focused on the given field, but the reading and vocabulary level is usually discernible to the layperson.

Then there is the *newspaper*—perhaps the publication most familiar to the reading public. Newspapers range from prestigious national dailies to weekly rural papers. They focus on reporting current events, weather, and sports, among other topics. Note that in the definitions above, newspapers are technically a serial, rather than a periodical. In practical usage in the workplace, newspapers are treated, processed, and housed much like the periodicals described previously.

It is important to note that, with the rapid growth of periodical publishing on the Internet, the distinctions between categories so obvious in the hardcopy counterparts are becoming blurred.

Hardcopy Needs

Because of their ongoing publication, relatively small size, and often time-sensitive value, hardcopy periodicals require much labor-intensive handling before they make it onto the library's shelves for patron access. In large library facilities, tracking the receipt of each issue, individual labeling, security tattle-taping, shelving, and eventual binding can employ dozens of library technicians and student assistants.

Some of the processing needs that often require a separate periodicals department include the following:

The currency of contents requires a very short turnaround time in making the periodicals available to customers.

The slim size makes periodicals vulnerable to theft, so care must be taken in attaching security targets to each issue.

The high use and vulnerability to theft often require a closed stack or reserve collection, which increases both space and staffing needs.

The ongoing publication requires the claiming of lost or missing replacement issues to maintain a complete title run.

The wear and tear on the paper copies often necessitates binding into annual volumes for durability and retention.

The temporary housing of current, high-interest issues in display shelving, rather than stacks, for customer convenience increases overall handling requirements.

In summary, periodicals add a vital element of timely material covering an incredible diversity of subject areas to any library collection. They do require labor-intensive processing and a high level of maintenance to ensure access and complete back files.

Even though today's libraries rely increasingly on electronic access to periodical indexes and full-text article databases for their current subscriptions, the majority maintain a mix of paper copies and electronic versions. In some cases, this translates into purchasing simultaneous subscriptions to the same title to ensure access to periodical archives or back runs. In other cases, publishers require a paper subscription to gain access to an e-subscription. The model varies, but hardcopy periodicals are still a major component of library collections.

Staffing

Larger libraries of all types may employ professionals whose primary responsibility is overseeing the periodicals collection. A periodicals, or serials, librarian will typically coordinate the selection, acquisition, processing, organization, and management of the library's periodicals collection. In large research libraries, which receive thousands of subscriptions, several serials assistants are employed in the check-in, claiming, and cataloging of periodicals to get them to the public as near to the time of arrival as possible.

New products, publishing trends, title changes, and emerging patron preferences in this rapidly changing area make such a job more dynamic and challenging than it was in the past, when emphasis was often centered on balancing tight budgets with collection needs as subscription prices spiraled upward.

Special Collections

Collections of original manuscripts, photographs, architectural drawings, diaries, first editions, realia, institutional archives, and other unique materials usually with an historical focus are often centered in a section of the library known as the Special Collections department. Such a department focuses on the acquisition, management, preservation, and user access of these special holdings, just as a general library unit operates its general book and multimedia collection. In the biggest of libraries there may be multiple Special Collections departments (e.g., Archives, Manuscripts, Rare Books, Local History). How these collections are differentiated depends on local needs. Typically, archives refer to documents generated by the organization itself in the daily course of doing business (e.g., by the college or municipality or corporation of which the library is a subordinate unit). Similar documents originating from outside the organization might be housed in an entirely separate unit called Manuscripts. Care and organization of the materials is very similar. Rare

Books and Local History departments are less distinct divisions and tend to blend many of the characteristics from general collections with those of special collections.

Even the largest of libraries severely limit the scope of the manuscripts they collect. For example, the library at the University of Illinois–Urbana is the third largest university research library in the United States. However, there are only about a half dozen topics for which it attempts to collect any scrap of information, regardless of the format. Among those topics earmarked for comprehensive collecting are materials by and about President Abraham Lincoln and author/poet Carl Sandburg. This is an example of the general practice where collecting policy is determined by the curriculum or research focus of the parent institution.

Sources for Acquiring Materials

Because of the unusual nature of the materials, the acquisition, processing, and cataloging aspects of special collections are handled very differently from more traditional library materials. In terms of acquisitions, an institutional archive will receive selected noncurrent records from other departments within its agency. For example, older publications, photographs, architectural plans, and presidential or mayoral speeches from the college, corporation, or municipality will be transferred to the archival repository.

The number of institutions that have substantial acquisitions budgets for manuscripts is usually limited to large, scholarly research and academic libraries. Materials may be purchased from manuscript vendors who work in the subject areas in which the department collects (e.g., Californiana, New Jerseyiana, Civil War, John Steinbeck, women authors, American children's literature). Often, dealers very familiar with a collection's focus will suggest relevant items of interest from their inventory to special collections staff for possible purchase.

Materials also frequently come from private sources, often as donations. As a result, the cultivation of potential donors plays an important role in the ongoing collection development efforts of a Special Collections department. Careful record keeping in the form of deeds follows each donation of materials. A deed documents the legal transfer of ownership, specifies any restrictions on use or reproduction, conveys literary and other rights, and verifies the provenance or origin of a collection.

Materials may be acquired in large collections, in small lots, or singly. The Special Collections department at Cal Poly University, San Luis Obispo, recently received the personal and business papers of a locally prominent, pioneering mercantile family. Before processing, the donation comprised some 100 cartons along with hundreds of loose ledgers, maps, drawings, and other oversized items. In contrast, the same department just purchased a slim, hand-written 1849 Gold Rush-era diary from a rare book and manuscript dealer.

MARC Format, Encoded Archival
Description, and Finding Aids

Another distinction of special collections is found in the accessing and cataloging of materials. Unlike book materials, each item is not individually indexed. For example, a manuscript or archival collection consisting of correspondence, historical photographs, and ephemera might contain 5,000 individual pieces; rather than devising a cataloging record for each scrap of paper or image, the bibliographic record describes the collection as a unit. A distinct MARC record protocol—MARC-AMC (Archival and Manuscript Control) was devised for cataloging archives and manuscripts, but it has since been superseded by MARC 21. All prior separate formats, such as the AMC bibliographic format, have been fully integrated into MARC 21. The ability of MARC format to handle archival and manuscript materials means that bibliographic records for these collections can be added routinely to a library's OPAC. Compiling such a record may be a joint effort between special collections personnel and cataloging staff. In the largest libraries, there may be staff whose sole job is to catalog rare books or manuscript materials.

In addition to the MARC record, special collections are accessed in more detail through an archival tool known as a finding aid or descriptive guide. This is typically a narrative describing the significance of the collection; its physical arrangement, size, and formats of materials; followed by a skeletal inventory of the holdings. In terms of physical and intellectual organization, each collection is broken down hierarchically into record groups, series, subseries, boxes, and folders. The organizational framework for each individual collection within the department reflects the unique contents of that collection, and, wherever possible, is based on the provenance or origin of the materials. Today, many libraries routinely publish their finding aids online to assist researchers in preparing for an on-site visit to their special collections.

Encoded Archival Description (EAD) using Standard General Markup Language (SGML) is rapidly becoming the new standard for use with archival finding aids. Like other markup languages, SGML prepares documents for publishing on the Web and can be completed with the help of an authoring program.

Thus, traditional book classification systems such as LC or Dewey are not applied to special collections materials. Because of their varying shapes, sizes, and often fragile condition, materials found in special collections are also housed differently than books, videos, CDs, DVDs, or other physical packages of information that can literally stand on their own. Manuscripts, photographs, and the like are placed inside special acid-free storage boxes, folders, and sleeves of varying sizes, which house them and also contribute to their preservation and stabilization. The original condition of each historical item is closely guarded; no library ownership stamps, sticky call labels, Post-it® notes, or colored dots are allowed on the materials. It is likely that the staff of the special collections department will handle all processing for these materials.

Emphasis on Preservation

Special collections departments take seriously their preservation mission. Controlling the environment within the department, much like a museum does, is an important element for ensuring long-term access to unique, historical materials. Temperature and humidity extremes are to be avoided because they can advance decay or deterioration of materials. Sophisticated air control systems or HVACs (heating ventilation and air-conditioning), along with the use of dehumidifiers, humidifiers, and meters that measure temperature and humidity, called thermohygrometers, are all used to monitor the environment. The use of acid-free storage containers, Mylar® sleeves, and other stable protective housing is standard procedure.

Research etiquette also emphasizes preservation. Special collections departments are closed stack areas where materials are paged or retrieved by staff for on-site review and study by researchers, one box or folder at a time. Patrons are often required to wear white, cotton gloves when handling original items. This prevents the transfer of oil from the hands to the historical materials. Writing implements are restricted to pencils only—again, to protect the special materials from any permanent damage or defacing. Materials are noncirculating, and there may be photocopying limitations to minimize handling of fragile original items or because of deed restrictions. Figure 5.2 depicts research etiquette.

Figure 5.2. In special collections departments, manuscripts or other fragile materials are housed in protective acid-free boxes and Mylar® sleeves. Research etiquette also emphasizes the careful handling of materials. Reprinted by permission of Kennedy Library, Cal Poly State University, San Luis Obispo.

Because of the unique nature of the materials and their potential value on the retail market, special collections items are especially vulnerable to theft, so greater security precautions and restricted user access are the norm. Photo identification, research credentials, or other documentation may be required of patrons prior to accessing materials. For some large, scholarly, independent institutions such as California's Huntington Library, or the Folger Shakespeare Library in Washington, DC, letters of recommendation and an application may be required of potential researchers before access privileges are granted.

Conservation Efforts

At times, conservation techniques must also be applied in an attempt to reverse water or smoke damage, to stabilize deterioration as from high acid content in paper, or to mitigate other problems with documents. In some cases, very large research and university libraries will have their own conservation labs on site—such as the Library of Congress, Los Angeles's Getty Museum, or Yale University. The majority of libraries send their conservation work to outside specialists because of the highly skilled and labor-intensive nature of such work.

It is tempting to think that the expensive and time-consuming effort of preserving original documents can be abandoned now with the ability to digitize information easily. However, every storage medium has a different shelf life, and, in many cases, that is not known until some time has passed. Although today we herald the wonders of computers, it remains to be seen what the life span of digital storage will be. On the other hand, high quality "permanent paper" buffered and with low acid content still remains the most durable and reliable medium, with a life span of approximately 500 years.

In addition to the breakdown of the storage medium itself, the obsolescence of the playback equipment (e.g., microfilm reader, computer programs and drives) can also prevent access to information and necessitate its transfer from one medium to another. After all, how many libraries still have film loop readers? And floppy disk drives are no longer standard equipment in many personal computers. Equipment for reading data stored on 8-inch and 5¼-inch floppy disks is already difficult to find; will the 3½-inch diskette be far behind? When considering the transfer of information from its original format (e.g., paper, photograph, 16mm film, floppy disk) to a newer medium, archivists are also aware that, for some scholars, the container is as much a focus for research as is the information within.

Staffing

Staff who work in special collections may be called librarians and library technicians, or they may be termed archivists and archival technicians. Thus, professional training requirements will vary accordingly. It is fair to say that a degree in history, or a least an affinity for history, is an important requirement for those considering a career in this area. A national certification program for archivists was implemented in 1989. The independent, not-for-profit Academy of Certified Archivists provides standardized certification through an examination process. For those interested in further exploring these specialties, the Society of American Archivists' Web site is listed in the resources section at the end of this chapter.

Although some would argue that librarians and archivists are entirely different breeds, the authors (both of whom have worked in special collections settings) choose to differ with that point of view. The careful selection of materials according to a plan, preparation of items for researchers' use, and access and reference services are all required in both arenas. Emphasis on electronic access to information, especially digital imaging, is very timely and is transforming special collections, just as it is other areas of library and information science.

Microforms

Microforms have come in many different sizes and variations since their initial use in libraries during the 1930s. Microfilm and microfiche remain the two types most commonly found in libraries, archives, and research centers today. Microfilm editions are photographs of each page of the original periodical, newspaper, thesis, or other document. The images are produced on rolls of film, typically 35 millimeters in size. To read the miniaturized document, which is not legible to the naked eye, the film must be loaded into a microfilm reader, which enlarges the tiny, reduced-size print to legible form. Microfiche editions are cards of 16-millimeter film. Common sizes include 3 inch by 5 inch, 4 inch by 6 inch, and 3 inch by 7 inch. They are also significantly reduced and must be placed in a microfiche reader machine to magnify the text. Most modern readers also produce photocopies of the document. Other types of microforms in use over the years have included aperture cards, microcards, ultrafiche, and other variations of microphotography.

For more than half of the twentieth century, microforms were a major storage medium in libraries and information centers of all sizes.[7] Advantages to this miniaturized format include the preservation of hardcopy data, reduction in shelving and space needs, and, in its high quality form, stability and a long life span as a reliable storage medium. Archival quality microfilm (also called silver halide microfilm) will last for approximately 200 years.[8] Microfilm is particularly well suited to interlibrary loan because its compact size makes it easy to ship, and playback machines are standard worldwide, thus eliminating concerns about incompatibility between libraries.

Making Microforms Accessible

For approximately 40 years, libraries building retrospective collections have purchased mainstream periodical and newspaper titles in microfilm from special microform vendors who work exclusively with that medium. For in-house or smaller local publications, they contract with a company to produce microfilm records of these unique titles.

Once received, the film requires special, labor-intensive processing before it is shelf-ready. This includes the insertion of stoppers at the end of each reel and the labeling of the film leaders and storage boxes. Special storage cabinets are used for both microfilm and fiche; they are rarely shelved on regular-sized book stacks.

As for user access, there is the need to provide patrons with multiple readers or printers and to keep them in good working order. Staff assistance in the use of the machines is also required and often results in an additional service desk devoted to microforms. In large microfilm reading rooms, such as those found in the National Archives's regional branches, trained volunteers are available to help with equipment use and problems. Student assistants and interns are also often posted in microform rooms to troubleshoot problems. And, of course, all of this requires dedicated library space. Figure 5.3 shows a Canon digital microfilm scanner.

Figure 5.3. The use of new technologies makes it possible to digitize microfilm and microfiche images for enhanced viewing and electronic storage. Reprinted by permission of Canon USA, Inc.

National cataloging standards call for a separate cataloging record to be made for different formats of a title. So, in theory, where microform holdings form archives or backups of hardcopy titles, they require additional work from a cataloging perspective. (In practice, many libraries cut corners on this standard by adding holdings data in different formats to the main bibliographic record.)

Patron Resistance

Although popular among staff, microforms have never been a favorite among patrons. For researchers, eye strain and repetitive use syndrome are physical discomforts that result from long hours in front of a reader. Another source of frustration (to the library staff as well as to patrons) is the breakage of microform reader parts, which occurs with frequent use. Also, poor quality film can be can blurry and illegible. Anyone who has done genealogical research and accessed early nineteenth-century newspapers and census records will empathize.

Most younger students today are unfamiliar with microforms, not having been exposed to the medium in junior or senior high school. In an introductory library skills module, it is not unusual for college professors to give students an assignment to locate the front page of a major newspaper for their birth date to introduce them to the mysteries of microfilm.

Future of Microforms

The Internet revolution has significantly impacted the longstanding practice of storing noncurrent periodicals and newspapers on microfilm, and, less frequently, on microfiche. As Web-based periodical archives begin to reach back more than a decade or two, many libraries are canceling their microfilm subscriptions and relying solely on their online holdings. Although *perpetual access* (that is, the guaranteed, continued access to retrospective holdings online) remains an unsettled issue, it is possible that microform publishing may decrease significantly. The distinct emphasis of the Web has been the provision of current materials. It remains to be seen whether the further retrospective conversion of microfilm holdings into online formats and databases will be lucrative enough for online publishers to pursue. Even if the demand is there and the numbers play out, it is likely that the oldest and most obscure titles will remain in library collections on their microfilm rolls and fiche cards. Historians and other researchers, as well as many library staffers, will continue to use microfilm for accessing retrospective titles.

Although not inexpensive, the capability exists for digitizing microform images. Special scanners can digitize microfilm or fiche images for distribution over computer networks to desktop computers. This conversion process combines photographic and electronic imaging technologies. Leaders in the use of this conversion technology so far have been corporate libraries and their record management centers. It will be interesting to watch the future direction taken by two large repositories with predominantly microfilm collections: (1) the National Archives, and (2) the Church of Jesus Christ of Latter-Day Saints (Mormons). Between the two, they house a major percentage of the world's genealogical and historical resources and are used extensively by professional and lay researchers daily.

For the average library facility with limited resources, their current microform holdings of retrospective titles represent a significant investment that will not soon be discarded. Because this format is still viable, and, for most collections probably represents low-use items, many libraries will keep their extant microform holdings but will look to new technologies to access current materials and to archive them as they become noncurrent.

Government Documents

Although they represent an enormous wealth of data on almost any subject imaginable, government documents tend to be overlooked by the average researcher as sources of information. "Gov docs," as they are nicknamed by library staff, are those publications produced by or for a government agency; this includes international, federal, provincial, state, county, parish, city, or other jurisdictions. In the United States, the Government Printing Office (GPO) is the agency charged with producing, distributing, and selling federal documents. As such, the GPO is one of the world's largest publishers. Through its distribution arm, the Superintendent of Documents, the GPO offers about 12,000 titles for sale to the public. Many of these tend to be of high interest to consumers.

Compared to commercially published books that often have attractive, attention-getting packaging and professionally designed covers, government publications are often plain and drab in appearance. However, the lack of frills also keeps the price down, and, as a whole, government publications are very reasonably priced—sometimes they are even free. The variety of topics covered and the diverse audiences for which these publications are written are wide ranging. A short pamphlet on good parenting skills, a checklist of resident bird species at a national park, a technical report from the Surgeon General on secondhand tobacco effects, or the multi-volume, annual *U.S. Budget* are all examples of documents emanating from national government agencies. Government publications are often a critical and sometimes sole source for detailed statistics on many aspects of life, from the population census to motor vehicle fatalities, to the number of fish netted, to precise rainfall tallies.

GPO Access Web Site

Creative and efficient dissemination of information has always been a point of pride and a mandate for the GPO. Over the years, this has meant using new technologies to package and distribute documents from federal agencies. The GPO has been producing publications in CD-ROM format for about a dozen years. Beginning in 1994, they implemented an information-rich Web site for the public called GPO Access (see Figure 5.4) and continue to improve and enhance its features. GPO Access provides links to many services including their *Catalog of Publications*, information on their regional bookstores, and a searchable database and ordering system for titles from the *Consumer Information Catalog*. The extensive site also serves as a gateway to many other federal government Web sites.

Figure 5.4. The Government Printing Office (GPO) Access Home Page provides links to many of the agency's services of interest to libraries, including online ordering of federal publications.

Federal Depository Program

Since 1813, the federal government has designated depository libraries to ensure consumers access to many of its publications. Today, the Federal Depository Library Program (FDLP) consists of about 1,350 participating libraries throughout the nation. These libraries are designated at one of three levels for the regular receipt of information in print, multimedia, and electronic formats: (1) full, (2) regional, and (3) selective. Materials are sent to the library at no cost. In return, the depositories provide organization, housing, and professional reference assistance for patrons, available to all citizens who want access. Publications received as part of the federal depository arrangement may have mandatory retention schedules, and they cannot be weeded in the usual fashion. Instead, they must first be offered to other depositories, and, if there are no takers, only then can they be discarded.

Through the depository libraries, the federal government disseminates key information to the public at large. Many state governments also have depository arrangements with libraries to provide convenient access to their documents for citizens.

Diversity of Formats to Process

A hallmark of government documents (especially those from the federal government) has been the diverse formats in which they are produced. Printed materials include monographs, technical reports, periodicals, booklets, pamphlets, brochures, maps; current microformats are microfilm and microfiche; multimedia ranges from videos to CD-ROMs to DVDs. The online publishing of government information dramatically increased in the 1990s, and the Web continues as a primary distribution channel for government data. Retrospective document collections with older materials may also include such now-obsolete media as film loops, 16-mm films, and 5¼-inch floppy disks.

From a processing point of view, this diversity can be a bit problematic. Irregular sizes, spiral bindings without spines for labeling, and the constantly changing formats for a single title require additional staff time and special handling before they are shelf-ready. In addition, there are depository status labeling requirements and retention mandates to which depository libraries must adhere.

The steady flow of depository products means a serious space commitment for the library, and the diverse formats need various styles and sizes of shelving to accommodate them all. Many government publications are new editions of standard titles that replace older versions, and, thus, constant weeding of superseded items is required.

Although publishing of many government documents on the Web is a major convenience in access and distribution, it presents a new question in terms of long-term, archival access. Currently, there is no policy for preserving or capturing digital documents, which can be very ephemeral in nature. Just as the federal depository system has provided a system for preserving public access to publications in print, microfilm, and other formats, a policy needs to be implemented to ensure permanent access for digital documents.[9]

Why House Government Documents Separately?

In many larger library facilities, government documents are housed separately from the main collection. There are a variety of issues that play into this decision. A significant one is that federal documents have their own distinct classification system called SuDocs, which is often used in place of the more common Dewey Decimal or Library of Congress codes. When the SuDocs classification is applied, a separate shelving sequence is required. If the collection of documents is large, then this requires a sizeable commitment of both floor space and shelving. Additionally, there are many special indexes produced, both commercially and by the government, that provide exclusive access to government documents. It is both convenient and practical to house a collection of documents in proximity to their accompanying special indexes and finding aides.

Cataloging issues also often argue for providing a separate reading room or department for government publications. Because they originate from hundreds of different agencies, there is no standardized format for producing government documents. And with each new presidential administration, there is often a reorganization or renaming of federal agencies, which further confuses the collection of publications. As a result, government documents are notorious for their lack of basic bibliographic data so critical for compiling library cataloging records; often, no author is cited, there may be several variant titles on the work, a publication date may be lacking, and so forth.

Federal documents are in the public domain; thus, no dated copyright statement is required on the work. (Copyrighting of state-produced materials varies for each state.) Hence, performing full MARC cataloging and adding each record to the library's OPAC is an expensive and labor-intensive task. In fact, government documents are often relegated to the last priority by the cataloging staff because of this. It is not unusual to have government publications in a sort of cataloging limbo, where they are put out on the shelves for public access and use but without being included in the OPAC. Although they may be inventoried in a departmental index, this practice obviously limits full access for researchers who believe that the library catalog is comprehensive.

New on the scene is the arrival of cataloging services specific to government publications. One such firm is Marcive. Drawing from a library's designated profile of government documents received, the company supplies the cataloging record and accompanying labels and processing data. The ability to rely more on this type of outsourcing service could make a great difference in reducing the traditional cataloging backlog of government document departments.

Another reason for maintaining a separate documents room is that it allows for specialization among staff. By focusing primarily on the complexities of the documents collection, professional and support staff are able to hone their expertise and provide high-quality service to customers using these specialized materials.

Proponents for integrating government documents into the main library collection argue that keeping them separate only contributes to their overlooked status. And the use of yet another mysterious classification system only further intimidates and confuses researchers, presenting one more obstacle to overall access. There is no argument that maintaining a separate department and another service desk is an added expense in the library's budget. With all of these considerations, both for and against separation, the trend is for larger collections of documents to be situated and managed as discrete departments.

Acquisition Choices

There are several approaches to obtaining federal documents. As with books and other more familiar library materials, there are jobbers who specialize in providing government publications, such as the long-time documents wholesaler Bernan. Participation in the depository library program, as described previously, is another option. Additionally, the GPO has a network of 20 "brick-and-mortar" bookstores in major cities around the country that sell some of the more popular hardcopy and electronic titles from its inventory directly to the public and to libraries.

Another acquisitions approach is to use the *Monthly Catalog of U.S. Government Publications* to locate relevant, new titles for purchase. This old standby is now available in various formats, including CD-ROM as well as a searchable index with online ordering on the Web. In all of its formats, the *Catalog* lists full cataloging and order data for recently released federal publications.

At the regional and local government level, library staff often acquire materials directly from the issuing agencies by being placed on a mailing list or by direct query. Although this approach may be necessary for local publications, any library with a significant collection of government documents will try to maximize the use of jobbers for acquisitions because it would be prohibitively labor-intensive to contact all levels of government agencies in this manner.

With any of these methods for gaining awareness of and eventually ordering government publications, there is very little reliance on reviewing media as there is with commercial book purchases. Only a few periodicals cover the release and review of government documents for librarians. A current leading title is the *Journal of Government Information,* a bimonthly periodical by Pergamon Press to which major academic libraries with large document collections subscribe. For an excellent overview to the world of government documents, Joe Morehead's *Introduction to United States Government Information Sources*, 6th edition, is a standard.

Diverse Job Opportunities

The library activities, such as acquisitions, cataloging, and processing, that take place behind the doors of Technical Services offer many interesting career paths; both at the technician and professional levels for those who excel in detailed work, possess strong computer skills, and prefer limited public interface.

Certain library materials, such as periodicals, special collections, microforms, and government documents, often require a separate department to properly handle the special needs that these formats bring with them. Such departments also afford diverse career opportunities—many of which are overshadowed by the higher profile public service jobs in Reference and Circulation. Those who enjoy variety in their daily work life—a blend of selection and acquisition, processing, and reference service to users—are encouraged to investigate these areas of specialization.

Associations such as the ALA have professional sections devoted to technical services areas, such as serials, acquisitions, and collection management, along with round table groups for government documents, federal government librarianship, and students. The Society of American Archivists supports member sections focusing on such issues as electronic records, preservation, and reference, as well as sections for students, college and university archives, business archives, and more. Connecting with working professionals as mentors is an effective way to explore an area of specialization within the field.

Study Questions

1. Check the current edition of the *Bowker Annual: Library and Book Trade Almanac* to see whether the number of hardcopy books being published is increasing or declining. What trends in the publishing industry do you think are affecting the production of hardcopy titles?

2. Outline the stages that a book passes through to get onto the shelves of your college library. What is the typical turnaround time from initial order to receipt? How does a video compare? A CD-ROM or DVD?

3. Find out the name of five jobbers active in the library trade. How are they different in the services they offer? How are they similar?

4. Choose a popular magazine title and a scholarly journal title of your choice. For each publication, find out in what formats it is currently available (e.g., hardcopy, full-image Web, full-text Web). How does the pricing of each compare?

5. Visit a special collections department, such as a university archives, a manuscript department, or a local history room. Describe some of their major holdings. What security precautions are in place?

6. Since the inception of the World Wide Web, catalogers, reference librarians, and other library staff have been discussing and experimenting with various methods for cataloging the Web. What current methods in this direction do you think are particularly effective?

Resources

Books

Cook, Michael. *The Management of Information from Archives.* 2d ed. Brookfield, VT: Gower, 1999.

Evans, G. Edward. *Developing Library and Information Center Collections.* 4th ed. Englewood, CO: Libraries Unlimited, 2000.

Modern Archives Institute. *Introduction to Modern Archives Administration.* Washington, DC: National Archives and Records Administration, 1993.

Morehead, Joe. *Introduction to United States Government Information Sources.* 6th ed. Englewood, CO: Libraries Unlimited, 1999.

Schellenberg, T. R. *The Management of Archives.* Rev. ed. Atlanta: National Archives Trust Fund Board, 1990.

Taylor, Arlene. *Wynar's Introduction to Cataloging and Classification.* 9th ed. Englewood, CO: Libraries Unlimited, 2000.

Yakel, Elizabeth. *Starting an Archives.* Chicago: Society of American Archivists; Metuchen, NJ: Scarecrow Press, 1994.

Periodicals

American Libraries. March 1999. (Issue on preservation topics.)

Kaplan, Karen. "A Vision for the Past," *Los Angeles Times* (16 February 1998): D1–D6.

Ketcham-Van Orsdel, Lee, and Kathleen Born. "Serials Publishing in Flux," *Library Journal* (15 April 1999): 48–53.

Noriyuki, Duane. "Pueblo, Colo., aka Catalog Country," *Los Angeles Times* (17 March 1996): E1–2.

Web Sites

- Bancroft Library, University of California, Berkeley
  http://www.lib.berkeley.edu/BANC/
  (Accessed November 21, 2001)
    One of the West Coast's leading primary source repositories has an extensive Web site and provides standardized electronic access to its many special collections.

- Introduction to the Dewey Decimal Classification
  http://www.oclc.org/dewey/about/about_the_ddc.htm
  (Accessed November 21, 2001)
    Forest Press, which publishes the Dewey Classification volumes, provides an overview of the Dewey Decimal system, summaries of the tables, and information on ordering their titles.

- Cal Poly University Archives/Special Collections
  http://www.lib.calpoly.edu/spec_coll/
  (Accessed November 21, 2001)
    An example of a university special collections department Web site. The department posts their mission statement, department hours, access information, a list of manuscript collections, reference services provided, and reproduction rules.

- Do We Really Know Dewey?
  http://tqjunior.advanced.org/5002/
  (Accessed November 21, 2001)
    This site was developed as a school project by students at the Nettleton Intermediate Center, Jonesboro, Arkansas. A playful overview of the Dewey Decimal system and correct shelving procedures geared for junior high level.

- Getty Conservation Institute
  http://www.getty.edu/conservation/institute/
  (Accessed November 21, 2001)
    Part of the J. Paul Getty Center in Los Angeles, the Getty Conservation Institute. Web site features a newsletter, publications information, and relevant links.

- GPO Access
  http://www.access.gpo.gov/
  (Accessed November 21, 2001)
    An information-rich Web site distributing federal government information to the public. GPO Access is an essential reference portal to GPO data as well as to other U.S. agency sites. Includes a Web version of their *Monthly Catalog* for identifying and ordering federal documents, information on their retail bookstores, and an online *Consumer Information Catalog* for buying publications from the Pueblo distribution center.

- How to Decipher Call Numbers: Tutorial
  http://www.lib.monash.edu.au/vl/callno/callcon.htm
  (Accessed November 21, 2001)
      Australia's Monash University has developed a site that describes the basics about Dewey Decimal system call numbers. The tutorial teaches users and staff what a call number is, how they are created, and how to use them in locating library materials.

- Internet Preservation Resources
  http://www.library.yale.edu/~lfors/preservation.html
  (Accessed November 21, 2001)
      Link menu compiled by Lynne M. Fors to leading conservation institutions and agencies, publications, and projects.

- Library of Congress: Conservation Division
  http://lcweb.loc.gov/preserv/conserv.html
  (Accessed November 21, 2001)
      Provides an overview of our national library's Conservation Division, which has been a world leader in developing many modern conservation practices. Programs featured include Environmental Housing of Rarities, Book and Paper Conservation Section, and Preventive Preservation Section.

- Society of American Archivists
  http://www.archivists.org/
  (Accessed November 21, 2001)
      The leading national archival professional association, SAA, provides a site that includes membership information, continuing education opportunities, employment links, and more.

- Understanding MARC Bibliographic
  http://lcweb.loc.gov/marc/umb/um01to06.html
  (Accessed November 21, 2001)
      Authoritative tutorial written by Betty Furrie and reviewed and edited by the Network Development and MARC Standards Office, Library of Congress. For those wanting a more thorough knowledge of the MARC record.

- United States Government Printing Office, Library Services
  http://www.access.gpo.gov/su_docs/fdlp/libpro.html
  (Accessed November 21, 2001)
      The largest publisher in the world, the GPO sells its products online and in bookstores throughout the United States. In addition, it administers the Federal Depository Library Program (FDLP), which ensures that the American public has access to federal government information.

Notes

1. *Bowker Annual: Library and Book Trade Almanac*, 46th ed. New Providence, NJ: R. R. Bowker, 2001, 485.

2.   *Literary Market Place 2000.* New Providence, NJ: R. R. Bowker, 1999, ix.

3.   E-collections listserv. E-mail to author, 3 April 2000.

4.   OCLC, Inc. *About OCLC.* Available: http://www.oclc.org/about/ (Accessed December 6, 2001).

5.   Joy Wanden. OCLC staff member. E-mail to author, 21 July 1998.

6.   Arlene Taylor. *Wynar's Introduction to Cataloging and Classification,* 9th ed. Englewood, CO: Libraries Unlimited, 2000, 503–4, 506.

7.   Allen B. Veaner. "Microforms," in *Encyclopedia of Library History.* Wayne A. Wiegand and Donald G. Davis, eds. New York: Garland Publishing, 1994, 435.

8.   Karen Kaplan. "The Culture's Immortal, But Not the Disk," *Los Angeles Times* (16 February 1998): D1.

9.   "Science Information in Peril," *Los Angeles Times* (1 March 2000): B6.

Chapter 6

Circulation and Access to Materials

Just as in a retail establishment, efficient inventory control and good customer service are important elements in managing a successful library. Each individual book, video, CD, DVD, map, pamphlet, or other material needs to be tracked as it circulates within a reading room, in and out of a department, or is physically removed from the library for use elsewhere. In addition to good products, friendly and professional assistance is also critical in generating satisfied repeat customers. It does not matter how well other areas of the library function; if the connection to the customer is not made successfully, the library has not served its purpose. Both inventory control and customer service largely fail or succeed based on the effectiveness of the circulation department.

The most visible sign of a library's inventory control or circulation efforts is the service counter, where the official charging and discharging of library materials takes place—and which, most often, is a hub of activity. Besides the obvious checkout transactions, many other activities go on at a circulation desk, including referral to other departments, answering directional questions, patron registration, fines collection, and more. As with the location of cashier stations in retail stores, the careful positioning of a circulation desk is a critical part of the inventory control operation. Strategic placement helps deter theft, provides the ability to count and view inbound and outbound traffic, and offers convenience to customers as they enter and exit the facility.

For many customers, regardless of the type of library, circulation desk employees are often the first and only staff with whom they come in contact as they visit the library. Thus, the public relations value of all interactions at the circulation counter should never be underestimated. And first impressions—positive or negative—leave a customer with lasting memories. As the old adage says, "You never get a second chance to make a first impression."

Most customers and novice staff see the circulation department as being synonymous with only those operations taking place at the service counter. But, in fact, there are other related responsibilities that come under the umbrella of this library department that take place away from the physical space of the service desk. These operations may include shelving, management of reserve collections, document delivery and interlibrary loan services, collection inventory and maintenance, and library security.

In small libraries, branch outlets, or other facilities staffed by a solo librarian or technician, the circulation desk also doubles as a reference counter or all-in-one service desk. Larger libraries have a separate service counter dedicated just to circulation functions and typically positioned adjacent to the main exit. Departmental collections, such as government documents, local history, children's room, and others, may handle their own circulation, and thus a large library may have several checkout counters on different floors or at locations in various departments.

Access to Library Materials

The designation *Circulation Department* is a popular one, but such a department may also be named Borrowers' Services, Loan Services, or Access Services, particularly in larger university, public, or research facilities. These latter names clearly reflect the department's emphasis on making library resources available to borrowers. Traditionally, that has meant physically loaning out materials to qualified borrowers so that they can take them home, to school, to the office, to work, and use them off site.

As electronic access to resources continues to grow dramatically, the actual loaning out of the physical item is only one type of access. Increasingly, libraries provide remote access to holdings data; e-books and electronic reserve collections (e-reserves); and databases, indexes, and full-text periodicals for their qualifying clientele. In some cases, access is free to all interested users; in others, access is limited to qualified borrowers who receive a password, subscription number, or other code that lets them log on to the electronic library holdings.

Circulation Terminology

When discussing the loaning out of library materials, there are several commonly used terms that tend to confuse library users. These terms define the circulation status of the book, video, government document, or other physical item. Materials that do not leave the premises of the library or information center include those designated as reference, rare books, and other specially identified items that, because of age, condition, or value, may call for restricted use. Available for in-house use only, *reference* materials tend to be multi-volume sets, handbooks, dictionaries, indexes, and other works that can be consulted briefly for facts or overview information. They may also be expensive, or frequently used, or both; the implication being that patrons can study them on site or photocopy the needed pages, whereas the volumes themselves remain in the library at all times to maximize their use by the greatest number of individuals.

In contrast to the restrictions of the reference status, materials designated as *circulating* may be checked out to registered borrowers. In the majority of libraries and information centers that stress full service and maximum access to materials, it is typical for the bulk of the collection to circulate. However, in the case of specialized materials, such as those discussed in chapter 5 (e.g., microforms, special collections, current hardcopy periodicals, maps, and other unique items), circulation may be very limited, or the entire collection may be for reference use only.

Reserve status is normally found in school media centers and academic library environments. Reserve materials are high-use items required for study by classes during a semester or school term; the number of copies is less than the number of students, so shared use must be enforced. Examples of reserve materials include copies of required textbooks, supplementary course readings, sample tests and assignments, or other curriculum-linked items. The materials may be part of the permanent library collection that has been transferred temporarily to reserve status, or they may be the property of an instructor who has loaned them to the library for the duration of the course. Public and special libraries will also, on occasion, classify materials as reserve to meet the requirements of seasonal school assignments or in-house training needs.

The electronic provision of reserve collections is growing, especially in academic libraries. Newer releases of OPACs feature an e-reserve module for seamless delivery of required readings, lecture notes, sample quizzes, and so forth to authorized users (e.g., enrolled students). Copyright permission must be obtained whether from the professor—in the case of quizzes, notes, and study packs—or from the commercial publishers of texts and other books.

Deciding on Loan Periods and Circulation Status

Library policies today are a far cry from the chained books and closed stacks of earlier times. Although total anytime–anywhere access is not yet a reality for most researchers, the current emphasis on maximizing access can be seen in innovative services such as extended operating hours, remote access to databases, e-books, OPACs, online renewals, electronic reserve collections, and e-mail reference assistance. However, there are legitimate reasons why the circulation of certain physical materials may need to be limited or denied. Some typical items with limited circulation include the following:

- Sets or series (e.g., multi-volume encyclopedias or print periodical indexes where a missing volume lessens the value of the set as a whole).

- One-of-a-kind items (e.g., the only copy of an out-of-print item).

- High-demand items (e.g., class required items).

- Reference materials (e.g., items not designed for reading cover to cover and can be briefly referred to or sections photocopied).

- Fragile or rare items (e.g., manuscripts, maps, or photographs that could be damaged by extra handling).

- Expensive items (e.g., replacement of the item would be costly).

- Items with a record of being stolen (e.g., these are certain topics in every library that are considered "hot;" anything dealing with these topics is prone to theft).

- Items with copyright and security issues (e.g., lending software may violate copyright laws and can also spread viruses).

- Items that require special playback equipment (e.g., in the case of microfilm, a special reader is required to view or print it).

Once a collection or an item has been reviewed, if it warrants checkout but with limitations, there are other options for limiting status in addition to the basic reference and reserve categories discussed previously. The library's standard loan period (e.g., two days, two weeks, or a month) can be modified so that material is returned earlier and is available sooner for other users. Limiting the renewal of materials is another option. For example, policies for certain materials may be that no renewals are allowed or that only one renewal is possible.

Restrictions by user type is another standard circulation policy. For example, in an academic environment it is not unusual to limit the borrowing of videos to instructors only or to restrict the checkout of reserve items to currently enrolled students. Also, in a college or university library, alumni or community cardholders may have only partial borrowing privileges, whereas current students and staff enjoy full privileges. Loan periods may also differ by user type. In a corporate setting, permanent employees may have longer borrowing periods for materials, whereas temporary or contract employees may only check out materials for short intervals. College professors are often able to borrow materials for an entire term, whereas their students are limited to a two- or three-week loan period.

Circulation restrictions according to a user's age may be in place in school media centers or in public libraries. Although a broad reading of the First Amendment, as is advocated by the ALA's "Free Access to Libraries for Minors: An Interpretation of the Library Bill of Rights,"[1] argues against such age restrictions, they are, in fact, common. Local public library systems in particular may limit the checkout of videos, CDs, DVDs, and CD-ROMs to those over 18 years old; the rationale for this type of policy may be based on content, on the need for special care of multimedia materials, or because of an item's replacement cost.

Though not frequently advertised, many libraries and information centers will modify loan policies at the discretion of the librarian on duty. These loans tend to be allowed on a case-by-case basis and usually consist of waiving the standard circulation status or extending the loan period of an item based on special circumstances.

With all of these circulation policy options, balancing the individual's access needs with those of the library's clientele as a whole is a key concern. Additionally, the security of library materials is a consideration in decision making. As with all policies, circulation rules need to be revisited and revised on a regular basis—especially as new formats or services come along—to keep them current with borrowers' needs and usage patterns. So, a healthy dose of common sense helps in keeping policies reasonable.

As the online renewal of books by patrons becomes more common-place, many libraries are revising their standing renewal policies to work in this new environment. In some cases, telephone renewal is being replaced by the online option, with an eye toward eventually completely eliminating phone-in renewals. Online renewal offers convenience to users and, once implemented, reduces the overall amount of staff time spent on renewals. However, a negative issue is that users do not always notice when an online renewal attempt has been denied. Denial of a renewal might occur because of a recall or hold on the title, outstanding patron fines on library materials, or other reasons. The result is that the patron keeps the book for an additional loan period, erroneously thinking that they are acting legally. Instead, the item accrues overdue fines, and, upon return, an unpleasant situation could arise.

Overdue Fines

Whether at the corner video store or local public library, a familiar practice is to charge borrowers a fee for the late return of materials. Although this may seem like an annoying penalty for the tardy customer, the rationale behind these fees is to gather materials back so that they are available to the rest of the user population. In other words, assuring timely access for all is the motivation behind the fines. Contrary to popular opinion, not many libraries get rich off of their overdue fines.

Overdue fine policies and fee schedules usually must be approved by the parent organization of a library, such as a school board, city council, board of supervisors, advisory board, or other governing body. Once approved, it is good customer service to clearly post and publicize these fee rates. As first-time borrowers are registered with a library, the overdue policies and fees should be explained, along with the borrowers' new privileges.

The collection of overdue fines is a time-consuming task. When a library or information center is able to link outstanding overdue fines to their parent organization's operations, the process becomes more efficient. University and college libraries track outstanding fines as part of a student's overall account at the institution. When fines remain unpaid, other key services, such as registration for courses, retrieval of grades, or transcript requests, are blocked, often resulting in timely payment of library fines. Although they seldom charge overdue fines, school library media centers often contact parents directly about overdue or lost material, meanwhile limiting library privileges and postponing the release of report cards.

An increasing number of library systems hire collection agencies to follow up on delinquent or long-overdue accounts. This get-tough stance represents a more efficient method than previous in-house efforts because collection agencies have access to customer data and credit records and are in the business of delinquent accounts collection.

At the other end of the policy spectrum, some libraries choose to waive overdue fees altogether. After calculating the cost of tracking, processing, and collecting overdue fines on their own or through a collection agent, they have decided to discontinue the practice. Rather, they emphasize the safe return of materials and charge only replacement costs if the item is lost. The positive public relations value of a no-fines policy is another consideration, which may convince some libraries and information centers to take that route.

In the past, amnesty weeks or fine-free weeks have been popular, especially with public libraries. These are often timed to coincide with National Library Week in late April or with an individual library's anniversary, new branch opening, or other special event. No questions asked; no fees assessed. "Just bring 'em back!"

Other Fines

Although library overdue fines get the most attention, there are other fines commonly assessed to borrowers. When patrons lose or damage library materials, they may either be charged the actual replacement value of the item (or, if out of print, something comparable), or the library may have set a flat fee for various categories (e.g., adult hardback book, $30; children's hardback book, $20; bound journal, $150). Many libraries add a processing fee to the replacement charge as a revenue recovery method for processing time and supplies. These fees typically can be as little as $5 or more than $30, with academic libraries on the high end. This type of charge is similar in concept to a restocking fee charged by some retail stores for returned merchandise.

Although the hard and fast rules surrounding library fines have been the butt of countless jokes and newspaper cartoons, in fact, many agencies employ alternative methods of accepting payment for those who cannot pay in cash. Volunteer time in the library or the donation of like material plus a processing fee may sometimes be accepted in lieu of outright payment.

Whether overdue fines and lost/damaged fees are recovered from patrons or not, all libraries need to build into their budgets regular, ongoing funds for replacement and repair of materials. To not do so is to be in a state of denial.

Patron Registration

Patron registration is the opening of a new account for qualifying library customers. It is a process very similar to walking into a department store, such as Macy's or Nordstrom's, and signing up for a store credit card. In this case, the library card takes the place of the charge card. Libraries vary greatly in the way they handle the registration process. Public libraries tend to have the most stringent procedures for registering new patrons and verifying their identification. This makes sense because their patron base is large, ever changing, and less intimately known to them. Many public libraries are experimenting with online patron registration forms that allow customers to fill out the required information, and then e-mail the form to the library. Library staff members process the form, then wait for the patron to appear in person with the appropriate photo identification before issuing the new library card.

Academic libraries may rely on official campus identification cards and draw from enrollment databases for patron verification. Special libraries may vary from not requiring registration at all, on the one hand, to a very formal process involving security clearance, on the other.

School libraries consult class lists supplied by teachers or the administrative office at the beginning of the academic term to open student accounts for that year.

In the case of some private research facilities or university libraries, community members with no affiliation to the institution may be able to purchase access privileges. In this case, the registration process involves payment of the fee in addition to the collection of name, address, and other identifying information.

Why Register Patrons?

There are many valid reasons for a library or information center to register its patrons. Some of the major reasons include the following:

To verify that a person qualifies to use the specific library.

To determine the level of borrowing privileges, once qualified.

To establish a record of who borrowed what items.

To have contact information to locate patrons with overdue materials.

To collect demographic information on customers for planning purposes.

To be able to recall items needed for reserve use.

Privacy of Patron Records

Once patron data have been gathered and becomes part of the library's database of customer information, it is very important for staff to realize that this personal data is private. Industry ethics and laws in some states advocate that such confidential information be afforded both internal and external privacy protection. This means that neither personal data gathered nor an individual's circulation records are to be shared with outside agencies; nor are they accessible to library staff other than those who are assigned to work with these records.

This issue and others relating to workplace ethics are discussed more fully in another section of this book in chapter 8, "Ethics in the Information Age."

Stacks Maintenance

Maintenance of the library's collections is crucial to an efficient operation. In most libraries, collection maintenance tasks are managed by the Circulation Department as an extension of their primary mission to provide access to and to track the loan of materials. Admittedly, these are housekeeping tasks and tend to be somewhat tedious chores that must be done to maintain quality library service.

Some of the key maintenance tasks include shelving and shelf reading; cleaning, repair, and rebinding items; and inventorying items. Although the accurate and rapid reshelving of all materials is an ongoing, daily activity in any library, the other tasks take place on a more periodic basic. Many libraries and media centers that are closed to students for holiday or summer breaks select that time to conduct an inventory of their collections. For those libraries and information centers that do not close for extended periods of time, collection inventorying may be done in phases, with parts of the collection temporarily unavailable to researchers while the process is underway.

Library Circulation Systems

Today the majority of libraries, information centers, and school media centers have an automated circulation system in place. Modern systems now link a database of bibliographic records with patron use records to form an integrated OPAC. Most of today's systems provide a module that is accessible on the Web, allowing anytime–anywhere searching by patrons and staff. In addition, those OPAC systems that are fully Z 39.50 compatible allow a user to simultaneously search catalogs from two or more different libraries, even if each catalog is running software from different vendors. Z 39.50 is a protocol by which one OPAC transfers a search inquiry or other data to another OPAC, without the user being required to reenter the information, using the precise search keys of the second OPAC.

For many larger academic and public libraries, the current system may be a fifth or sixth generation system. Early use of computerized library circulation systems began in the 1960s at large, academic facilities. Many of these libraries had been experimenting with key punch cards to tabulate circulation in the prior decade.[2] Before the advent of commercial software packages, some of these libraries developed their own homegrown automated circulation systems, usually in concert with campus or municipal computer departments. In the early 1970s, CL Systems, Inc. (later to become known as CLSI) was one of the first commercial vendors to begin selling turnkey library circulation systems. They were soon followed by many other companies offering software solutions for basic library circulation tasks.[3]

These early automated systems were limited to circulation control functions—check-in and check-out transactions, calculation of fines, printing of overdue notices, and placing items on hold—all of which are time-consuming, laborious, and repetitive, but necessary tasks for accurate inventory control and library operation. Typically, these early turnkey and homegrown systems were not integrated to include bibliographic "look-up" functions for the public. Thus, the wood card catalog, with its numerous drawers filled with index cards, remained the tool for patron access to the library's holdings. Maintenance of the card catalog required an ongoing effort of detailed, repetitive, painstaking work by cataloging department staff.

The first OPACs, which married the patron records with a detailed database of the library's holdings and were geared for public use, arrived on the scene in the early 1980s.[4] As OPACs matured and became commonplace in the next 15 years or so, that longtime staple of libraries, the card catalog, was superseded by a computer screen. Across the nation and around the world, libraries began closing their card catalogs. Even the venerable *New Yorker* magazine noted with mixed emotions this passing of a cultural icon. In a 1994 article, staff writer Nicholson Baker caused quite a stir in the library world as he mourned the closing of Harvard's card catalog and questioned the need for installation of its automated system, HOLLIS.[5]

Although there certainly have been growing pains associated with the transfer to OPACs, most library staff will overwhelmingly attest to the benefits that automation has brought both to patrons and to employees. For customers, this has meant improved, decentralized access and convenience, user-centered features, and the demystification of library processes. OPACs have also allowed customers to play a more active role by providing precise title location and availability data and enabling patron-initiated placement of holds. For library staff, integrated computer systems have automated many tedious, repetitive tasks associated with circulation's record-keeping functions and technical services' cataloging operations.

There are some patrons who still lament the conversion to computer access and feel at a loss. An older, longtime library user recently said to one of the authors, "I feel like I have lost the college library since the installation of computers. Without the card catalog, I don't even want to come to the library." A renewed effort to assist and train reluctant computer users is one approach to mitigating this discomfort, but realistically, there will always be some researchers who resist any change from the familiar.

Since the early OPACs of the 1980s, there have been many advances and improvements in the product, most parallel to developments in computer hardware and software technology overall. Currently, Web interfaces are the state of the art for automated library systems. These contemporary card catalogs are remotely accessible, often to the general public, with no special password required, and offer many convenient, value-added features, such as online renewal and account checking.

Automation of library systems does come with a hefty price tag. Installation of a new system is regarded by library agencies as a capital expenditure and often costs in the six-figure price range. For most public sector library agencies, this translates into a competitive bid process with vendors submitting complex responses to library-generated requests for proposals, or RFPs.

OPACS in Common Use

At the beginning of the new millennium, OPACS were in common use across the United States. Exact statistics for all types of libraries are not available, especially for schools and for special libraries, for which data gathering tends to be difficult. But trends are visible to practitioners in the field. One such observation by Dick Boss, a respected library automation consultant, estimates that nearly 100 percent of the nation's 2,000 largest libraries were automated by 1999.[6]

Those libraries that are still relying on a manual system for their circulation and other operations tend to be smaller, rural, poorly funded, and not belonging to any type of library network or consortium. These typically include smaller special libraries, such as those found in churches, museums, historical societies and archives, or obscure government agencies.[7] School libraries in smaller private or parochial schools, as well as those located in isolated and rural public school districts, are other examples of those often without an automated system. Because these libraries are without partners, minimally funded, often staffed by volunteers or temporary help, have limited telecommunications infrastructures, and have done little to convert existing paper records to machine-readable formats, the roadblocks to installation of an OPAC are many.

Two approaches that are helping isolated libraries and information centers to make progress toward automation are grant funding from private sources and membership in state-funded, multi-type library networks. Although no single grant will provide a ready-to-use OPAC on a silver platter, the receipt of specific grants can assist a library in laying the groundwork needed before conversion from a manual to an automated system can take place. Various state and national telecommunications measures have provided infrastructure funding for needy schools and libraries, and grants from the private Gates Library Foundation provide updated hardware, software, and staff training. By partnering with state-funded, multi-type library consortia, a once-isolated library can gain much needed expertise, access to consultants, and reduced pricing as part of a larger group.

Early Circulation Methods

Ledgers were the earliest method used in libraries for tracking information on the borrower and the item borrowed. For the system to function well, multiple ledgers were required. Each transaction for a business day was noted in chronological order in a daybook. Later, data from the daybook was copied into separate ledgers, which provided access by patron name and by book title.

The ledger containing the borrowing record of each patron was arranged alphabetically by the borrower's last name and allowed several pages to record ongoing entries. The third ledger listed each book in the collection with several pages reserved to record successive borrowers and their respective due dates. Between them, the three logs provided three different access points to circulation data. The daybook provided a daily transaction log, but to verify a patron's account, the alphabetical patron ledger needed to be consulted. To ascertain the whereabouts of a particular book, the book ledger needed to be viewed. Ledgers were in common use in American libraries until about the time of the Civil War.[8]

An earlier variant method, which eliminated the need for multiple ledgers, was the so-called dummy system. Wood dummies—that is, blocks with lined paper attached to them—were used to represent each book; as a patron checked out a book, his or her name and the book's due date were noted on the side of the book dummy. The dummy was then placed in the empty shelf space to indicate that the book was charged out. A variation of this was to have a dummy represent each patron. The correct block was then placed on the shelf as the book was removed; book title and due date were then written on the dummy.[9] An obvious limitation of this version was that each patron was limited to one book at a time.

These early tracking systems worked successfully only when dealing with small numbers of both borrowers and circulating items. Once the number of patrons, the volume of use, and the collection size increased, these methods quickly became cumbersome and inefficient.

Improvements on the ledger method of tracking circulation led to various systems using paper slips. These transaction slips functioned like receipts and were inserted into a book pocket attached to the inside of each tome. Further improvements on the slip system led to the two-card method. One pre-prepared card held key bibliographic information about the book, such as author, title, call number, and copy number, and was tucked inside the book pocket. The second card contained borrower identification and was kept at the charging desk for a borrower's signature at checkout. Both cards were stamped with the due date when an item was checked out.

The Newark System, so called because of its first use by the Newark, New Jersey, Public Library in 1896, became a popular example of the two-card system and was in widespread use for several decades. Approximately 30 years later, a refinement of the two-card system, known as the Detroit Self-Charging System, raised efficiency with the use of preprinted due date cards and library identification cards.[10]

Although these systems seem archaic today, in times of lengthy periods of electrical outages or computer malfunctions, library staff may need to revert to these manual systems to try to maintain some order over circulation. A library technician intern in a local school district encountered just such a situation recently. Besides the unfamiliarity of the manual system to the borrowers and to staff, not all of the elementary school children were able to sign their names, which presented further complications during the outage period.

In the later half of the twentieth century, many systems for printing due-date cards, book cards, charge cards, and borrowers' identification cards were developed to replace the earlier manual tasks of typing, stamping, and signing. Borrower identification cards ranged from paper to embossed plastic to the now common cards with optically readable barcodes.

The Library Card As a Symbol of Opportunity

Though the details surrounding the first borrower's card issued to a customer are lost to history, the concept of possessing one's own library card remains a symbol of opportunity and lifelong learning. A library card is the key to the free public library services that are a right for all citizens in the United States.

For residents, retirees, and immigrants new to a community, the initial trip to the public library to sign up for a user's card is a first step in accessing local programs and services. It is a fact well-known to public library staff that for ex-convicts and others returning to mainstream society, signing up for a library card in their new town is a recommended early step in their rehabilitation. A library identification card is equated with attaining literacy; the pursuit of pleasure reading; exploration of resources for study, research, and job search; Internet access; cultural programs; and more.

And for young readers, their first library card is a proud possession that encourages them to grow in their reading skills. A recent ALA promotional ad released in conjunction with National Library Card Sign-Up Month urges parents "to make sure your child has the most important school supply of all—one available free to every child—a library card." Such a campaign emphasizes the important and multifaceted community resource that a library is to its customers.

Characteristics of an Automated Circulation System

Upon examination, the key characteristics of a modern automated circulation system are not too different from the basic inventory control needs of the nineteenth century manual systems briefly described previously.

At minimum, a circulation system needs to do the following:

- Be efficient and easy to use for both staff and patrons in all of its modules. Just because library staff may think that a system is wonderful and efficient, does not mean that the public interface is equally convenient and intuitive.

- Record and track three key elements relating to collection circulation: (1) the person who borrowed the item, (2) the exact item borrowed, and (3) the time the item was borrowed and when is it due back.

- Track the status of all items in the collection individually. Accuracy and detail are important aspects of an efficient inventory control system and thus are primary needs in a library circulation system. The system must record, at a minimum, whether items are charged-out, overdue, lost, or missing; interlibrary loans; out of circulation for repair or binding; or on the shelf and available for use.

- Track the status of all patron accounts. This includes all registered borrowers, either active or inactive, and especially those with overdue items, outstanding fines, blocks, or other problems with their accounts.

- Match requests for holds with incoming items. Upon patron or staff request, the system must be able to flag the record of an item that is charged out and then acknowledge that the requestor is next in line to receive the desired title when returned.

- Provide statistics relating to the circulation of items. Key statistics include, at a minimum, the number of times a particular item has been checked out; overall circulation by week, month, or other period; circulation by individual library outlet, branch, department, or system wide; and circulation by call number.

Since the coming of the Internet, there is a new characteristic that is currently essential and can be added to the list above. A modern, integrated circulation system must offer a Web interface option in its OPAC module. Web access for an OPAC serves a very utilitarian purpose because it is the same platform upon which many other key library services and research tools are now delivered. In addition to taking advantage of all emerging Web technologies, such an interface provides customers the convenience of easy toggling between a library OPAC and other Web resources.

Other hallmarks of Internet access that provide added value and convenience to a Web-based OPAC include anytime–anywhere access, patron authentication, patron-initiated holds, interlibrary loan requests, and account tracking.

A rule of thumb for all library automation systems is that the current system should receive serious review at least every seven years, with replacement of the system and a change in vendors a possibility to be considered. In the interim period, there will probably be upgrades (e.g., new software releases) to the system provided by the vendor every year or two to reflect new features and capabilities.

Automation Resources

Although settling on an automation vendor is a daunting task, there are currently many reputable sources to help a library manager or other staff with the selection of vendors and products. For the past 20 years, Pamela Cibbarelli, a leading analyst and writer in the field of library automation, has published a bi-annual directory that lists software packages, Web sites, consultants, and other key resources related to the automation of North American libraries.[11] In addition, she also publishes annually user rating surveys known as "Cibbarelli's Surveys" that provide candid comments from the users of a specific library automation software product. These surveys are published in the trade periodicals *Computers in Libraries* and *Information Today.*

Another respected industry periodical, *Library Journal,* features the results of its own library automation marketplace survey in each April edition. The published results focus on the performance of major library automation vendors and include profiles on each company with data such as market niche, number of installations, market share, and new products and services. *Library Technology Reports,* a bi-monthly periodical published by the ALA, is another authoritative source for information on library systems and equipment.

Professional conferences aimed for the library generalist, as well as those specifically targeting technical staff, also provide an extremely valuable venue for data gathering, both from automation vendors and from library and information center colleagues. Examples include, but are by no means limited to, the Internet Librarian, annual meetings of state and regional library associations, the annual and midwinter sessions of the ALA, the National Online Meeting, and the Special Libraries Association conferences. Typically, at the exhibit hall of the conference, the major automation vendors host booths staffed by sales and technical representatives who are there to answer questions and demonstrate their software products.

User groups of a particular automation package (e.g., Endeavor, Winnebago, SIRSI) help provide a different perspective to balance the vendor's point of view. These groups are composed of customers, and they communicate through a listserv and often hold periodic regional workshops. Querying user groups before making a purchase decision or when drafting the specifications for an RFP can be a valuable way to evaluate products and customer satisfaction. Once a system has been chosen, participation in a user group provides support, shared expertise, and strength in numbers when lobbying the vendor for improvements. With Web access to most OPACs a given, another means of testing the performance of a potential system is to anonymously use it just as a patron would do. In addition, in-person visits to library sites provide a unique chance to watch multiple users at work on a system and to consult with technical services staff in detail.

With the great strides gained in computerized systems over the past four decades, library routines have become increasingly streamlined with each new generation of automated systems, especially in the area of circulation functions. The once standard tasks of manually date-stamping books or calculating overdue fines by hand are now seen as quaint and old-fashioned routines that show up in classic movies.

Library Security

Thieves in an archive? Violence in a library? How dare they! There are many patrons, members of the general public, and even novice staff members who cherish the concept of a library as a safe haven from the woes of the outside world. Unfortunately, libraries, archives, and media and information centers are prone to purposeful theft, vandalism, and other crimes. Just as there seems to be more news media coverage of violent events as a whole, libraries have their share of shootings, seemingly senseless attacks, and other crimes that make the evening news.

Because the circulation or loan services department is focused on the safe return of the library's materials, the broader issues of library security and crimes also tend to fall under their jurisdiction. Generally, there are two categories of security issues. The first category is offenses involving library property. This includes the theft of library materials or equipment; mutilation or intentional damage to library materials or equipment; and vandalism to the building. The second category is offenses against people—staff or patrons—that take place in the library building. Examples of such offenses include abusive conduct, assault, and indecent exposure.

Security in libraries is not a new concern. During the Roman Empire, it was the custom for a conquering army to pillage library buildings as they swept through a city, taking library books as spoils of war. In more modern times, a notorious library thief, Stephen Blumberg, was convicted in the 1990s and served a prison term for the theft of approximately 24,000 volumes from libraries in 45 states.[12]

Theft

The most common incidents of crime are theft or mutilation of library materials. The perpetrator may be a student with no money for a photocopy machine, a kleptomaniac, a self-appointed censor, or a professional thief out to make a profit. It could also be a library employee.

Electronic theft detection systems were first installed in libraries in the 1960s. By the 1980s, all but the smallest libraries and information centers were using some type of security system to deter theft. Once the library market was saturated, vendors targeted retail stores to find additional customers for their security product. Known in the industry as *materials control systems*, the most commonly used systems are found in libraries, supermarkets, and retail stores. Although not foolproof, they do lower losses through the concept of deterrence. Many would-be thieves, seeing a security gate or locking turnstile at an exit point, will be discouraged from attempting to steal an item. Setting off an alarm and being confronted with possession of an unauthorized item in a public place is embarrassing at the least.

Such systems in and of themselves are by no means infallible. But when combined with vigilant staff efforts, security systems have generally reduced pilferage by about 80 percent over that experienced by a library with no security devices in place, according to 3M, a major vendor of such systems.[13] Figure 6.1 depicts a library patron passing through a security portal.

There are various models of materials control systems; some work on radio frequency, others on electromagnetism. Typically, a screen or gate detects sensitized items. Each item—such as a book, magazine, videocassette, or DVD caddy—carries a hidden or disguised target. When properly checked out, the item is desensitized and the target turned off, and the patron passes through the security gate uneventfully. When an item has not been checked out properly and desensitized, passing it through the gate triggers an alarm and locks the gate or turnstile. Options to the turnstile include the addition of flashing red lights or loud, recorded messages to increase the visibility of an unauthorized exit. Larger library facilities may place gates on every floor or at all reading room exits. When in use, these detection system turnstiles and gates must comply with the Americans with Disabilities Act (ADA) so as not to present a physical barrier to access for those in wheelchairs.

Figure 6.1. Security equipment can help discourage library theft when positioned at checkout counters and building exits. Reprinted by permission of 3M Library Systems.

Pass around systems are another variation on security arrangements. This alternative, which is used in large video stores such as Blockbuster and other chains, is most likely to be used in nonacademic library settings where patrons are unlikely to bring items back into the building until they are ready to relinquish them. In such a system, the item is never desensitized. Instead, it is passed around the security gate by a staff member after being checked out and handed to the customer who is standing outside the security zone.

Preventive Measures

Attention to overall library security increases the effectiveness of materials control systems. A good place to begin is with a survey of the library's security. Conduct the survey with security or police personnel to gain their expert input. Assess vulnerable areas, such as unsecured windows and unalarmed delivery or staff entrances, which allow one to circumvent the secured entrance. Controlling all exits with gates, alarms, locks, cameras, electronic keypads, or guards helps to minimize such security gaps.

Internal library procedures should also be considered. For example, how long do new materials lie around in the technical services area before a security or tattletape target is applied to them? Who has access to the new, unprocessed materials? Don't overlook library, custodial or other building staff. Taking active measures, such as locking down computers and peripherals, TV monitors, VCRs, and other property can help prevent equipment loss.

When building a new library from scratch, staff have the advantage of taking security issues into consideration with the architect and designing a facility to deter theft and crime. Attention to preserving visual corridors in reading rooms and stack areas that allow for surveillance by personnel from service counters can increase the security of collections, staff, and patrons. Minimizing the presence of poorly lit stack areas and dark, remote corners in the library is also very important. Such safety and design concerns apply to the library building itself and to adjacent parking areas. Although not often discussed in the literature on library security issues, the safety of these adjacent areas is an important issue. If unsafe, it can provide a barrier to patron access to the library and its services.

Within existing library structures, there are various methods for augmenting security, such as increased lighting, installing video surveillance cameras, hiring a library security guard to patrol the building, increasing staff visibility at all service points, and enhancing materials controls systems. Attempting to offer reasonable loan periods on library materials is another consideration that could impact theft and mutilation. For example, if an item can be checked out for only two days and a patron needs the material for a longer period, then they may think that stealing it is the best answer to satisfy their needs.

Realistic Policies

As with other security systems, a determined or practiced thief will find a way around them. So the bottom line for library staff is that losses to the collection will occur. Therefore, realistic administrators need to allow for some shrinkage in the collection and to budget funds for the replacement of stolen or damaged items. Also, setting aside funds to periodically upgrade or replace security systems is a necessary planning strategy. To be cost-effective, the overall cost of the security measures should not exceed the amount saved by having those procedures in place.

Have a policy in place with the library's parent organization for penalizing a perpetrator once caught. Typically, in an academic library, students can be fined, placed on probation, or at least sent to the dean's office for a warning. In school settings, disciplinary action can be taken and parents notified. Public libraries will want to have good working relations with their local police department to provide them needed support with security issues. Library staff should not attempt to physically restrain suspected thieves or perpetrators, but should summon the assistance of trained security personnel.

As with many other elements of a library or information center (relevancy of collections, helpfulness of staff, public hours, and so on) the library's reputation for safety will be known in the community and will affect patron satisfaction and usage levels.

Mutilation

The purposeful act of mutilation may involve cutting out a section of a book or magazine with the intent of taking just those pages needed by the irresponsible patron. Or it may involve destroying pages or tearing whole volumes from their spines in an effort to eliminate offensive photographs or text. Because mutilation typically occurs inside the reading room or library building, security systems are of little help in catching perpetrators in the act. If a security target remains attached to the pages that were removed and the perpetrator attempts to pass through the exit gate, they can be caught at that time and dealt with. Sadly, however, the damage to materials is already done. Sometimes the purpose of the mutilation is simply to defeat the security system.

In a school or academic setting where much usage is linked to topical assignments, informing faculty of the problem can help catch a potential mutilator. Some libraries periodically mount displays of damaged and mutilated materials in an attempt to educate patrons and perhaps deter would-be mutilators.

People Problems

Those libraries that are open to the general public are the most apt to encounter the so-called "problem patrons." Because these facilities are open for long hours (often including evenings and weekends), and provide warm, comfortable shelter, they are inviting places of shelter for homeless and other needy people. No identification is required to enter, and there is an abundance of free entertainment available, along with restrooms and hot, running water.

Most problem patron behavior can be characterized as falling into the following categories: nuisance behavior (e.g., lonely or elderly people who monopolize reference personnel or carry on long-winded monologues); criminal behavior (e.g., vandalizing materials, stealing materials, performing sexually lewd acts); and various types of behavior that are often bizarre, unpredictable, and threatening. These acts are often exhibited by mentally disturbed patrons.

Many libraries provide special staff training conducted by outside experts or local law enforcement personnel in dealing with problematic individuals. Such training usually includes conflict resolution, safety issues, defusing difficult situations, and other techniques. Dealing with problem patrons in the course of a workday is a genuine issue for most library staff, and they deserve access to this training to best prepare them for handling such interactions.

Disaster Preparedness

Another aspect of library security is disaster preparedness. Also referred to as emergency preparedness, this is a related but much larger security issue that focuses on making ready a library facility and its staff in the event of a natural disaster, such as flood, fire, earthquake, tornado, or the like. Disasters perpetrated by criminals, such as bombs, arson, and hostage-taking, are also included in emergency preparedness. Just as with theft, libraries do not have a special immunity from disasters.

To have a viable disaster plan, much advance footwork, preparation, and coordination is needed. An up-to-date, written library disaster plan is probably part of a larger campus, school district, corporate, city, or other agency's overall plan. Typically, a disaster plan should specify the chain of command for decision making and include data such as maps and floor plans, evacuation routes, and procedures. Highest priority collections for removal or safeguarding should be indicated. Computer data backups, especially all OPAC files, should be housed at an alternate, remote location in case on-site files are unrecoverable.

A thorough discussion of disaster preparedness is beyond the scope of this textbook. Many comprehensive books have been written about this topic, and certain library industry Web sites provide helpful emergency checklists. The ALA Web site features a Disaster Preparedness Clearinghouse developed by the Association for Library Collections and Technical Services with links to many key emergency response or conservation agencies (Web site address: http://www.ala.org/alcts/publications/disaster.html).

Whether the responsibility of a library director managing a multi-branch system or of the solo librarian operating a small, special library, disaster preparedness training is a topic to be taken seriously.

Interlibrary Loan Services

Interlibrary loan (ILL) is an important service whereby individual libraries agree to share their collections and to supply materials on demand to one another for patron use. Upon the receipt of a patron's request, the borrowing library asks another facility to supply a needed book, video, or copy of a periodical article for a minimal fee (typically $10 to $20) or sometimes free of charge. Often, agreements are drawn up among member libraries belonging to regional networks or consortia that formalize this cooperation. But, typically, those libraries that receive public funds—state colleges and universities and public systems—will automatically accept requests from another library without a formal cooperating agreement, though they may impose fees or restrictions. In contrast, special libraries that are part of private corporations or institutions, such as those in law firms and businesses, and that do not belong to any networks, are under no obligation to loan out their materials. And, in fact, for reasons of competitive intelligence, they may not want to do so because it might assist a rival business.

In state-funded library networks, all libraries that want to receive services must provide some level of access to their own collections as a prerequisite to membership. This may take the form of providing on-site use, ILL services, access to specialized reference services, or even direct borrowing to qualifying customers affiliated with the network.

Often, ILL services are under the umbrella of a circulation department because each external loan, though requiring special handling and attention, is just another type of borrowing transaction. The net result of this sharing of materials is better service for library customers. Specifically, patrons have access to a much-expanded resource base. Even in the information-rich age of the new millennium, no single library can have it all. Through the use of ILL, the boundaries of a single library's collection, or even a system's, are extended far beyond its own hardcopy and electronic holdings.

The *National Interlibrary Loan Code for the United States,* a document compiled by the Reference and Adult Services Division of the ALA, serves as a guideline for libraries in general and for any systems or networks that want to develop their own ILL policies.

As the Code states:

> Interlibrary Loan has been described as an adjunct to, not a substitute for, collection development in individual libraries. Changes in the last decade have brought increasing availability of materials in alternative formats, an abundance of verification and location information, and a shift in the very nature of interlibrary cooperation. Interlibrary borrowing is an integral element of collection development for all libraries, not an ancillary option.[14]

Regarding the reciprocity implied in such a nationwide effort, the Code notes:

> The effectiveness of a national resource sharing system depends upon the responsible distribution of borrowing and lending. Libraries of all types and sizes should be willing to share their resources liberally so that a relatively few libraries are not overburdened. Libraries must be willing to lend if they wish to borrow.[15]

For researchers in the know, ILL is one of the best-kept secrets of libraries. There are rarely big, bright signs offering this extended service. Rather, it has always been suggested to patrons on a case-by-case basis as the reference interview progresses or when the request for information cannot be filled locally. The ILL service is similar to a special order in a retail store. When the color, size, and label of the jacket you want (say, burgundy, size 12, Liz Claiborne) is not available, your local department store might offer to call other regional branches to see if they stock the exact item desired and can then send it to your local store.

The first formal mention of ILL in America was in a letter to the editor in *Library Journal*'s premier issue in 1876. ILL became common in the 1920s, although cooperative loaning between libraries had already been taking place for some time prior to that.[16] With the adoption of the first ALA *Interlibrary Loan Code* in 1919 and the growing number of union or shared catalogs of library holdings, ILL became firmly established.[17] Standardized forms were developed mid-century and were in common usage until the advent of OCLC's ILL model, faxing, and then e-mail in the 1990s rendered the multipart paper forms obsolete.

Limitations on ILL requests

Certain types of library materials may not be available for interlibrary loan because of their physical size, shape or condition, copyright restrictions, or local demand. Typically, these materials include, but are not limited to, computer software; rare, very old, or valuable books; most new books; the hardcopy issue of a journal in its entirety; audiovisual materials; and reference books. Each library sets its own limitations on what materials it will and will not loan out. In addition, copyright law restricts the number of articles that can be photocopied from the same journal without paying royalty fees.

An important concept of ILL is that the service is to locate and obtain a specific book or article citation; thus, ILL is not a subject search for materials but a search for a supplying library that owns a precise title not available at the local level. The ILL service is considered to be a supplement to the on-site collection. On the other hand, ILL should not be mistaken as a substitute for collection development in individual libraries. If an item is repeatedly requested through ILL, it is an indication that there is a local need for that item, and purchase for the permanent collection should seriously be considered. Repeat requests for ILL may also provide data for cooperative collection development efforts among libraries.

When requesting an item through ILL, there is a direct correlation between the accuracy and completeness of the book, video, or journal article citation provided and the likelihood of the material being located. Staff from the borrowing library search large databases such as OCLC to locate an item that matches the citation provided by the customer. So when a patron submits a citation with the author's name misspelled or omitted, incomplete publishing data, or other inaccuracies, the chances of locating the material are diminished substantially.

Once a supplier is located, the borrowing library queries the potential lender as to the availability for loaning out. It may take queries to several libraries that own the item before a successful loan actually happens. There are many reasons that multiple queries may be required, including the following: the item in question may be checked out or may have been sent out to the bindery; if it is an older publication, it might be in a remote storage facility and require a longer delivery time; ILL departments in academic libraries are often closed for two to three weeks during holiday or semester breaks. Many times, diligent library technicians processing ILLs will shop around until they find a free supplier so they can save the patron from having to pay a service charge.

Patrons frequently ask, "How long before my ILL request will come in?" The reality of ILL is that the turnaround time for receiving the desired material varies with each specific request. For researchers and students using this inexpensive but often slow service, the caveat is "submit your request as early as possible," before a project deadline. Anecdotal evidence and the disclaimers on many library Web sites indicate that, for libraries using modern methods of ILL processing, the bulk of requests arrive within a two-week period. But on a case-by-case basis, the turnaround time can be unpredictable. And, certainly, international loan requests may take considerably longer to fill.

Abuse of the ILL Service

No discussion of the benefits of interlibrary sharing would be complete without mention of the so-called abuses and imbalances that can arise. Many libraries have limits on the number of ILL requests that a patron can have "in the pipeline" at any one time. One of the authors of this text remembers an eager nursing student at a community college who, during a single library visit, submitted requests for 25 articles from specialized health periodicals. From that time on, that small college library instituted a limit of 10 ILL items at once, per patron.

Staff time is a consideration when setting reasonable limits on ILLs, as is the estimated cost of each ILL transaction. One estimate conducted at a metropolitan public library put the minimum cost in staff time for processing an ILL request to borrow an item at an average of $10 per unit.[18] Calculating the cost of an ILL transaction can provide a basis for determining a fee schedule in an effort to recover the costs of the service. One source for computing costs is Boucher's *Interlibrary Loan Practices Handbook.*[19]

Another consideration is that completed ILL requests often lie on the hold shelf of the requesting library, never to be picked up by the patron. The reasons why a library patron neglects to pick up the item vary, but it might be that he or she found another supplier for the item, refused to pay any ILL changes, simply forgot, or lost interest in the material that was once so urgently needed. Placing a limit on the number of simultaneous ILL requests per patron helps balance the needs of borrowing and supplying libraries. Remember that in the case of a borrowed book or video, when it is sent out on loan, the item remains unavailable to local readers for three to four weeks.

Because of their vast resources and the breadth of their collections, large university and research libraries traditionally have been deluged with requests for technical, medical, and other materials not available in small, generalized library collections. This can create quite an imbalance, with large facilities constantly being asked for material, while small libraries rarely receive loan requests. For this reason, the ILL Code recommends, "The requesting library should avoid sending the burden of its requests to a few libraries. Major resource libraries should be used as a last resort."[20]

As a means of remedying this transaction imbalance, some states have set up a system of ILL reimbursement within their boundaries. This means that a public library receives a set dollar amount as reimbursement for supplying an ILL requested for a library patron from outside its jurisdiction. According to a study in January 2000 by Himmel and Wilson (library consultants on such reimbursement programs), of the 45 states responding to the survey, 22 states received some type of state reimbursement for ILL, whereas the same number did not. (One state did not respond to this question.)[21]

The widespread use of automated library catalogs, especially union catalogs that delineate holdings of multiple libraries, along with other advances in technology in the latter years of the twentieth century, have greatly enhanced the process of identifying a potential ILL supplier. Locating those libraries holding a desired title is now faster and easier overall. Plus, the ability to identify various libraries—small or large, well-known or lesser known, in state or out of state, helps to spread the resource sharing more equitably.

How It Works

Here is a recent illustration of how the service works typically. One of the authors just received (through ILL) a request for an obscure local history book, *The History of the County of Guysborough, Nova Scotia.* The request was placed with the college library's loan services department, using its new Web-based ILL form. The request form (see Figures 6.2 and 6.3) is part of the library's Web site and is accessible to campus students, staff, and faculty (http://library.cuesta.cc.ca.us/illoan.htm). Because the college subscribes to the bibliographic utility OCLC, its expansive international database of members' holdings was then searched for this title. More than 15 potential supplying libraries were identified. Several libraries were queried unsuccessfully before the University of Windsor in Ontario, Canada, agreed to supply the title. A hardcopy volume was shipped fourth-class library rate to the borrowing library, along with an invoice of $10. The patron was allowed to check the book out for two weeks and promptly paid the fee directly to the loaning library.

Cuesta College

Learning Resources

Interlibrary Loan Request

<< Back

Materials unavailable at the Cuesta College Libraries may be available from other libraries. All Cuesta faculty, staff, and students may use this service. For additional information, please see the Information Desk librarian or contact the Interlibrary Loan Department (805) 546-3155 x2469.

Fields followed by an * are required fields and must be filled out in order for your request to be processed.

Processing time for most requests is 7-10 working days.

Borrower Identification

Name: [   ] *   Date of request: [12/12/2001] * (mm/dd/yy)

Library card #
Student body card # [   ] *   Need before: [   ] * (mm/dd/yy)
or SSN:

Phone: [   ] * (i.e. 805-123-1234)   E-mail: [   ]

Willing to pay:* ○ Yes ○ No   If yes, limit:* ○ $1-5 ○ $6-10 ○ over $10

Please indicate who you are? *   Where would you like to pick up the item? *
○ Cuesta College Employee   ○ San Luis Obispo Campus
○ Cuesta College Student   ○ North County Campus
○ SLO County Community User

Book Request

Author: [   ]   Title: [   ]

Publisher: [   ]   Edition: [   ]

Publication
Date: [   ]   Series: [   ]

Magazine or Journal Article

Journal Title: [   ]

Figure 6.2. Many college, university, and public libraries now provide online interlibrary loan forms as a convenience for patrons. This one is from Cuesta College in San Luis Obispo, California. Reprinted by permission of Cuesto College Library.

Paul V. Galvin Library

Illinois Institute of Technology

| SERVICES | ABOUT | RESOURCES | COLLECTIONS | HOME |

ACCESS
SERVICES

REFERENCE

WORKSHOPS

ASK A
LIBRARIAN

INTERLIBRARY
LOANS

PROXY
ACCOUNTS

LAPTOP
AREA

Interlibrary Loan Request for Books & Conference Proceedings

1. Fill in all requested fields (*indicates a required field) in order for your request to be processed.
2. When you are done, click on "Send your Item Request" to send your request to the Access Services Department.
3. Or, if you wish to start over, click the "Start Over" button. This will clear the form, and you can start over or cancel at this point
4. Missing information will result in the delay or rejection of your request.

Before submitting a request, please make sure that the Galvin Library does not own the item by checking Voyager or ILLINET Online.

Patron Information

ILL services are available to IIT faculty, staff, students, and affiliates. If you are not IIT affiliated, your request will not be processed.

What is your status?	Undergraduate ▼
*Name:	
*IIT ID Number:	
*Email Address:	
*Telephone:	
*College or Department:	
Select a Location to pick-up your item:	Paul V. Galvin Library Circulation Desk ▼

Item Information

| *Tell us the latest date this item would be useful to you: | Two Weeks ▼ |
| * Title: (No Abbreviations) | |

Figure 6.3. Interlibrary loan form; Galvin Library, Illinois Institute of Technology. Reprinted by permission of the Paul Galvin Library, Illinois Institute of Technology, December 2001 (www.gl.iit.edu).

Compared to the expense of trying to obtain a copy of this out-of-print title, or, even more costly, having to journey cross-country to read the book in a Canadian library, the small fee was well worth the convenience of having the book shipped to the customer's library.

Initiating an ILL Request

For many patrons, an ILL request is prompted by a visit to their library. Often such a request begins at the circulation desk when a patron realizes that a desired item is not held locally. Frequently, it may also develop as the final step of a reference interview, as local resources are explored and found to be inadequate. For patrons who search a library's OPAC remotely and are familiar with the ILL service, a request might be submitted as an e-mail request or a telephone request. Conveniently, many libraries now have complete ILL forms available on their Web sites. Again, each library will determine how it accepts an ILL request. Often, ILL services are limited to valid, card-carrying patrons, so that whatever form the request takes—an e-mail inquiry, a completed ILL form submitted from a Website, or an in-person request—some verification of accounts is performed.

Historically, an important aspect of ILL is that the transaction is library to library. It is true that changes are now on the horizon that will make online, customer-initiated ILL requests more commonplace within official library networks, but patrons will still need to be members in good standing at one of the participating libraries. Authentication of their status will be part of the log-on interface. At the current time, at the majority of libraries in the United States, patrons cannot initiate a request on their own, independent of a home library affiliation. The borrowing library places the request and, in effect, vouches for the patron's careful use of the item. This also helps to ensure the prompt return of borrowed items to the lending library and the collection of any service fees charged. In many cases, the loaned item—once delivered—does not leave the borrowing library. For example, loaned microfilm must be used on site in the requesting patron's library. Often, unique or older books, such as local history titles or reference books, are loaned with the understanding that the customer must read them on site.

Direct Borrowing

Direct borrowing is a variation on the interlibrary loan services described previously and one that many seasoned library users have yet to experience. In library consortia where direct borrowing is an agreed-upon service, patrons from one participating library can walk into any other member library and check out items. The computer system of the lending library verifies that patrons are in good standing with their home library before authorizing the transactions. The home library generally is responsible for enforcing loan periods. In some arrangements, the patron must return borrowed items to the lending library. In others, the items can be returned to any participating library.

One of the authors had the opportunity to use direct borrowing when he worked at an engineering university in Chicago, the Illinois Institute of Technology (IIT). That university participated in a consortium with more than 30 other academic libraries in Illinois. Because the author's personal research interests were centered in the social sciences, the library resources meeting his needs were more likely to be found in the collections of other consortium members than they were to be located on the shelves of the library at his own institution.

The OPAC of IIT was linked with those of the other libraries in the consortium. Therefore, the author could easily check to determine which members of the group held the desired titles. Because the circulation systems were also linked, it was possible to determine if any of those titles were missing, checked out, or restricted from circulation by virtue of being categorized as rare, reference, or reserve materials. Generally, the author found titles of interest to be available at the libraries of two comprehensive universities that were both along his daily commuting path. With this as the case, he had three options:

1. Stop at a holding (lending) library on his way home, hoping that no one had checked out the book in the meantime.

2. Request that the item be pulled from the shelf and immediately charged out to him and held at the lending library until he could pick it up.

3. Request that the item be charged out to him and delivered to his home library by means of a state-funded delivery service, if he could wait a few days for the item.

Although direct borrowing has never been nearly as commonplace as the library-to-library loan method, the current growth in distance education courses may see both of these services become a staple for the far-flung, off-campus student who needs anywhere–anytime access to course-required materials or supplemental resources.

Document Delivery Services

There are a variety of sources that provide what is referred to as *document delivery*, a service similar in concept to interlibrary loan. Most of these sources are commercial firms, although many larger, university libraries also offer such a service to the general public on a fee basis. Document delivery differs fundamentally from traditional interlibrary loan in four ways:

1. The service is not restricted to library card holders; any individual with a valid credit card can patronize a document delivery firm.

2. The service uses a broader array of suppliers including libraries, private firms, individuals, publishers, and others to procure the desired item.

3. The emphasis is on speed in procuring the requested item.

4. The service can be costly.

Document delivery firms are often located in communities with large academic or research libraries and they may employ regular as well as contract employees in their effort to quickly locate, retrieve, photocopy, and deliver the desired materials. Examples of large, established document delivery vendors include Ingenta (http://www.ingenta.com/), U.S. Dept. of Commerce National Technical Information Service (NTIS; http://www.fedworld.gov/onow), ISI Document Solution (http://ids.isinet.com), and Information Express (http://www .ieonline.com/docdel.html). A scan of the Yellow Pages in most telephone or business directories will often reveal smaller, local document deliveries firms as well.

Like many other vendors in the library business, document delivery companies may be specialized. Some may supply only medical sources, others may specialize in patent data, and other firms may provide access to a wide range of subject area materials, ranging from newspaper and periodical articles to monographs to foreign language materials.

Special libraries such as those in law firms and corporations—where competitive intelligence and other time-sensitive business decisions often influence rush information requests—have traditionally been frequent users of document delivery vendors. In these scenarios, whenever possible, the cost of document delivery transactions is billed to a client or charged back to a specific department within the organization.

Well-funded academic libraries often have accounts with commercial document delivery firms and pay all or part of the fees to supply items to their faculty, currently enrolled students, or both. In this case, the end user cannot distinguish between an item acquired through the traditional ILL process or one procured through a commercial firm. The cost and means are transparent to the satisfied patron.

Future of ILL

Although interlibrary loans to date have been a service primarily used by serious researchers, faculty, genealogists, and seasoned library patrons, there are many indications that the service may soon undergo a renaissance as a result of the Internet's many applications.

ILL may soon be discovered by new groups of students and researchers. Distance education, where students (regardless of geographical location) use the Web to access course materials online and never meet in any physical classroom or visit a "bricks-and-mortar" library, is projected to be a growth industry for colleges and universities. These academic institutions must make required and supplementary materials available to their far-flung students in a convenient manner. This often means providing them with full ILL services and subsidizing all or part of any costs. Requested books or videos might be physically delivered to the student's home or office; or articles and readings may be delivered via e-mail or viewed on the Web with password access. Commercial document delivery firms may also be used to provide materials to students in a speedy manner, with the cost absorbed, or at least subsidized, by the university.

The increase in multi-type library consortiums with shared holdings lists will also encourage interlibrary loan activity by making holdings data more readily available to patrons. After checking a holdings list online, qualified researchers then turn to an ILL request form that is also online. Quickly, conveniently, and at the point of need, the patron can then submit a timely request for a needed ILL item.

In another interesting development, the Library of Congress is experimenting with using the Internet to provide digital ILLs for certain short, fragile works from its collection that are in the public domain. Rather than photocopying or mailing out such an item, the Library of Congress scans the contents and notifies the requesting library agency that the item will be available for online digital viewing at a specific time.[22]

Commercial document delivery may also benefit from technological advances and from a general increased awareness of such services. The need to supply distance education students with required materials may also impact the fee-based alternatives to the traditional library-to-library transactions.

Study Questions

1. In your college library, what is the name of the department that handles circulation and interlibrary loan? How many people are employed in this department and at what job levels (e.g., student assistants, pages, library technicians, librarians, managers)?

2. What is the distinction between the designations *reference* and *reserve* for library materials?

3. What are some of the considerations that must be balanced when setting circulation policies for the loan of a library or information center's materials?

4. What is your opinion about limiting access to library materials according to a patron's age? In a public library? In a school media center?

5. Are overdue fines a necessary evil in the management of a library's collection? Explain why or why not.

6. Name the key functions of a modern automated circulation system. What are some additional features that provide added value?

7. Why are libraries, media centers, archives, and information centers vulnerable to theft? Name some basic preventive measures that can be taken to deal with theft problems.

8. Have you placed an interlibrary loan request in the past year? If so, were you satisfied with the materials obtained and the service? Explain why or why not.

9. How do interlibrary loan and document delivery services differ? How are they alike?

Resources

Articles

Bishop, George. "Library Security At Its Best," *Media & Methods* (September/October 1998): 16.

Crawford, Walt. "The Card Catalog and Other Digital Controversies," *American Libraries* (January 1999): 52–58.

Hamilton, John Maxwell. "Is There a Klepto in the Stacks?" *New York Times Book Review* (18 November 1990): 1, 48–49.

Jones, David, and Geoffrey Larkin. "Securing a Good Design: A Library Building Consultant and an Architect Consider Library Security," *APLIS* (December 1993): 164–70.

Khong, W. K. "A Security Flaw in Barcode Self-Charging Systems," *Library & Archival Security* 15, no. 1 (1999): 91–94.

Linderfelt, K. A. "Charging Systems," *Library Journal* (June 1882): 178–82.

Manzano, Roberto J. "Library Guards Await Limited Police Power," *Los Angeles Times* (15 July 2000): B7.

Nelson, Jesse. "Security in the Schools," *Media & Methods* (May/June 1997): 12, 14.

Plummer, Mary W. "Loan Systems," *Library Journal* (July 1893): 242–47.

Scott, Janny. "No Longer a Refuge for Readers," *Los Angeles Times* (10 August 1993): A-1, 14.

Shuman, Bruce A. "Designing Personal Safety into Library Buildings," *American Libraries* (August 1996): 37–39.

Thompson, Amy. "The Next Chapter in Library Security," *Security Management* (August 1997): 61, 63–64.

"3M Introduces Digital Identification System, Model 3500 Detection System; Demonstrates Pikiosk," *Information Today* (September 1999): 47, 49.

Vogel, Brenda. "Making Prison Libraries Visible and Accessible," *Corrections Today* (April 1994): 120, 122–24.

"With Millions of Dollars in Overdue Items, Librarians Get Tough," *New York Times,* Late Edition (East Coast), 21 May 1995, sec 1, 18.

Books

Boucher, Virginia. *Interlibrary Loan Procedure Manual*, 2d ed. Chicago: American Library Association, 1997.

Kahn, Miriam. *Disaster Response and Planning for Libraries.* Chicago: American Library Association, 1997.

McNeil, Beth and Denise J. Johnson. *Patron Behavior in Libraries: A Handbook of Positive Approaches to Negative Situations.* Chicago: American Library Association, 1995.

Morris, Leslie. *Interlibrary Loan Policies Directory,* 6th ed. New York: Neal-Schuman, 1999.

Shuman, Bruce A. *Library Security and Safety Handbook: Prevention, Policies, and Procedures.* Chicago: American Library Association, 1999.

Switzer, Teri R. *Safe at Work? Library Security and Safety Issues.* Metuchen, NJ: Scarecrow Press, 1999.

Willis, Mark. *Dealing with Difficult People in the Library.* Chicago: American Library Association, 1999.

Web Sites

• Lyall, Dr. Jan. "Disaster Planning for Libraries and Archives: Understanding the Essential Issues," *Provenance: The Electronic Magazine* 1 (2): 1996. Http://www.netpac.com/provenance/vol1/no2/features/lyall1.htm (Accessed January 18, 2001)

Videos

Keller, Daniel P. *Managing the problem library patron.* (35 min.). Goshen, KY: Campus Crime Prevention Programs, 1990.
    Presents practical guidelines and conflict resolution techniques for dealing with a variety of common problem patron situations encountered in libraries.

Notes

1.   "Free Access to Libraries for Minors: An Interpretation of the Library Bill of Rights." Chicago: American Library Association, 1991. Available: http://www.ala.org/alaorg/oif/free_min.html (Accessed October 31, 2000).

2.   Wayne A. Wiegand and Donald G. Davis, Jr., eds. *Encyclopedia of Library History.* New York: Garland Publishing, 1994, 143.

3.   Ernest Muro. *Automation Services for Libraries: A Resource Handbook.* Annandale, NJ: Vendor Relations Press, 1991, 5, 6, 14, 24, 25.

4.   Ibid. 25, 26.

5.   Nicholson Baker. "Discards," *New Yorker* (4 April 1994): 64–86.

6.   Dick Boss. E-mail to the author, 15 March 1999.

7.   Arlene G. Taylor. *Organization of Information.* Englewood, CO: Libraries Unlimited, 1999, 24.

8.   Nevada Wallis Thompson. *Circulation Systems for School Library Media Centers: Manual to Microcomputer.* Littleton, CO: Libraries Unlimited, 1985, 4–12.

9.   Wayne A. Wiegand and Donald G. Davis, Jr., eds. *Encyclopedia of Library History.* New York: Garland Publishing, 1994, 142–43.

10.   Ibid.

11.   Pamela Cibbarelli, ed. *Directory of Library Automation Software, Systems, and Services, 2000–2001 Edition.* Medford, NJ: Information Today, 2000.

12.   Laurie Becklund, "Man Writes Novel Chapter in Annals of Library Thefts," *Los Angeles Times,* Home Edition, 28 April 1991, A-1, 36, 38.

13.   *3M Quality Guaranthree.* St. Paul, MN: 3M Library Systems, 2001, 1.

14.   ALA RASD MOPSS Interlibrary Loan Committee. "National Interlibrary Loan Code for the United States, 1994." Last modified March 28, 2000. Chicago: American Library Association. Available: http://www.ala.org/rusa/stnd_lnc.html (Accessed October 6, 2000).

15.   Ibid.

16.   Arthur Curley and Dorothy Broderick. *Building Library Collections,* 6th ed. Metuchen, NJ: Scarecrow Press, 1985, 174.

17.   Wayne A. Wiegand and Donald G. Davis, Jr., eds. *Encyclopedia of Library History*. New York: Garland Publishing, 1994, 285–86.

18.   Nancy O'Neill. Santa Monica Public Library E-mail to author, 28 September 2000.

19.   Virginia Boucher. *Interlibrary Loan Practices Handbook*, 2d ed. Chicago: American Library Association, 1997, 220–32.

20.   ALA RASD MOPSS Interlibrary Loan Committee. "National Interlibrary Loan Code for the United States, 1994." Last modified March 28, 2000. Chicago: American Library Association. Available: http://www.ala.org/rusa/stnd_lnc.html (Accessed October 6, 2000).

21.   *Supporting Interlibrary Loan and Direct Loan Services in California's Multi-type Library Environment*. Milton, WI: Himmel and Wilson Library Consultants, 2000, 7.

22.   "Library of Congress Interlibrary Loans Delivered Online," *Ancestry Daily News*, 4 December 2000. Available: http://www.ancestry.com/library/view/news/articles /2999.asp (Accessed December 15, 2000).

Chapter 7

Reference Service

What is reference service? The centerpiece of reference service is an individual reference transaction. The transaction occurs when highly trained staff provide walk-in, telephone, or e-mail consultation with a library customer. The consultation is generally one-on-one and therefore can be specifically targeted to resolve the information or research needs of individual patrons. Thus, the primary activity of a reference unit is to directly aid specific customers in their quest for information and in the effective use of resources.

Although all divisions of a library or information center ultimately serve the customer, reference service is one of the most direct and visible efforts, regardless of the type of library environment. A 1998 Gallup Poll of public library usage conducted for the ALA showed that 64 percent of adults have library cards, and, of that group, 65 percent consulted a librarian for assistance during a recent in-person visit. Thus, reference is also a well-used service.[1]

A reference service counter may also be called Research Services, the Information Desk, the Help Desk, or other similar names, all connoting the provision of assistance. In most libraries these terms are used interchangeably. However, in very large libraries there may be multiple service desks, each with a very specific function. For example, in such a library, the Information Desk may be found in a very visible and readily accessible location where general and directional referring occurs. More specialized problem-solving would then take place in subject-oriented locales (e.g., the Fine Arts section or the Science and Technology section), often as a result of a referral from the Information Desk.

In such arrangements, the rationale is for the Information Desk staff to screen patron requests, answer the routine questions, and refer the more complex ones to more highly trained and often subject-specialist librarians. In some ways this would be similar to nurses screening patients and referring the more serious problems to doctors while handling routine matters themselves. However, in most libraries, all reference activities take place at one service point.

Each community of information seekers has its own distinct set of needs. Whether that community is an affluent suburban population, attorneys in a legal firm, middle school students, or a university campus, they will interact uniquely with the reference department serving them by requesting different information. Because of the ongoing interaction between reference staff and patrons, this department often has a hand on the pulse on those local information needs—at least those that are articulated and expressed to the staff.

In addition to providing research guidance, a secondary goal of reference service in many libraries is to teach users how to conduct searches and to use resources in an effort to become self-sufficient in their investigations. Reference staff spend much of their time instructing customers on how to navigate their way through the virtual sea of information. This may be achieved through one-on-one tutoring or by more formalized classroom-like education.

The goal of helping customers become self-sufficient is both a necessity and a mission of the institution for most libraries. Academic and school libraries, like their parent institutions, have a teaching mission. Information literacy, as well as literacy in the traditional reading, writing, and arithmetic, is critical to students' success in all aspects of their lives. In addition, libraries are not generally staffed at levels that allow reference staff the luxury of actually doing the research for each customer, even if it would be faster and more enjoyable for all concerned. The needs of other customers must also be met. Also, once customers have learned one information skill, they may be able to perform it unaided the next time they need similar data. They will then return to the reference staff with more complex and more interesting challenges, having been able to solve the more mundane problems on their own.

In contrast, within many special libraries, this logic does not apply. In this setting the primary customers are highly specialized and highly paid professionals. It is more cost-effective for the library staff to collect and synthesize the information than it is to train the specialists to do their own research. For example, in a law firm library, the library staff time spent on a particular case may be billed directly to the client instead of just being absorbed as overhead. Even if the client is being billed $60 to $100 per hour for library research, this is considerably less than the billing rate for attorneys in the firm. In addition, the library staff can probably find the information more efficiently than the attorneys can. Thus, the clients save money and perhaps get better service as well.

The Evolution of Reference Service

Up until the last decade of the twentieth century, the mark of a superior reference librarian was a comprehensive, working familiarity with sources—knowing standard titles, their contents, scope, frequency of publication, and their counterparts on various free and fee-based databases. With the phenomenon of the World Wide Web and the proliferation of electronic sources, this ability to "know it all" has changed significantly. Because of its very nature, the contents of the Web are limitless, highly dynamic, and defy memorization. Some reference books may have an online edition similar to or the same as their print version; some have an interactive, continuously updated version online; and some refuse to have a Web presence, remaining available in print form only. Information publishing has changed dramatically and will continue to move in new directions that we can't yet predict.

The Modern Reference Desk

Despite an active industry watch against negative and demeaning stereotypes of librarians, the image of a stern, white, middle-aged, single female with glasses and dowdy clothing is a perennial one in the media. In reality, library reference workers are a diverse group, technologically savvy, and very people oriented.

Reference technicians and librarians typically staff a service desk where the tools of the trade consist of several formats. A computer workstation with a Web-based library catalog and periodical databases, full Internet access, a fax or data modem, and e-mail, all networked to the local area network is the centerpiece of the reference desk. A telephone, of course, remains an essential resource. Ready reference print resources are often very close at hand, too, with access to a larger reference collection of print materials in an adjacent area.

Surrounded by an ever-changing array of resources, reference librarians or technicians spend their workdays adeptly toggling back and forth between electronic tools and physically moving from computer workstations to print or microform materials as each question demands. Today's reference worker is equally at ease in the worlds of print and electronic information.

Although the reliance on electronic tools increases as we speak, computers do "crash" occasionally, and there are days when power outages mean relying solely on print sources. And for those patrons still reluctant to use computer-based resources because of disabilities, reticence, or learning style preference, print tools may be the preferred medium.

No Question Too Trivial

Seasoned reference librarians and technicians attest that a major stimulus of the job is the wide spectrum of reference questions they encounter each day. During the course of one week in the authors' county, the following questions were asked at the local reference desk of public, academic, and special libraries:

> I want to start a muffin company. Can you help me research the market for such a venture?

> Do you have Cliff's Notes for *Hamlet*?

Do you have a repair manual for a 1976 Ford Mustang?

My child is doing a report on Kwanzaa. What do you have?

I'm trying to find the original street names in our city's downtown area.

Where do I find current census data for the tri-counties, especially breakdowns by ethnicity?

I'm doing a stock market report and need the beta for Pepsi.

My term paper is on the history of sewers and water management systems on campus and in town. Where do I start?

Although an unusual or difficult request may be memorable because of the challenge it poses or because of its novelty, within each type of library or information center there will be well-defined patterns to the reference questions asked. And some degree of predictability or recurrence can be expected for a certain percentage of the queries. For reference staff, it is this mix of the familiar and the exotic queries that keeps them on their toes.

Job Skills for Reference Service

What are the job skills needed to effectively perform reference services in a library, school media, or information center? The following combination of communication skills, personal attributes, and technical competency are highly recommended for reference staff.

- *Interpersonal skills.* With a high level of customer interaction in reference, it is essential to have strong "people skills," enjoy public contact, and be approachable and patient.

- *Knowledge of information sources.* Keeping current with print and electronic resources and keeping pace with their many rapidly changing formats and contents is critical.

- *Perseverance.* Searches often require sustained efforts and creative thinking in the hunt for information.

- *Sense of curiosity.* It may seem low tech, but a good reference librarian should enjoy playing detective and be motivated by the hunt for information, regardless of the specific query or subject.

- *Team player.* As one member of the reference team, most staff will likely work independently as well as with others. Collegiality in sharing information, techniques, referring patrons, or training assistants makes the job go more smoothly.

- *Training skills.* Providing on-demand instruction for customers in the use of various print or technology-based tools is an important and ongoing task.

- *Verbal communication skills.* Many patrons are researching sensitive topics and may be hesitant or unable to articulate their information requests clearly. An ability to deal sensitively with customers while ferreting out their needs is a must.

Evaluating Information

Along with instructing library customers and helping them locate data, reference librarians and technicians also assist them in evaluating the credibility and relevance of what they have found. This role is becoming increasingly more visible in the era of instantaneous electronic information and the easy self-publishing environment of the Internet. Many industry leaders see this as the most significant role of the librarian in the future. As with the old saying, "Just because it's in print, don't believe it," even more scrutiny must be applied to digital sources. Many of the traditional elements relied upon for evaluating a book; for example, a publisher's name and location or an author's credentials, may not be present on a Web site. The very act of "publishing" on the Web is accessible to anyone with no editing or review process at all.

Another important distinction in assisting researchers locate or evaluate information is whether the material is a primary or secondary source. *Secondary* source materials are probably most familiar to novice researchers and students. Compilations and summaries of information, such as encyclopedias, fact books, almanacs, and textbooks, are considered secondary sources. This is because the information is a generation or more removed from the original source; it may have been abridged, paraphrased, abstracted, critiqued, translated, or otherwise interpreted by various authors and editors. To those unfamiliar with a subject area, secondary sources can be easier to understand because another person has tried to place the material within a meaningful context.

In contrast, looking at a *primary* source enables the researchers to study firsthand accounts and to draw their own conclusions from these original documents. Primary materials are especially favored by historians, other scholars, and professional writers as they often refer directly to original letters, diaries, maps, scientific studies, speeches, photographs, and the like for study or perusal. Consider the difference between browsing George Washington's actual words and thoughts as conveyed in his personal letters and reading a summary of his point of view in a biographical account; studying an original, hand-drawn town site map and reading a textual description of the location of an ancestor's property; consulting the actual data table in a scientific study versus reading a newspaper account or hearing a TV news sound bite summarizing it.

Therefore, primary sources carry greater credibility than do secondary sources because people have not filtered their content.

Whether with print, multimedia, or electronic sources, or whether the sources are primary or secondary, reference staff guide users through the evaluation process. Questions to ask when evaluating information include the following:

Credibility:

Can you find an author's name, a group name, or other sponsor credited on the document?

Can you clearly identify the credentials or authority of the author or publisher?

Is contact information for the author or publisher provided?

Are they affiliated with an established publisher, business, university, or other organization?

Does the URL of a Web site provide any clues as to the sponsoring group?

Do they have a print/Web counterpart to the information at hand?

Is the information supported with a bibliography, works cited page, or footnotes?

Bias:

Can you detect any political, philosophical, religious, or other bias to the information presented?

Are all points of view presented on the topic or only a single view?

Is the source trying to sell you a product, an idea, or a service?

Currency:

Does the document have a date on it? Can you locate when it was published, posted, last updated, or created?

Does it seem that the information is updated regularly?

Appropriateness:

Does it meet the customer's need?

Is the reading level appropriate for the customer?

Is the level of technical information appropriate?

Is the coverage or length adequate?

The Best Source for the Job at Hand

With the prevalence of personal computers at home, work, school, and in the library, many users (especially younger patrons) think that the Internet is the only tool available or the only source needed for all possible research. Patrons may also assume that the first computer they walk up to houses all the programs and tools that the library has to offer. This may or may not be the case.

These common scenarios reinforce the importance of another advisory role of the reference librarian: recommending the best tool for the research need at hand. The wonderful explosion of information access can also translate into a confusing welter of options for a customer: "Do I check the Web, the electronic card catalog, the local area network, subscription databases, or something else?" As an information advisor, the reference librarian or technician is well equipped to direct a user to the best tool, which means saving time and a less frustrating research experience for the customer.

Reference Interview

Step back for a moment and think of the all-too-common frustration level that consumers face when they come away empty handed or unsatisfied from a visit to a retail store, a municipal agency, a physician's office, or other service venue. With their information quest unsatisfied or perhaps only partially filled, they go away thinking, "They didn't give me any answers. That was a waste of time. I still don't have what I need." The same situation can apply to many when patronizing a library or an information center.

But reference librarians are not psychics. Thus, before they can advise customers on the best source or train them to use electronic tools, a crucial exchange must take place: the reference interview. This interview is a unique interaction between the reference librarian or technician and the library user. In many cases, the successful outcome of the user's visit to the library will be based on a careful reference interview. Often, this conversation determines not only where the answer can be found, but also what the specific question or need is. Respected library educator and author William Katz defines this interaction as a dialog "between the librarian with expert knowledge and the layperson in need of information." [2] Ideally, this dialog takes place before beginning a search, thus providing the librarian with key data for interpreting the question in terms of library resources.

Reference Interview Steps

The following outline delineates the typical sequence of a reference interview. This is not always a linear model; it may be necessary to return to the second step if no appropriate answer is located.

1. *Initial question*: Customer poses query to reference librarian or staff.

2. *Clarification of the question*: Staff initiates a dialog to attempt to clarify the actual needs of the customer and to try to elicit more information, such as the level or format required, amount of data, deadline, and so forth. This conversation between reference staff and the customer may be brief or it may continue throughout the search itself.

3. *Translating the question into potential library sources*: Library staff take the lead by suggesting potential sources and finding out what has already been consulted, then they formulate a search strategy.

4. *The search*: The reference librarian or technician guides the patron through the physical search of appropriate sources. Simultaneously, they implement point-of-use instruction with each tool consulted so that the patron gains some knowledge for future independent searching.

5. *Follow-up*: This is an important closing element that is often overlooked but essential from a customer service point of view. As the search progresses, the librarian should query the patron, "Is this what you needed?" to be sure that the search is on track. As patrons are left to evaluate the located material on their own, reference staff should make the offer, "Let me know if you need more help." This leaves the door open for a renewed search or other additional help.

Categories of Reference Questions

When is a reference interview necessary? To answer this, it is first helpful to consider the types of questions typically encountered. Although there are many methods for analyzing queries, the following all-purpose division devised by William Katz is logical.[3] This scheme classifies queries into four general categories: directional, ready reference, specific search, and research.

Directional Category

These are straightforward questions dealing with location or existence of a service or resource. Typically, it is not necessary to spend time delving further than the question as posed. Staff knowledge of the building, services, and policies are sufficient to answer these queries.

Examples of directional questions include the following:

"Where is the photocopy machine?"

"Do you have Internet access?"

"Where is the children's department?"

"Where do I get a library card?"

Ready Reference Category

Quick, single-fact queries, ready reference requests are reminiscent of questions from Trivial Pursuit® board games or TV quiz shows. They are often an isolated statistic or fact that requires verification and fact finding. To answer these queries, turn to online and print sources such as encyclopedias, almanacs, statistical compendiums, directories, dictionaries, as well as quick Web searches using regular or meta search engines. Some ready reference queries may require a reference interview for clarification.

Examples of ready reference questions include the following:

"Which U.S. president was never married?"

"I need the Web address for the National Archives."

An example of a ready reference question with a reference interview is as follows:

* * *

Patron: I need the current population of New Jersey.

Staff: How current does the population figure need to be?

Patron: The most current available.

Staff: Do you need a total population or breakdowns by county, sex, or ethnicity?

* * *

Specific Search Category

This is a more involved and more time-consuming level of inquiry, rather than the isolated fact finding required of ready reference questions. The gathering of an overview or background information may be the first step, followed by further delving into the subject. A patron may want to browse materials and read about their topic to become familiar with it, then they will eventually refine it further. Specific search queries require a reference interview to elicit facts and identify a direction for the search. Sources used may range widely from encyclopedias at the start to books, periodicals, government documents, and Web sites as the search progresses.

Examples of specific search questions are as follows:

"What do you have on swimming pools?"

"I'm doing a term paper on Julia Morgan, the architect. Do you have information on her?"

"Do you have information about the history of the AIDS epidemic?"

"We need cultural guidelines for business travelers in Indonesia."

"I need everything there is on our competitor's new CEO."

Examples of a specific search question with a reference interview are as follows:

* * *

Patron: I need information on becoming a ranger.

Staff: What kind of information do you need? Do you need a job description or perhaps a job exam study book?

Patron: Hmm. Maybe both.

Staff: What type of ranger? Park ranger, forest ranger, Texas Ranger, or something else?

* * *

Research Category

Although the word *research* is often used quite loosely (e.g., "I want to research the phone number for this company"), it is used here to convey a sophisticated level of inquiry that implies in-depth study of a topic or issue. Research queries may require ongoing investigation, with multiple trips to the reference desk. They will probably entail using a variety of primary and secondary sources and may use interlibrary loan or document delivery services. Accessing technical and fee-based databases may be appropriate. After in-house sources have been exhausted, referrals to other information centers or agencies will be needed. The research level of investigation is characterized by the synthesis and analysis of information, not merely the copying of it. A reference interview at this level could be fairly lengthy because the librarian will need to ascertain the topic, previous research or sources consulted, technical level of information needed, and other details.

Examples of research questions include the following:

"I'm studying the effects of sun exposure on skin cancer and need recent scientific studies about it."

"What are the latest theories on the disappearance of Amelia Earhart?"

"I'm writing a journal article on the medical uses of aromatherapy."

Reference Interview Techniques

There are several straightforward techniques that practitioners can employ to help carry out a successful reference interview with customers. The following is a brief overview of these techniques. For more in-depth coverage, refer to works listed in the resources section at the end of this chapter.

Open-Ended Questions

Whenever possible, ask open-ended questions to allow for more than a staccato "yes" or "no" answer. By engaging a customer in a dialogue, clues about their information needs should emerge to help carry out the search.

* * *

Patron: I want something for a paper on Shakespeare.

Staff: What kind of project are you working on?

Patron: It's a term paper on *Hamlet.*

Staff: How long does your paper need to be?

Patron: Ten pages with fifteen sources cited.

Staff: Where have you looked so far?

* * *

Asking the two-part question can be also helpful. For example:

* * *

Patron: I need something on Amelia Earhart.

Staff: Are you interested in her life story or in a particular flying record?

* * *

Active Listening

Whether on the job or in our personal lives, the art of listening is a skill that we often take for granted. Active listening takes a conscious effort, and, when used effectively, is a technique that can be vital to anyone staffing a service desk or involved with customer interaction. Active listening means paying close attention to the comments of the speaker and hearing the speaker out, rather than jumping in or cutting the person off. In the interest of saving time, it is easy to feel compelled to second-guess a need and quickly recommend an appropriate source without fully hearing the query. An active listener resists that temptation.

The trained reference employee applies active listening to the reference interview by giving the patron full attention and maintaining eye contact. While directing the interview, they indicate their understanding by responding to the patron's explanation with nods and short "yes" and "OK" responses. Then it is useful to paraphrase the query back to the patron to ensure both parties that they are on the same wavelength.

Putting the Customer at Ease

Asking for assistance in a library setting is not something that everyone feels comfortable doing. Putting into play some basic tenets of good customer service can help alleviate some of that discomfort. When staff present a friendly, informal, yet businesslike demeanor, people sense that they are there to help them. Moving out from behind the reference service counter and walking to the computers or stacks with the patron removes the physical barrier of a desk or counter. Keeping the reference desk clear and free from clutter also sends the message that staff are available and not otherwise distracted. Many reference librarians and technicians wear name tags indicating their job title and company logo while on duty. This encourages customers to approach them, instead of a student aide, volunteer, or other library staff not specially trained in reference assistance.

Nonverbal behavior, or body language, also plays an important part in putting the customer at ease. A pleasant, even tone of voice—not too loud or condescending—is optimal. A patient and courteous manner is much more welcoming than an abrupt, easily annoyed demeanor. Unconscious gestures such as placing hands on the hips or folding the arms can be interpreted as negative, aggressive gestures. Prefer a neutral stance, with both hands to the side or placed behind the back in the "actor's grip."

Maintaining eye contact is an important cue that expresses interest and a willingness to assist. In contrast, averting eye contact with a customer conveys the distinct feelings of inattention or boredom. When a staff member and a patron are at different levels, making eye contact can be difficult, for example, when the staff member is seated at a desk and a customer is standing, or, conversely, when a staff member walks up to assist a wheelchair patron or a customer seated at a computer. Computer screens themselves—though indispensable—can also present a barrier to eye contact. Instead of directly communicating with one another, all eyes are on the monitor. Selecting both reference desks and computer carrels to be counter height is one method of putting both parties on the same eye level.

Being aware of cross-cultural differences is of growing importance as the library-using community increases in diversity. Issues such as personal space, reluctance to approach strangers for help, and other cultural customs or behaviors can prevent direct communication. Some libraries with distinctive ethnic populations provide cultural sensitivity training to staff as a means of breaking down such barriers.

Burnout is a problem in any public contact job. At a busy reference desk it is important to schedule staff for shifts that reduce the chance for burnout. Usually shifts of two hours without a break or without the mixture of a variety of other tasks are about the longest that most staff can maintain the highest level of service orientation. Occasionally, longer shifts may be tolerable, but, over the long haul, prolonged shifts will lead to stressed staff members and less than optimal service.

Reference Service Policies

Having clear-cut policies for reference services is another facet of offering good customer service. Among the policy issues to consider are which level of staff (professional or paraprofessional or both) answer reference requests; which format of inquiry has priority (e.g., walk-in, e-mail, telephone, fax); and what time limitations, if any, are imposed per individual question. As with all policies, these issues should be re-evaluated as reference tools, habits, and customer preferences change. Unless your library has a specific policy to the contrary, walk-in customers should get first priority over telephone or other electronic requests. But, perhaps in the future, e-mail requests will be of such volume that they take priority over walk-in traffic. Then staffing patterns and service policies would need to be adjusted accordingly for a new customer preference.

Learning the Reference Interview

One of the best methods for novices to learn the ins and outs of the interview process is to observe reference librarians in action. If possible, "shadowing," or following the librarian and patron interaction from the initial query to the completion of the search, is particularly helpful. Afterward, discussing the search strategy chosen and its pitfalls or successes will reinforce the actions observed. Shadowing more than one staff person is especially valuable because each individual has a unique approach. Role playing in a classroom or workshop situation and viewing training videos are two other effective instructional methods.

Several Library Technology student interns from the authors' college were recently based in academic library reference departments for fieldwork and spent their initial days shadowing seasoned staff interacting with students. Their comments on reference training bears out the effectiveness of this method:

> "The concept of the reference interview is becoming more clear as the students come in with their questions. Even a simple directional question, such as "Where are the current periodicals?" may need some clarification."
>
> "It's interesting to see the different approaches each librarian takes to a search and what their favorite databases and search engines are."
>
> "While covering reference [with the college librarian], I found out how much I enjoy helping people narrow down their huge, expansive topics. They often start with something completely unmanageable."
>
> "I am feeling more and more comfortable in assisting students with their search needs. I get started by conducting the Reference Interview, get them started on Polycat or appropriate databases and then seek further assistance, if necessary."
>
> "These [business] questions are once again a reminder that it is vital and time-saving if you can query the student and qualify their exact needs. One student started out wanting to know information about "the restaurant business in California." As it turned out, he needed the numbers of wine and beer licenses issued in California and pursued this upstairs in Government Documents."

Reference: Art or Science?

Is good reference work an art or a science? Actually, it is a combination of both. Certain core elements are present in any successful reference transaction. Success is based on a skillful reference interview combined with an efficient and appropriate matching of the customer's needs with available or attainable information sources.

The *science* of reference is in the ability to understand and characterize the inquiry by subject category and the amount and type of information sought. For example, is the patron's request really regarding sociology or social work, social policy, or religious teaching? Does the person want a definition, an overview, a list of sources, everything on the topic, or only one specific fact? The right referral might be to a dictionary of social work or a religious encyclopedia, a specialized bibliography, a general almanac, or a Web site.

The *art* of reference is in the conduct of the interview. Personal style that is comfortable for the interviewer is important. The other end of the process, recommendation of a source, is also an art based on the experience of the staff member. There really is not a single "right" way to do it. That is why even very experienced reference staff like to observe other staff members. Each person develops pet information sources that work well for them. They also specialize by subject areas and personal interests. It is not a sign of weakness to turn to another staff member for collaboration in the process of trying to answer a patron's query. In fact, it is a sign of confidence and maturity. No staff member can know everything in every subject.

Reference Reality Check and the Future

Of course, quality reference service is always dependent on adequate staffing and funding. Expectations of service must be adjusted when these resource levels are not optimal. For example, with limited numbers of workers, reference staff may be too busy to return to patrons for follow-up assistance. In that case, staff should use common sense shortcuts: get patrons started on their search and recommend that they check back if they need more help or find a staff member if they need further assistance. Another technique is batching reference requests. For example, a staff member shows two or three people at once how to use the library catalog. In understaffed libraries, strong emphasis needs to be placed on the goal of teaching patrons how to be more self-sufficient in their library skills. The use of trained library science or library technology interns, docents, or other seasoned volunteers should be considered to augment permanent staff.

Especially in facilities open to the general public, problem patrons frequenting the reference desk are a daily reality of life. Problem patrons require patience and special attention whether they are the homeless, lonely seniors, people with mental illness, latchkey children, or other populations. Here again, staff training is commonplace to prepare and educate library workers in techniques for diffusing difficult, awkward, or potentially violent situations. Information centers and libraries often develop policies specifically to deal with recurring problem-patron issues. Having security staff on site and cultivating a good rapport with the local police are also common approaches.

As for the future, reference service in libraries and information centers will continue to be very visible and staff will continue to have high levels of interaction with customers, though more may be in a virtual setting rather than primarily face-to-face. The anticipated growth in distance education courses and training with its anytime–anyplace philosophy and capability is already impacting existing reference service traditions. And the concept of serving users who live within a local political or geographical funding area may also be challenged with the growth in electronic communication and research.

Study Questions

1. Do you use the reference department of your local public library? Why or why not? If yes, how would you characterize the service you've received?

2. As a student, do you use the reference department of your college library? How does it compare to the local public library? What kind of a reputation does it have among students on campus?

3. To see firsthand how a typical reference department operates, visit the reference department of a large, local library, preferably a university, college, or central public library. Spend about 30 minutes to an hour observing the reference desk operation. Summarize your observations in a one- to two-page report. Some things to discuss in your summary include the following: the number of personnel staffing the desk, the physical layout, the amount and type of customer activity, print and electronic reference materials on hand at the desk, and the proximity to larger reference collections in the library. If possible, note sample questions asked during your visit.

4. Nonverbal communication plays a subtle but important role in the reference interview. List five positive nonverbal cues that are helpful to exhibit when working the reference desk.

5. What approach would you suggest for dealing with a patron who repeatedly poses reference queries that perplex the librarian?

6. Is there an archives or special collections department in your college library or hometown? If so, visit it and observe the level of reference service provided. How does it differ from the general information desk in your college library?

Resources

Articles

Abels, Eileen G. "The E-mail Reference Interview." *RQ* 35 (Spring 1996): 345–58.

"Active Listening." *Public Management* (US) 79 (December 1997): 25–27.

Brody, Marjorie. "Listen up! Do You Really Hear What People are Saying?" *American Salesman* (June 1994): 14.

Hoskisson, Tam. "Making the Right Assumptions: Know Your User and Improve the Reference Interview." *Reference Librarian* 59 (1997): 67–75.

Books

Berkman, Robert I. *Find It Fast: How to Uncover Expert Information on Any Subject.* 5th ed. New York: Harper Collins, 2000. (Available both in print and online.)

Jennerich, Elaine Z., and Edward J. Jennerich. *The Reference Interview As a Creative Art,* 2d ed. Englewood, CO: Libraries Unlimited, 1997.

Katz, William A. *Introduction to Reference Work,* Vol. II, 8th ed. New York: McGraw-Hill, 2002.

McDaniel, Julie Ann, and Judith K. Ohles. *Training Paraprofessionals for Reference Service: A How-To-Do-It Manual for Librarians.* New York: Neal-Schuman Publishers, 1993.

Wynar, Bohdan S., ed. *Recommended Reference Books for Small and Medium-Sized Libraries and Media Centers.* 21st ed. Englewood, CO: Libraries Unlimited, 2001.

Web Sites

- Tillman, Hope N. "Evaluating Quality on the Net." 19 March 2001. http://www.hopetillman.com/findqual.html (Accessed November 29, 2001)
    Tillman's seminal essay on evaluating resources on the Internet, updated periodically.

- Arizona State Library, Archives and Public Records. "Selection of Library Resources–Internet Resources." n.d.
http://www.dlapr.lib.az.us/cdt/slrir.htm
(Accessed November 29, 2001)
    Funded by the Arizona State Library, this page is part of their Collection Development Training for Arizona Libraries (CDT) site which was developed with the goal of meeting the collection development training needs of Arizona's small and rural public libraries.

Notes

1. Gallup Organization for the American Library Association. *Usage and Perception Study*. Lincoln, NE: Gallup Organization, 1998.

2. William A. Katz. *Introduction to Reference Work, Vol. II: Reference Services and Reference Processes*. 8th ed. New York: McGraw-Hill, 2002, 125.

3. William A. Katz. *Introduction to Reference Work, Vol. I: Basic Information Services.* 8th ed. New York: McGraw-Hill, 2002, 16–19.

Chapter 8

Ethics in the Information Age

Ethical ideas should apply to all aspects of our lives. "Almost all (92%) workers report that maintaining honesty and integrity at work is very important, and 90% report that taking individual responsibility and having a good work ethic is important"—a greater emphasis than they gave "specific skills such as computer skills (50%)".[1] There are a lot of different opinions as to what really constitutes ethics. This chapter addresses one very specific slice of applied ethics—the ethics of access to information in a library setting.

When one of the authors mentioned that he was thinking about teaching a course called "Ethics in the Information Age," a colleague commented, "Oh that sounds interesting. I don't really know much about copyright law." Another responded, "Good, I should take that. I need to know more about computer law." In both cases, the person equated law with ethics. Law and ethics are not *un*related. If they were the same there would be no reason to study ethics. Ethics can demand a higher standard than the law. At other times ethical beliefs have caused individuals to break the law. Twentieth century examples include the nonviolent civil disobedience campaigns led by Indian leader Mohandas Karamchang Ghandi (later to be known as Mahatma or Great Soul Ghandi); Martin Luther King, Jr., during the 1950s and 1960s U.S. civil rights movement; persons attempting to preserve the environment; and those on both sides of the abortion issue. In many cases, the law is merely society's attempt to codify elements of ethical beliefs.

If the law is not the only guiding principle in making ethical decisions, then what else is to be considered? Fair treatment of others? Religious teachings? How does one arrive at truth? One explanation is that each person determines truth in one or in a combination of the following methods:

Six Ways of Knowing Truth[2]

1. *Rational thought*. Truth comes from logically correct thinking. (Everything grows out of Rene Descartes' observation, "I think, therefore I am.")

2. *Common sense*. Truth comes from what we all know in common.

3. *Sensory observation*. Truth comes from what we can see, touch, smell, taste, and hear.

4. *Intuition*. Truth comes from within the individual—a sort of sixth sense, an inner voice or consciousness.

5. *Scientific method*. Truth comes from rigorously testing hypotheses.

6. *Authoritarian faith*. Truth comes from an authority in which we have faith (e.g., the Pope, *The Bible*, Rush Limbaugh, Dr. Laura, Dr. Martin Luther King, Jr., our parents, Osama bin Laden, the government, a professional body, a mentor, Confucius, etc.).

Only if a person relies on authoritarian faith in the government as the way to know truth will truth as defined by law and by ethics be identical. If one relies on any other way of finding truth, ethics and the law, on occasion, will lead one to different, however not necessarily contradictory, conclusions. It is the application of these various "truths" in the practice of the information professions that are explored here.

Of particular relevance in ethics for information professionals are the following values, often called "rights," which sometimes conflict with each other:

right to know;

right to privacy;

right to property; and

right to protect children.

Most information workers would agree enthusiastically with each of these "rights" in the abstract. However, in many real-world situations, they are faced with dilemmas created by what the preamble to the *Code of Ethics of the American Library Association* (see Appendix C) describes as "ethical dilemmas [that] occur when values are in conflict."[3]

Ethical values are discussed within the context of whether they increase or impede access to information. Some values, such as intellectual freedom and the right to know, are generally values that increase access to information. Other values, such as the right to privacy, the right to property, and the right to protect children tend to restrict information. Certain values, such as the right to crime-free communities, sometimes restrict, and at other times, increase access to information.

For decades, libraries have been in the forefront on many of these issues. Recently, the advent of the World Wide Web has made it appear that many new ethical issues have been added. At the very least, this event has caused us to reassess and redefine these values in new terms. However, for the most part, the ethical issues library workers face today are a continuum of "old" ethical issues.

The Value of Information

The critical mission of libraries is to acquire rights to information on behalf of their clientele. Traditionally, we have thought of this in terms of buying containers of information (e.g., a book, a video, or a periodical). Although we often thought of what we were doing in terms of acquiring the physical item, what we were in fact doing was acquiring the information embedded within that item. This distinction may seem to be an abstract one. However, in understanding our role in the Information Age, it is a very important distinction. It has always been the information we were "buying" and not just the container.

Perhaps that distinction can be more clearly understood by considering what a book really is and how its value is determined. A book is, at the most basic level, pages of paper with some ink on them fastened together with glue. One way of determining the economic value of a book would be to weigh the ounces of paper and the amount of glue and ink contained in each copy of the book. Next, one would determine the unit values for paper, ink, and glue. With this information in hand, one should be able to establish the market value of that book. Were it only that simple.

Of course, there was value added in the cutting of the paper and in applying the ink to the pages. And, what about the fancy cardboard or leather that was used for the outside protector or cover of the book? Still, establishing a fair price for a book is a fairly objective process. What really gives the book value in the marketplace is the *pattern* of the ink on the pages and not the *amount* of ink on the pages. It is the ideas behind the words, pictures, and other graphical presentations. Unfortunately, establishing a fair price for these ideas is far more complicated. On the other hand, this process of setting a price for books is one to which we have become accustomed throughout our lifetimes and now take for granted.

In the electronic age, this process of setting a fair price is quickly developing an entirely different dimension. Technological innovation has significantly tipped the balance in the marketplace, at least temporarily, in favor of the producers. Social forces have not yet reacted sufficiently to force a new equilibrium, where all interests are in a rational, if delicate, balance. In this stage of technological advance, the publishers have seized the initiative and are attempting to define the price of *access* to their advantage. At the same time, consumers are reluctant to pay the legitimate cost of production and distribution of something as intangible as information.

Intellectual property is a term that library workers understand intuitively. We all mouth platitudes such as "information is power." Most of us really believe this or we would be in some other line of work. However, the term "intellectual property" is relatively new in our vocabulary. Even though intellectual property law has been the fastest growing area of law for some time, the phrase "intellectual property" appeared for the first time in 1999, in that venerable shaper of legal discourse *Black's Law Dictionary*. Until then, this concept had been found in that treatise only in general terms under the discussion of "intangible property."

In the twenty-first century, our economy is rapidly becoming one in which the value of corporations is based more on the value of their intellectual property than on their physical property. Some in the corporate world very clearly understand this; but many are still struggling with the concept of whether, or how, intellectual property should be entered into a balance sheet or a profit-and-loss statement.

One would think that librarians would be well prepared to navigate this new world on behalf of their clients. Some are, but many of us are only beginning to appreciate how the rules of the game have changed and where we are heading. Before further discussing the ethics of information in the twenty-first century, we need to understand what professional consensus had emerged within the library arena by the end of the twentieth century.

The ALA Code of Ethics

The following sections are arranged under topic headings provided by the articles of the ALA Code. The full Code is in Appendix C.

> I. We provide the highest level of service to all library users through appropriate and usefully organized resources; equitable service policies; equitable access; and accurate, unbiased, and courteous responses to all requests.

The defining ethic for librarians and other library workers should be the compulsion to provide information to clients. This driving force of librarians is only slightly different than the role of those who work in bookstores, publishing houses, the broadcast media, and other related occupations. However, that difference in role is significant. The librarian's focus is on the consumer first and then on the information needed by that customer. Also, neither the librarian nor the library directly profit monetarily from each successful transaction that benefits a customer.

Free, democratic societies are based on the premise that informed citizens are capable of governing themselves. Libraries, particularly American libraries in the twentieth century, have been an embodiment of this belief. Public libraries have seen to it that their mission is to help create and maintain an informed citizenry. Other libraries have similarly tried to foster a culture of access to information for their specific clientele.

If this ideal is to be achieved, some level of information must be available to all residents who are citizens or are striving to become citizens. Particularly in tax-supported libraries, all residents should be treated the same, and all should have access to the same information resources and services. No single customer should be treated as being more important than another.

Access to information and the right to know are basic premises upon which democracy, libraries, and the Internet are based. However, are these without limits? It is generally assumed that a person's right to swing his or her arms stops somewhere short of another person's nose. In a similar fashion, a person's right to know is limited by another person's right to privacy and right to property. The *Declaration of Independence* proclaims the right to life, liberty, and the pursuit of happiness. The *United States Constitution* substitutes the right to property for the right to pursue happiness.

These rights are espoused not just in the United States. *The Universal Declaration of Human Rights* was adopted by the United Nations General Assembly in 1948. The Preamble of this document states that

> . . . recognition of the inherent dignity and of the equal and inalienable rights of all members of the human family is the foundation of freedom, justice, and peace in the world . . . [and] . . . the advent of a world in which human beings shall enjoy freedom of speech and belief and freedom from fear and want has been proclaimed as the highest aspiration of the common people. . . .

And, Article 19 states: "Everyone has the right to freedom of opinion and expression; this right includes freedom to hold opinions without interference and to seek, receive and impart information and ideas through any media regardless of frontiers."

> II. We uphold the principles of intellectual freedom and resist all efforts to censor library resources.

Intellectual freedom is defined by the ALA as "the right of every individual to both seek and receive information from all points of view without restriction. It provides for free access to all expressions of ideas through which any and all sides of a question, cause or movement may be explored."[4]

The *Freedom to Read Statement* was originally drafted in 1953 by librarians and publishers and was last revised in 1991. The full text is in Appendix D. This statement has been endorsed by numerous organizations interested in reading and in the freedom of access to information. An abstract of its main points is outlined below:

1. It is in the public interest for publishers and librarians to make available the widest diversity of views and expressions, including those which are unorthodox or unpopular with the majority.

2. Publishers, librarians, and booksellers do not need to endorse every idea or presentation contained in the books they make available. It would conflict with the public interest for them to establish their own political, moral or aesthetic views as a standard for determining what books should be published or circulated.

3. It is contrary to the public interest for publishers or librarians to determine the acceptability of a book on the basis of the personal history or political affiliations of the author.

4. There is no place in our society for efforts to coerce the taste of others, to confine adults to the reading matter deemed suitable for adolescents, or to inhibit the efforts of writers to achieve artistic expression.

5. It is not in the public interest to force a reader to accept with any book the prejudgment of a label characterizing the book or author as subversive or dangerous.

6. It is the responsibility of publishers and librarians, as guardians of the people's freedom to read, to contest encroachments upon that freedom by individuals or groups seeking to impose their own standards or tastes upon the community at large.

7. It is the responsibility of publishers and librarians to give full meaning to the freedom to read by providing books that enrich the quality and diversity of thought and expression. By the exercise of this affirmative responsibility, they can demonstrate that the answer to a bad book is a good one, the answer to a bad idea is a good one.

Links to a number of policies related to censorship of various types of materials are listed at the end of this chapter. These include policies about videotapes, materials for children, electronic information, meeting room scheduling, information on sexual orientation, exhibits and bulletin boards, and the labeling of materials as to their suitability.

Librarians have the greatest personal difficulty when it comes to issues related to what information sources are suitable for children. In this regard they mirror the society in which we live. In our communities there are very vocal citizens who will demand that young people (and often all people) be protected from ideas and expression with which they do not personally agree. On the other hand, ALA policy is stated in absolute terms in Article V of the *Library Bill of Rights*:

> A person's right to use a library should not be denied or abridged because of origin, age, background, or views. The "right to use a library" includes free access to, and unrestricted use of, all the services, materials, and facilities the library has to offer. Every restriction on access to, and use of, library resources, based solely on the chronological age, educational level, or legal emancipation of users violates Article V.[5]

More will be said later in this chapter about how this conflict has been taken to whole new levels by public access Internet stations in libraries.

> III. We protect each library user's right to privacy and confidentiality with respect to information sought or received and resources consulted, borrowed, acquired or transmitted.

Information seekers have the right to use library materials and services, including consultation with staff without having the nature of their inquiry broadcast to anyone. With respect to materials read, this policy has led to the confidentiality of circulation records that would disclose what any individual might have read. This right is not a constitutionally protected right such as that enjoyed by legal counsel or the clergy. However, the ALA has long been on record in recommending that all libraries develop a policy that states that

> such records shall not be made available to any agency of state, federal, or local government except pursuant to such process, order, or subpoena as may be authorized under the authority of, and pursuant to, federal, state, or local law relating to civil, criminal, or administrative discovery procedures or legislative investigative power.[6]

The ALA policy goes further to state that the library should "resist the issuance or enforcement of any such process, order, or subpoena until such time as a proper showing of good cause has been made in a court of competent jurisdiction."[7]

Most libraries have adopted such policies. Staff, particularly those at public service desks, need to be oriented so that they will not be taken unaware and be intimidated if someone carrying a badge or another authority figure demands to see the circulation records of a given patron. The same would apply to requests for the names of anyone who has checked out books on a given subject (e.g., bomb making or computer hacking).

Library staff should also treat such patron information on a "need-to-know" basis within the staff. Library staff members should not have access to such information unless that information is needed to perform a legitimate library function (e.g., processing of overdue notices). In addition, library staff members need to be vigilant about protecting other personal information about customers. They have no business giving out telephone numbers, addresses, or social security numbers to anyone and may be placing the library in jeopardy of legal liability of invasion of privacy by doing so.

Confidentiality of inquiry applies equally when customers consult staff about how to locate information. To the extent possible reference inquiries should be conducted in an environment in which questions can be asked and answered in a confidential manner. The classic stereotype of inappropriate behavior is for a staff member to say in a loud voice to a teenager, "And why do you need to know about birth control?"

One other element of confidentiality is that researchers may be investigating a potentially marketable idea. If this is the case, then it is inappropriate to share with anyone else even the fact that another person is researching that topic.

IV. We recognize and respect intellectual property rights.

Intellectual property rights have existed for hundreds of years. Although, as mentioned previously in this chapter, *Black's Law Dictionary* did not give the term its own definition until 1999:

> A category of intangible rights protecting commercially
> valuable products of the human intellect. The category
> comprises primarily trademark, copyright, and patent
> rights, but also includes trade-secret rights, publicity
> rights, moral rights, and rights against unfair competition.[8]

This definition has not evolved far from an 1845 court case, the date of the first recorded usage of the term: "Only in this way can we protect intellectual property, the labors of the mind, productions and interests as much a man's own . . . as the wheat he cultivates."[9]

Within the library environment, the most common manifestation of intellectual property is copyrighted materials. It is not the purpose of this book to make readers conversant in the vagaries of this topic. However, a level of awareness as to where some of the associated legal minefields may be planted can be useful. Library staff members are often expected to be resources within their organizations for advising others as to what is permitted under the copyright law. It is useful to be able to direct colleagues to information about the subject.[10] On the other hand, it is dangerous to make pronouncements in an area in which even intellectual property lawyers are hesitant to make definitive statements.

Simply stated, copyright is "legal protection provided to authors and/or publishers which protects them against unauthorized copying of their work."[11] Attorney R. Delgado-Martinez defines it in a little more detail:

> Copyright is a protection that covers published and unpublished works of literary, dramatic, musical, artistic, pictorial and certain other intellectual creations, provided such works are fixed in a tangible medium. This means that if you can see it, hear it and/or touch it—it may be protected. If it is an essay, if it is a play, if it is a song, if it is a funky original dance move, if it is a photograph, HTML coding or a computer graphic that can be set on paper, recorded on tape or saved to a hard drive, it may be protected. Copyright laws grant the creator the exclusive right to reproduce, prepare derivative works, distribute, perform and display the work publicly. Exclusive means only the creator of such work; not just anybody who has access to it and decides to grab it.[12]

Copyright is balanced by the right of fair use. Any users of a copyrighted work are allowed to make fair use of that work. Fair use is a widely discussed but much misunderstood concept. Fair use means that the work is being used in a legally acceptable manner that does not require the specific permission of the copyright holder or payment of royalties to the author or publisher. For it to apply, the use generally must be personal or educational and not for profit.

The most common example of legitimate fair use is to make a single copy of a work for one's own personal use. Personal use means the copy will not be shared with others in any way. Any shared use or further dissemination of information in the copy is restricted in the same manner because use of the original document would be restricted by the copyright law. This provision is the basis for the common library practice of having self-service copiers for patron use. Although the patron has the right to make a copy for personal use, the library does not have the right to systematically make multiple copies for the use of patrons. Basically, the liability of complying with the copyright law is shifted from the library to the patron by the omnipresent warning sign posted near public copy machines in libraries.

Additional factors that determine whether a use is fair use include the nature of the work, the amount and percentage of the original to be used, and the effect of the use on potential sales of the original.[13] The most important issue is whether the proposed use of the work will diminish the commercial value of the copyright for its holder. If it would replace sales that otherwise might take place, then the owner of the copyright deserves compensation. If the use is so inconsequential that no sales could be reasonably expected to be affected, then this would suggest a fair use of the item. Other specific guidelines apply if the use is for classroom use or for library reserve desk use. Copyright holders are often very generous in granting permission for clearly specified and limited educational use of their materials. However, one should never presume that this will be the case. Authors deserve recognition that their works are being used even if they are willing to forego compensation.

Technology is now adding a layer of complexity. Electronic publishing is making it possible to sell works on a per-use basis. Journal articles or individual issues of journals can now be downloaded on demand. The publishers do not have to guess in advance what the demand for a particular item will be. Royalties can be collected and the text and graphics downloaded as demand occurs. Not only is this changing the landscape of copyright and licensing, it has the potential for changing the role of the library as a warehouse. In the twentieth century libraries had to try to anticipate future need and acquire items just in case someone would want access to it at some future time. Now it is increasingly possible by electronic downloading to acquire the information needed at the time it is requested.

> V. We treat co-workers and other colleagues with re-
> spect, fairness and good faith, and advocate conditions
> of employment that safeguard the rights and welfare of
> all employees of our institutions.

This article of the code is not specific to libraries or to information professionals. However, it is important that all library workers know that they are expected to treat colleagues with respect. The second part of this article reflects the "do-gooder" nature of library workers—one of the refreshing qualities of most in this occupational group. Library work seems to attract employees who have an active concern for the welfare of others.

> VI. We do not advance private interests at the expense of
> library users, colleagues, or our employing institutions.

As with Article V, there is nothing particularly unique in libraries that raises this particular ethical admonition. All employees need to monitor their behavior to make sure that they are not taking advantage of their customers or employers for personal gain. This whole area will probably expand as more attention is paid to use of employer-provided e-mail for personal use. Liability concerns are causing employers to pay attention to how e-mail is being used. Courts have held that any e-mail, however frivolously intended or by what level of staff it was authored, has the potential to subject employers to harassment and other claims. Again, though, libraries do not have special concerns beyond those held by organizations in general.

> VII. We distinguish between our personal convictions and professional duties and do not allow our personal beliefs to interfere with fair representation of the aims of our institutions or the provision of access to their information resources.

Herein lies one of the greatest professional dilemmas for many librarians and other library workers. Although most are able to hold to the fairness suggested in this article, it is often personally traumatic to offer unbiased information on topics on which they have very strong personal views. It is difficult not to let personal feelings slip out, even with the best of intentions. Continual self-monitoring is needed to ensure that personal beliefs do not color fair and balanced information that allows the customers to find the information they need to allow them to make decisions and to further their ends.

> VIII. We strive for excellence in the profession by maintaining and enhancing our own knowledge and skills, by encouraging the professional development of co-workers, and by fostering the aspirations of potential members of the profession.

Most libraries support staff education in some form—either formal or informal. It is only natural that libraries and library workers have a special commitment to encouraging lifelong learning. Building on the foundation of commitment to education, library workers and libraries have a mutual responsibility to ensure that staff develop the new knowledge and skills that are needed now and those that will be needed in the future. Without a major commitment to staff development, library customers will not receive the continuing high level of service that they have come to expect. In addition, we constantly need to attract the best possible employees at every level of library employment. All of us need to be ambassadors for librarianship.

And What to Do About the Children?

Advocates of restricting access to library materials frequently do so with the best of intentions. Most often, they justify their actions on the basis of the need to protect children. Sometimes the justification is to protect everyone. Other times, the rationale is to prevent the misuse of public funds.

In these arguments there is a parallel with another contentious public policy issue of our generation—abortion. Protection of the unborn, protection of the mother, and protection of tax dollars from inappropriate threats are the most commonly voiced reasons for allowing or not allowing access to abortions.

For most people, it is easier to discuss these issues in the abstract than it is to deal with their application in public policy. Those on the two extremes of these sensitive socio–political issues do not feel ambiguity between theory and practice. However, for those less doctrinaire, such issues are not so clear cut.

Protecting children is a legitimate goal of civilized society. However, is it the responsibility of the state, through its schools and libraries, to determine what each child should have access to? ALA's position is that a library should not restrict the access of all children, strictly because of their chronological age, from information that some might find offensive or inappropriate:

> Libraries are charged with the mission of developing resources to meet the diverse information needs and interests of the communities they serve. Services, materials, and facilities that fulfill the needs and interests of library users at different stages in their personal development are a necessary part of library resources. The needs and interests of each library user, and resources appropriate to meet those needs and interests, must be determined on an individual basis. Librarians cannot predict what resources will best fulfill the needs and interests of any individual user based on a single criterion such as chronological age, level of education, or legal emancipation.
>
> Librarians and governing bodies should not resort to age restrictions on access to library resources in an effort to avoid actual or anticipated objections from parents or anyone else. The mission, goals, and objectives of libraries do not authorize librarians or governing bodies to assume, abrogate, or overrule the rights and responsibilities of parents or legal guardians. Librarians and governing bodies should maintain that parents— and only parents—have the right and the responsibility to restrict the access of their children—and only their children—to library resources. Parents or legal guardians who do not want their children to have access to certain library services, materials or facilities, should so advise their children. Librarians and governing bodies cannot assume the role of parents or the functions of parental authority in the private relationship between parent and child. Librarians and governing bodies have a public and professional obligation to provide equal access to all library resources for all library users.[14]

What Type of Books Are Challenged These Days?

Between 1990 and 1999, 5,718 challenges were reported to or recorded by the ALA Office for Intellectual Freedom. These complaints about the appropriateness of items in library collections can be categorized as follows:

1,446 were challenges to "sexually explicit" material;

1,262 to material considered to use "offensive language";

1,167 to material considered "unsuited to age group";

773 to material with an "occult theme or promoting the occult or Satanism";

630 to material considered to be "violent";

497 to material with a homosexual theme or "promoting homosexuality;" and

397 to material "promoting a religious viewpoint."

Other specific challenges were to material that deals with "nudity" (297), "racism" (245), and "sex education" (217), or were thought to be "anti-family" (193).[15] Ninety-seven percent of the challenges were to material in schools, school libraries, or public libraries. Of these, almost three-fourths were in schools or school libraries.[16]

During the last year of the twentieth century, the most frequently challenged books were ranked in the following order:

1. Harry Potter series, by J. K. Rowling, for its focus on wizardry and magic.

2. Alice series, by Phyllis Reynolds Naylor, for using offensive language and being unsuited to age group.

3. *The Chocolate War*, by Robert Cormier (the "Most Challenged" fiction book of 1998 dropped two positions in 1999), for using offensive language and being unsuited to age group.

4. *Blubber*, by Judy Blume, for offensive language and being unsuited to age group.

5. *Fallen Angels*, by Walter Dean Myers, for offensive language and being unsuited to age group.

6. *Of Mice and Men*, by John Steinbeck, for using offensive language and being unsuited to age group.

7. *I Know Why the Caged Bird Sings*, by Maya Angelou, for being too explicit in the book's portrayal of rape and other sexual abuse.

8. *The Handmaid's Tale*, by Margaret Atwood, for its sexual content.

9. *The Color Purple*, by Alice Walker, for sexual content and offensive language.

10. *Snow Falling on Cedars*, by David Guterson, for sexual content and offensive language.[17]

Current Issues

Ethical issues on the "front burner" in the early twenty-first century continue to involve the protection of children. The new element is Internet access. Access to the Internet is also the basis for an even more far-reaching social and political issue that is being called the "digital divide." At their core, these are not totally new issues. Instead, they are extensions of old ones.

For libraries, the Internet opens up a world of information. Much of it is good, but some is bad and some is downright ugly. As the World Wide Web continues to mature and increasingly delivers on its promise to transform our economy, its rough edges become more widely known. "Life in the gutter of the Information Superhighway" is the way one report described this area of cyberspace.[18] According to this report of children who have gone into an online chat room, one in four has been solicited for sex, and one in five has been sent provocative pictures through a Web contact.[19] Without knowing more about how this survey was conducted, the actual numbers may be suspect. However, no matter what the exact numbers are, it is clear that the Internet can be a dangerous place—especially for unsuspecting children.

Unease about such perils have led concerned citizens to pursue solutions on two separate fronts. One attempted remedy has been through the development of filtering software that attempts to ensure that offending sites or messages are blocked. The second effort has been through the enactment of laws that restrict what can be communicated over the World Wide Web.

Internet Filtering

Filtering software has been highly touted as a way to protect children from the perils of cyber space. So far it has met with only limited success, both legally and functionally. As an aid to parents in managing home computers, filtering software has matured significantly in the past few years. Even so, it may give parents a false sense of security if they rely on software alone to protect their children from exposure to unwanted sites. As a device to "protect" the users of public access Internet workstations, it is far from successful.

Filtering software uses a variety of methods to identify potentially objectionable sites. Some ask information specialists, parents, and teachers to classify and rate sites. Others identify harmful material by searching online content and Web site addresses for keywords such as *sex* or *breast.* Others use a combination of the above methods. Some provide updates as often as daily, as they try to keep in touch with dynamically evolving Internet content.

Other approaches taken by authors of filtering software are to provide

> a time management function that allows parents to control the time of day that children are able to access the Internet; control the total number of hours per day or week spent online; [and tracking of] the sites that their children have visited.[20]

Parents can subsequently decide whether any of these sites should be blocked.

Parents clearly have the right and the responsibility to protect their children. However, the issues change significantly when the state attempts to mandate a solution that will apply to all. Public libraries have become battlefields for the resolution of the issue of state-mandated limits to inquiry. Public libraries often serve very diverse communities, different segments of which have very divergent views of what information is acceptable and what is unacceptable.

Two Representative Cases

The most highly publicized battle over this issue was at the Loudoun County Public Library in Virginia. The first shot in this battle was fired in 1997, when the library board adopted a very restrictive Internet blocking policy, mandating the use of blocking software on adult terminals. "The issue is whether pornography will get into the library," said board president John Nicholas. "Our task is to protect our children."[21] The policy, adopted "after six public hearings and over the objections of library staff,"[22] stated in part, "Site-blocking software . . . will be installed on all computers. To the extent technically feasible, such software will . . . [among other criteria] block material deemed Harmful to Juveniles under applicable Virginia statutes."[23] The board then selected software, "despite the revelation a few weeks before that the product (which claimed to block only illegal obscenity) blacklisted the Quaker Web page and the American Association of University Women, among numerous other innocent sites."[24] A local group, Mainstream Loudoun, filed suit in federal court alleging that the library's Internet policy was unconstitutional.[25]

Mainstream representative Elaine Williamson, in a press release, stated

> Rather than designing an Internet use policy that restricts
> all users based on fear that a few may abuse it, we believe
> that there are more responsible and legally sound ways to
> deal with the issues that come with Internet access. . . .
> Our major concern is who has the right to control what
> patrons access on the Internet in public libraries, indi-
> vidual adults and parents, or a government agency?[26]

"The library board . . . argued that blocking Internet content was equivalent to a decision not to purchase a book, rather than being similar to a decision to remove one from the shelves."[27] This position was not accepted by Judge Leonie Brinkema who held that, "Although defendant is under no obligation to provide Internet access to its patrons, it has chosen to do so and is therefore restricted by the First Amendment in the limitations it is allowed to place on patron access." She found that the Loudoun library board's policy restricted "the access of adult patrons to protected material just because the material is unfit for minors." She went on to say,

> By purchasing Internet access, each Loudoun library
> has made all Internet publications instantly accessible
> to its patrons. Unlike an interlibrary loan or outright book
> purchase, no appreciable expenditure of library time or
> resources is required to make a particular Internet publica-
> tion available to a library patron. In contrast, a library must
> actually expend resources to restrict Internet access to a
> publication that is otherwise immediately available.[28]

After the decision was handed down, all Internet access was canceled while the board reviewed its options. It was soon reinstated under a new policy that made filtering optional for adults and allowed parents to decide what access their children should have.

A mirror-image legal challenge came from the other side of the country. In a Livermore, California, case a mother challenged the right of the City of Livermore to offer unrestricted Internet access in its libraries. "She alleges that, at various times in 1997, Brandon [her minor son] went to the library, accessed sexually explicit images on the Internet, downloaded them onto a floppy, printed them out at a relative's home, and allowed other minors to see the prints, all without the consent of Brandon's parents."[29]

In a response on behalf of the library board the city attorney stated, "the Board of Trustees of the Livermore Public Library recognizes that freedom of speech and expression are central to the successful maintenance of a free society."

The Board of Trustees "supports the idea that all members of the community have free and equal access to the entire range of library resources, regardless of content, approach, format or amount of detail. These rights extend to all users of the public library including minors."[30]

The mother subsequently filed suit.[31] Considerable legal scrimmaging followed during which the plaintiff asserted, "The library is integrally involved in providing pornography and should be considered the actual source of it. Imagine that, pursuant to policy, the library installs an obscene pornography display terminal in which patrons simply push a large red button and obscene pornography is displayed on the screen."[32] The City countered, "any alleged harm which may have been caused was caused by Brandon himself, not by the City."[33] The court twice dismissed the suit; the second time in effect ruling that "the Court believed that Plaintiff could not allege a set of facts which would entitle her to legal relief."[34] As of this writing, the matter is still under judicial appeal.

From a legal perspective these two cases were far more complex than represented here. This discussion has focused only on some of the major information ethics issues involved. Other issues of law that were adjudicated in these cases were deliberately ignored and left for discussion in legal treatises.

Be Prepared

Internet use policies are necessary in all types of libraries before a challenge is received. They are absolutely critical in public libraries. Special and academic libraries for the most part serve only clients who are chronologically adults. The primary focus of school libraries is to serve the needs of children. Policies can be crafted for one age group or the other much more easily than can policies that attempt to meet the needs of both groups.

Excerpts from a recent press release from the ALA suggest that most public libraries are now prepared. Results of a survey conducted by the Library Research Center, University of Illinois at Urbana-Champaign, found that

> 95 percent of public libraries have a formal policy in place to regulate public use of the Internet and that most others are developing such policies.
>
> To ensure that people are using the Internet responsibly, 80 percent of respondents say they purposely locate computer terminals in open spaces and often near a staff person's desk.
>
> The survey's results on children's access to the Internet showed that nearly 64 percent of respondents require permission from parents before children can use the Internet.
>
> Almost 50 percent have received informal complaints about Internet access, but only 7 percent were about content. Most were about faulty equipment or a slow response time.[35]

Legislative Remedies

On the political front, two major legislative initiatives were enacted into law during the last years of the twentieth century. Both the Communications Decency Act and the Child Online Protection Act, as their names imply, were crafted and marketed as measures to protect children. However, key provisions of the first were overturned in a landmark Supreme Court decision that went a long way toward defining permissible free speech on the Internet. The second, at this writing, is currently under judicial review with key portions of it at least temporarily stayed until this process is completed.

Communications Decency Act (CDA), 1996

The Communications Decency Act was Congress's first attempt to regulate online speech. "The CDA prohibited posting 'indecent' or 'patently offensive' materials in a public forum on the Internet—including web pages, newsgroups, chat rooms, or online discussion lists."[36] The act attempted to extend to the Internet controls similar to those common to broadcast television. Key parts of the act were struck down by a unanimous three-judge federal panel, which was subsequently upheld by the Supreme Court. In his opinion, Federal Judge Stewart R. Dalzell wrote, "The Internet may fairly be regarded as a never-ending worldwide conversation. The Government may not, through the CDA, interrupt that conversation. As the most participatory form of mass speech yet developed, the Internet deserves the highest protection from governmental intrusion."[37] "In fact, while that decision was indeed momentous, all that it really held was that government regulation of the Internet must be consistent with First Amendment principles, and that the CDA was not, because it restricted far more speech than was necessary or appropriate to deal with the problem of minors' access to 'indecency.' "[38]

Child Online Protection Act (COPA), 1998

After portions of the CDA were declared unconstitutional, Congress attempted to craft a somewhat narrower version, having the same intent. It was sometimes called CDA II or Son of CDA. Its title, like that of its predecessor, suggests the intent to promote decency and to protect children. "COPA makes it a crime for anyone, by means of the World Wide Web, to make any communication for commercial purposes that is 'harmful to minors,' unless the person has restricted access by minors by requiring a credit card number."[39] Possession of a credit card is thus presumed to be an indicator that the holder of that card is an adult—a questionable assumption in today's society.

Free speech advocates find this law flawed in many of the same ways the courts found CDA to be deficient. According to these groups, COPA creates problems in the following areas:

Imposes serious burdens on constitutionally-protected speech, including materials such as the Starr report, movies, and television programs, when disseminated through popular commercial Web sites such as CNN, Yahoo!, or MS-NBC. Medical sites such as OBGYN.net and sexual awareness sites such as PlanetOut also risk restriction under COPA.

Fails to effectively serve the government's interest in protecting children, since it will not effectively prevent children from seeing inappropriate material originating from outside of the U.S. available through other Internet resources besides the World Wide Web, such as chat rooms or email.

Does not represent the least restrictive means of regulating speech, according to the Supreme Court's own findings that blocking and filtering software might give parents the ability to more effectively screen out undesirable content without burdening speech.[40]

Early in 1999 in federal court in Philadelphia, Judge Lowell Reed temporarily blocked the implementation of COPA until a full trial could be held to determine its constitutionality. Unlike the CDA judicial process, which was given "fast track" status, this review may take years to work its way through the almost inevitable appeals process. In his ruling, Judge Reed wrote, "[I]t is not apparent to this Court that the defendant can meet its burden to prove that COPA is the least restrictive means available to achieve the goal of restricting the access of minors to this material."[41]

While this judicial review is underway, many in Congress attempt to mandate Internet filtering for children by attempting to attach such provisions to other bills to achieve this end. One of the more recent examples was the effort of Senator John McCain to require that any school to which E-rate funds were allocated would need to filter its Internet workstations to which children would have access.

The final word has yet to be spoken on how best to protect children from the hazards of the online world. Improvements in the ability of filtering software continue to evolve. On the legal front, legislation continues to be proposed, adopted, and subjected to judicial review. In these processes we get closer to the goal of our society: To protect children while preserving the rights of adults to exercise their rights to engage in free expression of constitutionally protected discourse. And libraries remain on the front line of the battle as they have for decades in the skirmishes over free expression through print works.

Digital Divide

The *digital divide* refers to the polarization of our society into two extremes: (1) the "information haves," and (2) the "information have nots." This kind of division in our society is not new. However, in some ways, the digital divide seems to have the potential to widen the traditional gap between the rich and the poor and to make it more difficult for the poor to have an opportunity to take part in the new digital economy. Not only have women and some ethnic minorities been slow to become consumers of the Net digital opportunities, they have also been greatly under-represented in the new jobs created in the past decade.

At least on the basis of gender, there is evidence that the digital divide is beginning to dissolve. As late as the mid-1990s, women made up less than 10 percent of the users of the Internet. By the late 1990s, with the wide diffusion of the graphically oriented World Wide Web, the ratio of female users jumped almost overnight to about 40 percent. Gurnwald Associates reported that, by the last quarter of 1999, "The Internet gender gap [had] disappeared. For the first time, girls [were] on the Net in proportions equal to or greater than boys; and mothers [seemed] poised to outnumber fathers online."[42] It remains to be seen if this seeming parity in use will translate over time into a more gender-balanced workforce in information technology jobs.

The picture is less rosy for other segments along the "digital divide" (see Table 8.1). "Indeed, the gap in PC ownership between the most-and least-educated has been growing dramatically in recent years. And in a similar vein, the gap between high-income and low-income households with Internet access has also expanded enormously since 1995."[43]

Table 8.1
Computer Access at Home

COMPUTERS AT HOME		
Households	**1998**[44]	**2000**[45]
Caucasian	47%	50%
African American	23%	37%
Latino	26%	49%
Asian American	55%	69%
ONLINE FROM HOME		
Households	**1998**[46]	**2000**[47]
Caucasian	30%	35%
African American	11%	25%
Latino	13%	38%
Asian American	36%	59%

This "racial ravine," as it was called in a recent federal report,[48] has profound implications for those of us committed to providing access to information as a means to empower all persons to participate as productive members of our society. Although recent evidence continues to show these different patterns of Internet use, the root causes do not appear to be racial. Rather,

> "income is the main driver of Internet adoption . . .
> younger people are more likely to be online . . .
> educated people are more likely to be online . . . [and]
> technology optimists are more likely to be online."[49]

Once these variables are taken into account, the effect of race on Internet use all but disappears. In addition, there is little difference in behavior between the ethnic groups once they do get online.[50]

It is clear that African Americans, Latinos, residents of city ghettos and isolated rural areas, and those from low income families have thus far not had the same level of access to the opportunities of cyberspace as have other Americans. This disparity has attracted much rhetoric from political leaders in the opening days of the twenty-first century. But, so far, no solutions have emerged to significantly equalize access to education, vocational information, and opportunities that are increasingly available on the World Wide Web.

Now, as much as ever, libraries have a role to play in helping extend the political and economic benefits of our free society and economic prosperity to all residents of our country. Libraries, particularly public libraries, are one of the few avenues of access to the World Wide Web for many who have yet to be able to afford a computer or online connections. Clearly, the "ostrich approach" of "burying our heads in the sand" is not a viable option for libraries. Even though, as Judge Brinkema stated in the Loudoun case, the library "is under no [legal] obligation to provide Internet access to its patrons,"[51] it certainly has an ethical obligation to do so. As larger amounts of government and private information are distributed online, libraries need to make sure that their policies of acquiring and disseminating information help shrink rather than help widen this gap. Free and unfettered access for all to this information is critical to the strengthening of our democracy.

More outreach is needed if the "racial ravine" is to be bridged. It appears that those who have computers at home are the ones most likely to use computers at work, at school and at libraries as shown in Table 8.2.

At the same time, libraries have a role to play in ensuring that the privacy of the inquirer is not compromised. However, as can be seen, that access is by no means ensured because of other often conflicting values held by a substantial number of our citizens. The struggle continues.

Table 8.2
Where People Connected to the Internet in January 2000[52]

Households	Home	Work	School	Library
Caucasian	35%	19%	3%	5%
African American	25%	17%	4%	6%
Latino	38%	23%	5%	7%
Asian American	59%	41%	10%	12%

That struggle is to reach and maintain the appropriate balance points between

- the public's right to know;

- the intellectual property rights of authors and publishers, so they can continue to create and distribute the very information the public needs;

- the right to privacy of consumers of information; and

- the appropriate protection and guidance of our children so that they can develop into creative and productive citizens.

These are not "new" ethical values. However, the application of them in the environment in which libraries of the twenty-first century function often makes it seem that these balance points are shifting under our feet.

Study Questions

1. Which of the six ways of knowing truth listed in this chapter do you use in determining what is the right thing for you to do?

2. Why is access to information particularly valuable in a society like ours?

3. Why is privacy valuable in a society like ours?

4. Why should individuals be able to profit from their ideas?

5. Under what conditions should details about the information sought by library patrons be made available to others?

6. What does "fair use" have to do with copyrighted materials?

7. Do parents, or does the state, know better how to protect children from harmful influences?

8. Why were the Harry Potter titles challenged as to whether they should be in schools and libraries?

9. Is filtering appropriate and effective to protect children using the Internet?

10. Is resolution of the "digital divide" important to our society?

Resources

Intellectual Freedom

- American Civil Liberties Union, *Briefing Paper 10 "Freedom of Expression"* http://www.aclu.org/library/pbp10.html

- American Library Association, *Policy Manual 53*, "Intellectual Freedom." http://www.ala.org/alaorg/policymanual/intellect.html

- Freedom to Read Statement. http://www.ala.org/alaorg/oif/freeread.html

- Library Bill of Rights. http://www.ala.org/work/freedom/lbr.html

Code of Ethics

- American Library Association, *Code of Ethics*, Adopted June 28, 1995.

Privacy

- American Library Association, *Policy on Confidentiality of Library Records.* http://www.ala.org/alaorg/oif/pol_conf.html

- cookiecentral.com, *Cookies and Privacy FAQ.* http://www.cookiecentral.com/content.phtml?area=4&id=10

- Robert Emmet Long. *Rights to privacy.* New York: H.W. Wilson, 1997. "The Reference Shelf," 1–20.

- John Schwartz. "Giving Web a Memory Costs Its Users Privacy," *New York Times* (4 September 2001): A-1.

- John Weckert and Douglas Adeney. "Privacy," *Computer and Information Ethics.* Westport, CT: Greenwood Press, 1997, 75–87.

Intellectual Property

- Kenneth D. Crews. *Copyright Essentials for Librarians and Educators.* Chicago: American Library Association, 2000.

- R. Delgado-Martinez. *What Is Copyright Protection.* http://www.whatiscopyright.org

- Liam B. Lavery. "Rights and Wrongs: A practical guide to Internet content," *CIO Web Business* (1 December 1999). http://www.cioi.com/archie/webbusiness/120199_gray.html

- Stanford University Libraries. *Copyright & Fair Use.* http://fairuse.stanford.edu/

- United States Copyright Office. http://www.loc.gov/copyright/

- University of Texas System Administration Office of the General Counsel. *Copyright Management Center.* http://www.utsystem.edu/OGC/IntellectualProperty/cprtindx.htm

- John Weckert and Douglas Adeney. "Intellectual Property," in *Computer and Information Ethics.* Westport, CT: Greenwood Press, 1997, 57–73.

Digital Divide

Kim Nauer. "The Information Revolution could create information haves and information have-nots," in Paul A. Winters, *The Information Revolution: Opposing Viewpoints.* San Diego, CA: Greenhaven Press, 1998, 131–39.

Steve Gibson. "The Information Revolution will not create information haves and information have-nots," in Paul A Winters, *The Information Revolution: Opposing Viewpoints.* San Diego, CA: Greenhaven Press, 1998, 140–46.

Notes

1. John J. Heldrich Center for Workforce Development and Center for Survey Research and Analysis, *Work Trends: Americans' Attitudes About Work, Employers and Government: Making the Grade? What American Workers Think Should Be Done to Improve Education.* Rutgers University, June 14, 2000, 2. Available: http://www.heldrich .rutger.edu (Accessed January 5, 2002).

2. Roughly paraphrased from a class lecture by Gregory D. Pritchard, Philosophy 101, Oklahoma Baptist University, 1962.

3.   *Code of Ethics of the American Library Association*, adopted by the ALA Council, June 28, 1995.

4.   Intellectual Freedom and Censorship Q & A (American Library Association, 2000). Available: http://www.ala.org/alaorg/oif/intellectualfreedomandcensorship.html (Last modified February, 3, 2000).

5.   Free Access to Libraries for Minors: An Interpretation of the Library Bill of Rights, adopted by the ALA Council, June 30, 1972 and amended July 1, 1981. Available: http://www.ala.org/alaorg/oif/free_min.html

6.   American Library Association, Policy on Confidentiality of Library Records, 1971. Available: http://www.ala.org/alaorg/oif/pol_conf.html

7.   Ibid.

8.   Bryan A. Garner, ed., *Black's Law Dictionary*, 7th ed. St. Paul, MN: West Group, 1999, 813.

9.   J. A. Simpson and E. S. C. Weiner, *The Oxford English Dictionary* Vol. VIII, 2d ed. Oxford: Clarendon, 1989, 1068.

10.   Two very useful sites for finding out more about copyright basics are http://fairuse .stanford.edu/ and http://www.utsystem.edu/OGC/IntellectualProperty/cprtindx.htm

11.   Stella Keenan, *Concise Dictionary of Library and Information Science*. London: Saur, 1996, 173.

12.   R. Delgado-Martinez, *What Is Copyright Protection*. Available: http://www .whatiscopyright.org (Accessed January 29, 2002).

13.   The University of Texas maintains a very helpful tutorial on copyright and fair use for those who want to understand how to apply these concepts in more detail: http://www.utsystem.edu/OGC/IntellectualProperty/cprtindx.htm

14.   ALA, *Free Access to Libraries for Minors: An Interpretation of the Library Bill of Rights*, adopted June 30, 1972, amended July 1, 1981; July 3, 1991, by the ALA Council.

15.   ALA, OIF, Banned Books Week: http://www.ala.org/bbooks/challeng.html#mfcb. Works are often challenged on more than one ground. Therefore, the number of reasons will exceed the number of challenges.

16.   Ibid.

17.   Ibid.

18.   CBS News, *Children, Sex & The Web*, June 10, 2000.

19.   Ibid.

20.   Center for Democracy & Technology, Amicus Brief Child Online Protection Act (COPA), January 11, 1999. Available: http://www.cdt.org/speech/copa/990111amicus.html (Accessed November 30, 2001).

21.   "Censor's Sensibility: Are Web Filters Valuable Watchdogs or Just New Online Thought Police?" *Time* (11 August 1997): 48.

22.   Ibid.

23.   The Censorware Project, *Loudoun County, VA Censorware Lawsuit*. Available: http://censorware.org/legal/loudoun/ (Accessed August 3, 2000).

24.   Ibid.

25.   *"Mainstream Loudoun v. Loudoun County Pub. Library,"* 2 F. Sup.2d 783 (E.D. Va. 1998).

26.   "MainStream Loudoun Files Suit Against Library Board's Unconstitutional Internet Policy," December 22, 1997. Available: http://www.censorware.org/legal /loudoun/971222_pressrel_ml.htm (Accessed August 3, 2000).

27.   The Censorware Project; ibid.

28.   Ibid.

29.   The Censorware Project, *Livermore, CA Lawsuit*. Available: http://www .censorware.org/legal/livermore/#Timeline (Accessed August 4, 2000).

30.   Thomas R. Curry, letter to Michael Millen, Esq. Re: Access to the Internet at the Livermore Public Library, April 17, 1998.

31.   Kathleen R. v. City of Livermore. *Tech Law Journal*. Available: http://www .techlawjournal.com/courts/kathleenr/Default.htm (Accessed February 5, 2002).

32.   *Opposition to Demurrer of Defendant City of Livermore to Amended Complaint,* January 13, 1999.

33.   The Censorware Project, *Livermore, CA Lawsuit*; ibid.

34.   Ibid.

35.   ALA News Release, "New survey shows 95 percent of public libraries have policies to manage the Internet," July 2000. Available: http://www.ala.org/news/v5n25 /internetsurvey.html (Accessed August 5, 2000).

36.   Center for Democracy and Technology. Available: http://www.cdt.org/speech /cda/ (Accessed August 4, 2000).

37.   Thomas J. DeLoughry and Jeffrey R. Young, "Federal Judges Rule Internet Restrictions Unconstitutional: In striking down law that many said violated academic freedom, the jurists call for "the highest protection" for the Internet," *The Chronicle of Higher Education,* June 21, 1996. Available: http://chronicle.com (Accessed August 4, 2000).

38.   Steven McDonald, "Point of View: The Laws of Cyberspace: What Colleges Need to Know" *The Chronicle of Higher Education,* October 31, 1997. Available: http://chronicle.com/ (Accessed August 4, 2000).

39.   Center for Democracy and Technology; ibid.

40.   Ibid.

41.   Ibid.

42.   Gurnwald Associates, *Children, Families and the Internet 2000*. Available: http://www.grunwald.com/survey/survey_content.html (Accessed November 30, 2001).

43.   Thomas E. Cavanagh and Christy Eidson, "The 'Digital Divide' in PC Use. *Across the Board* 37, no. 4 (2000): 55.

44.   Ibid.

45.   Ekaterina O. Walsh, "The Truth About the Digital Divide," *The Forrester Brief* (11 April 2000).

46.   Cavanagh; ibid.

47.   Walsh; ibid.

48.   Cavanagh; ibid.

49.   Walsh; ibid.

50.   Ibid.

51.   The Censorware Project, *Loudoun County, VA Censorware Lawsuit*. Available: http://censorware.org/legal/loudoun/ (Accessed August 3, 2000).

52.   Walsh; ibid.

Chapter 9

Job Search Basics

The array of professional knowledge and skills you possess are of no value to you or anyone else unless you can find an appropriate setting in which to put them to use. Generally, this will be within an organization. Finding the appropriate setting requires a well-planned and carefully executed job search strategy.

Getting Ready for the Job Search

According to personnel experts, current American workplace trends include fundamental change, outsourcing of staff, and increased dependence on technology.¹ As a backdrop to these identified trends, workers can expect multiple job changes throughout their careers and a resulting need for continually updating of their skills. The days of working solely for one employer until retirement are as passé as amber computer screens.

These general workplace trends are true in the library and information center sector as well. Whether a new graduate or a seasoned professional, you should keep your job-hunting skills honed; you will most likely put them to use several times during the course of your working life.

Early Twenty-First Century Library and Information Center Job Markets

The field has entered a very dynamic period, such that the librarian or library technician of today can only speculate on how the profession will continue to change with future technological innovations. For those uncomfortable with change, this pattern may cause dissatisfaction or a departure from the field.

According to the U.S. Department of Labor's *Occupational Outlook Handbook for 2000/01* (see Figure 9.1), the job outlook for the field overall is mixed, with slower-than-average job growth predicted for librarian-level positions in traditional environments, but with employment growth in related occupations with a strong emphasis on computer and organizational skills, such as private corporations, consulting firms, and information brokers.

For library technicians, jobs are expected to grow as fast as the average for all occupations through the year 2008. The increasing use of library automation may be one of the factors to spur job growth among library technicians. Here again, special libraries present the largest potential employment growth for library technician-level openings.

Regardless of the level of employment, technological competency is mandatory for entering the library and information field, and, once employed, workers can expect the demand for ongoing learning in this area to continue.

Who Am I, Professionally Speaking?

Before embarking on a job search or compiling a resume, serious job hunters need to spend time thoughtfully taking stock of their own skill sets and considering what an ideal job situation would be. This self-assessment may well be the hardest part of the job search process, even though filling out multiple-page application forms with tiny lines and too-small spaces is always onerous.

Before beginning your search, consider the following logistical issues:

Do you have a preference for working in a particular type or size of library or information center?

Are you willing to relocate? If not, what are your geographical limitations?

Are you seeking part-time or full-time employment?

Are you able and willing to work out of your home or to telecommute?

Do you prefer traditional office hours? Are you willing to work evenings, weekends, or variable hours?

Are you an entrepreneur? Would you enjoy starting your own business?

Are several steps needed to reach your ultimate career goal?

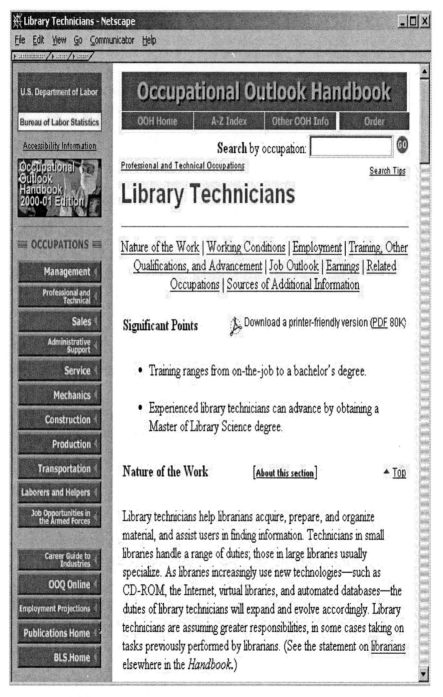

Figure 9.1. Both in print format and on the Web, the annual Occupational Outlook Handbook *is a useful tool for those seeking an overview of the job outlook in libraries and information centers, as well as other related fields.*

Your Skill Set

Try to enumerate your unique set of skills. For what are they best suited? Designing and maintaining Web pages? Teaching? Instructing and working with elementary school children? Some of each? Is a lot of public interaction appealing to you or a turnoff? For guidance in taking stock of your skills and interests, browse the current print edition or the interactive software version of the perennial favorite, Richard Bolles's *What Color Is Your Parachute?*

A recommended source for stretching your mind as to the varieties of employment within the library and information business is *What Else You Can Do With a Library Degree: Career Options for the 90's and Beyond,* edited by Betty-Carol Sellen. Many careers outside the familiar—such as working for outsourcing companies or vendors, serving as an independent consultant, and technical writing and teaching—are featured here in short articles written by people employed in these collateral areas.

The Other Side of the Job Market

Filling a position is very costly both in time and money. Employers do not take this lightly. Too often job seekers focus almost exclusively on their own needs and give short shrift to the point of view of the employer. Making an effort to understand and respond to the reasons why employers seek to fill positions may provide the job seeker with some competitive insight.

Even though most library employers are caring individuals, they do not make hiring decisions based on whether you are behind on your rent, your daughter needs $3,500 worth of orthodontic work next year, or whether you need just six more quarters to qualify for full social security benefits. Although these may be powerful motivators for you, these are not convincing reasons, in and of themselves, for an employer to hire you. In fact, sharing these needs too early in the employment process may prove to be counterproductive.

A more productive job-seeking strategy is to look at the situation from the perspective of potential employers. Why are they looking for new employees? Do they need to add new knowledge and skills not currently present in their organization? Do they need additional people with the same skills as existing staff? How much of the needed knowledge and skills can the employer afford for you to learn on the job? Which must be present in the new staff member on day one? Is the employer attempting to maintain current operations or to go in new directions?

Some investigation will help you be realistic about how you match up with the needs of the employer. This is an opportunity to demonstrate your research skills and to involve your network of friends in assisting you to achieve your goal. In addition, most employers will appreciate the thoughtful initiative and analytical ability that you demonstrate by exploring their situation in advance.

First, collect all the "public data," such as the position posting or advertisement, information about the library agency, and data about employment conditions and benefits with the organization of which the library is a part. Next, contact your network of friends and colleagues who might know something about the position and the library. After you have absorbed this information, you may want to contact the immediate supervisor, either by telephone or e-mail. Do this with care. Some supervisors may be reluctant to have contact with applicants outside the formal selection process. Others will welcome the opportunity to do some recruiting. Remember that the impression you make will carry over to the formal selection process. Nothing is "off the record." Therefore, call with a specific purpose—ask some questions that, when answered, will affect whether you apply or how you target your formal application. Do not call just to chat or to "shoot the breeze." The underlying purpose is to establish the foundation of a business relationship.

Once you have a good idea of what expectations the employer has for the prospective employee, you will have a more realistic view of your suitability for the position. If it appears that you match up well with the expectations for the position, then you will have a good starting point for how best to present yourself as the candidate who can solve the problem that led to the current recruitment.

Carefully analyze the posting. Is it specific to an individual position, or is it for a class of jobs? Stated another way, is this an application process to fill a specific opening or is it merely to establish eligibility to be placed on a list (possibly in order of priority) for any hiring decisions made during the next six months or the next year?

The Competition

As you start to enter the next step in your marketing plan, you need to focus on another element in the employment process—the competition. Your competitors are not potential employers. Rather, they are other potential employees who look, walk, and talk a lot like you. When you write your cover letter to introduce yourself as the solution to an employer's problem, you need to think about who your competition is likely to be for this specific job. It's not good enough to simply be qualified for the job. You must appear better qualified than the other "qualified" candidates. Of all the people who may apply for the job and meet the minimum qualifications, why should employers think that you are a better solution to their problem than any of the other candidates? Is your education more relevant? Have you demonstrated better skills? If so, which ones? Do you have more applicable experience? Find at least one area where you should have an advantage over most other applicants for the job and start building a convincing application package to sell to potential employers.

Internships and Volunteer Experience

If related work experience is not one of your most competitive job assets, then you may want to consider the benefits of an internship or volunteer stint before completing your formal educational program or as you prepare to embark on a job search. An internship can offer a valuable "sneak preview" into the world of work. As an intern in a library or information center, you can sample various working environments, network with library personnel in your geographical region, and gain valuable hands-on experience. Interning in the field can be quite eye-opening and can provide a very different learning experience than the traditional classroom venue. A successful internship can also serve as a source for job referrals and letters of recommendation in the future. Remember that each experience should be a building block to your ultimate career objective. It should be taken seriously so that you not only learn all you can, but also leave behind an advocate who will want to help you succeed in future steps down your chosen career path.

Internships typically come in two forms: (1) paid internships, and (2) practicums. Paid internships are when a business or government agency has set aside funds to hire students for summer or other short-term periods as a learning experience. Often, these are not widely advertised, and the hiring agencies may rely on word of mouth to recruit candidates. Professors, counselors, and job placement personnel are good sources to contact about potential paid internships. Querying library-related listservs can also be productive.

Unpaid internships or practicums are set up as an academic course with enrolled students earning college credit for their field hours. Practicums are a frequent and valuable component in both community college level library/ media technician programs and in graduate library and information school curricula. Many programs require them. Others will be willing to try to set up such opportunities.

In the event that no formal internship opportunities are available, serving as a volunteer staffer in a library or information center can provide some beneficial work experience for the novice, student, or re-entry worker. Many public library agencies and academic facilities have ongoing placement of volunteers. Begin by discussing your career goals and educational background with the department head or branch librarian where you would like to volunteer to explore what opportunities might best serve their needs and yours. Internships and volunteer situations can provide relevant experience to place on resumes when entering a field or changing careers.

The Job Hunt

Job openings are advertised in a variety of media: newspapers, Web sites, hotlines, and industry newsletters, as well as informally through word of mouth. Subscribing via e-mail to listservs focusing on your special area of employment interest—for example, law libraries, business information centers, or school media centers—is one way to find out about openings nationwide and beyond. Traditional job classified ads are published in local and regional newspapers, both online and in print.

Agencies such as city and county public libraries, universities, colleges, museums, and private companies often post their openings on their organization's Web site, as well as recruiting through flyers, newspapers, listservs, mailing lists, and so on. Resume submission via e-mail is becoming commonplace in high-tech private industries.

Trade publications such as *Library Mosaics, Library Journal, American Libraries, Chronicle of Higher Education*, and many others carry regular job announcements in their print editions as well as posting them on their Web sites.

Librarian positions tend to be advertised over a wider area than do library technician positions. It is generally assumed that paraprofessionals must be recruited from within the local commuting area but that librarians may be willing to relocate for the right job. Whether or not these presumptions are correct, most employers will formulate their recruiting efforts on this basis. Therefore, paraprofessionals who are willing to relocate may have to exercise greater initiative to locate job listings than do librarians.

For example, library technicians may need to subscribe to a local newspaper in an area they want to relocate to, or have a friend there carefully watch the job ads to become aware of appropriate openings. The advent of the Internet has created another avenue for locating jobs that are not advertised beyond the local area—that of browsing through the classified ads of newspaper Web sites in targeted cities.

Proactive Job Searching

Scanning the classified ads in any medium is one approach, but creative and energetic job searchers will also want to target and directly approach agencies for which they are interested in working. Tools such as the annual *American Library Directory* are indispensable for locating major library agencies in a given geographical area and gleaning some very basic information about their collections, budgets, staffing, and so forth. Most state libraries also produce a directory of library agencies within their borders. However, neither of these tools will include all of the smaller, private companies or agencies with internal information centers or libraries.

Visiting the Web sites of library agencies provides a fresh means of learning about the organization and how they present themselves to their clientele and the world at large. For agencies open to the public, there is still nothing like an in-person visit to observe, explore, and get a feel for services, staffing, and facilities. In addition, many part-time or temporary positions are not formally advertised and may be discovered only through an on-site visit or inquiry.

Any prospective library or information industry employee should be well equipped with the research skills needed to locate background information on a potential employer. This situation provides a test case for putting your reference skills to work by searching company or agency profiles, statistics, news coverage, press releases, floor plans, or mission statements to help yourself in your job search.

Outsourcing

Although many first-time employees will tend to seek full-time, traditional positions as staff in library agencies, private industry, government information centers, and schools, jobs with outsourcing firms are also an area of growth in the field.

What is outsourcing? Basically, it is supplementing the in-house workforce by hiring outside contractors from the private sector. Outsourcing may mean hiring a freelance consultant, turning to a temporary employment agency for staff, or going out to bid for a private company that will perform certain services. Historically, libraries have used automation, architecture, public relations, and management consultants, and contracted out services such as book approval plans and cataloging.

Contracting out library services has gone on quietly since at least the 1960s, especially in military and government libraries. But two large and notable projects have garnered a lot of media attention and industry discussion. The first was the controversy regarding the State Librarian's plan in 1996 to outsource all technical services to jobber Baker and Taylor for the Hawaii State Public Library System. Under the $11.2 million contract, the North Carolina-based company was to handle 100 percent of the system's selection, acquisitions, cataloging, and processing. Local public service librarians were subsequently dissatisfied with the materials selection aspect of the plan, as delivery time, quantity, and quality of materials proved inadequate.[3]

After a year of much public outcry and discussion, the Hawaiian legislature canceled the contract. Fallout from the canceled contract resulted in multiple lawsuits, the firing of the State Librarian, and the return of selection duties to the system's 49 branches. In addition, a new state law was passed requiring librarian input on materials selection. This sequence of events underscores the strong need for local input and involvement with a task, such as materials selection, which can be a very customized library service.[4]

The second high-profile case was the privatization of the Riverside County Public Library, in southern California. Because of ongoing economic woes during the 1990s and resulting major cuts in hours and services, the city of Riverside chose not to continue its 85-year-old partnership with the county to run the system. The county then went out to bid for a private firm to operate the library agency. As a result, Library Systems & Services (LLSI) of Maryland contracted with the county to run the entire library system beginning mid-1997. Initial published observations indicate satisfaction with the arrangement.[5] Because it is unusual to have a contractor running a public library, this situation will continue to draw much discussion and media coverage.

Despite these controversial examples, libraries of all types regularly turn to outside sources for short-term employee needs, consulting, or special skills. Some commonplace examples of outsourcing include the operation of special libraries, such as those on military bases, providing manpower to relocate a collection to a new facility, or hiring a consultant to prepare a specialized report.

In terms of employment options, outsourcing translates into diverse opportunities for entrepreneurs. Freelance librarians and library technicians, information brokers, consultants, Web masters, Web page designers, and others may serve as independent contractors to library agencies, private industry, or consumers. Typically, they work independently, supply their own work space and equipment, and are paid per hour or per project. The U.S. Bureau of Labor estimates that in total there are nine million freelance workers in the United States as of 1998. Although there are no definite figures available for the library and information field, outsourcing trends and the growing reliance on telecommuting indicate continued opportunities here. *The Burwell World Directory of Information Brokers* (1998) listed about 1,000 firms or individuals in business.

Temporary employees, on the other hand, may be hired by the library through a personnel agency specializing in supplying trained staff for short-term or temporary needs—such as the startup of a new branch, a move to new quarters, conducting an inventory, or staffing weekend hours of operation.

The Appeal of Outsourcing

Outsourcing appeals to a library because it means a cost savings on fringe benefits for personnel; it allows a company or library to meet a sudden or unusual demand; it provides flexibility in staffing; and it allows permanent staff to focus on interactions with patrons or other customized services that do not lend themselves well to outsourcing.

What does outsourcing offer to the employee? For those who prefer flexible or part-time hours, a variety of changing work venues, or a steady stream of new challenges, outsourcing may be the answer. It can also be an effective way to sample or preview the field when considering a career change or shifting to a different focus within the profession. For those with lifestyle needs such as retirement or parenthood, outsourcing can be an attractive option.

Conferences

Whether searching for outsourcing opportunities or for a permanent job with a library or information center, attending conferences is another means of networking and data gathering in your job search.

State and national library industry trade associations (e.g., Council on Library/Media Technicians [COLT], Medical Library Association [MLA], Special Library Association [SLA], American Society for Information Science and Technology [ASIST], ALA) typically have free job information centers or placement services as part of their annual conventions where applicants can list resumes and employers can post positions. While job-hunting, consider attending such a conference in your state or region to tap this service as well as to sit in on presentations and hear the issues under discussion by practitioners. One of the biggest reasons for attending trade conferences for workers at all levels is the networking value in making new professional contacts.

Many of these same associations maintain free telephone hotlines with information on current job openings, as well as posted career leads on their Web sites, as mentioned previously. *American Libraries* provides a list of many such hotlines.

Job Search Tools

There are three standard documents that typically comprise the job application packet: (1) the resume, (2) a cover letter, and (3) the application form. Each is different in format and in the data they convey about an applicant; effectively done, each should complement one another.

Resume

The resume is a canvas upon which you paint a portrait of those demonstrated skills and knowledge you are offering to employers. Each brush stroke (i.e., word) should be added for a purpose—to convey to employers a particular message about how you will be able to solve their problems after you are employed. Keep it focused on what they want to know; not what you want to brag about.

In general, your resume should not be changed every time you apply for a job. It should represent you. However, if you are applying for very different positions, you may want to consider tailoring various versions of your resume.

Data Sheet, Vita, or Resume?

In this chapter, the term *resume* is used in its broadest connotation. As Goldilocks had a choice of three sizes of chairs, there are actually three different resumes that vary in length: (1) the data sheet, (2) the vita, and (3) the resume. The data sheet is a bare bones outline with no embellishments. It usually comprises less than a page and gives little flavor for you and your style. An example of information on a data sheet would be "A.A., Library and Information Technology, Cuesta College, 2000." Because your purpose in creating a resume is to communicate your attributes in a way that makes you stand out from your competitors in the job market, the data sheet, as Goldilocks would say, is not nearly long enough to accomplish your purpose.

At the other extreme, the curriculum vita is too much information for most library positions. On the other hand, if you are applying for a librarian position in a university, many colleges, and some private research organizations, this is exactly what is expected to be competitive. You should list professional papers you have presented, articles you have published, committees you served on, and funded or in-progress research. The vita cannot be too lengthy if each item is legitimately professional and verifiable. However, if the job does not fall into the above categories, such activities—no matter how relevant in your mind—should be summarized or limited to only the most recent. An overly lengthy resume outside of the academic or research environment could actually work against you. You may be viewed as not genuinely committed to libraries outside the academic or research sector or too "nerdy" to relate to the clientele at hand.

For most positions, the true resume or summary is the appropriate model to follow. In using the resume, unless you have considerable professional experience—generally, more than 5 or 10 years—you should keep this summary to one page. As mentioned previously, this is the place to describe yourself in terms that will encourage employers to see you as a solution to their vacancy.

To Include or Not to Include Information

When crafting your resume, the real question you should be addressing is what knowledge and skills you are trying to market at this point in your career. You may possess knowledge and skills that you do not want to pursue at this stage in your life. Focus your attention on where you want to go, rather than where you have been. For example, if you are going through a career change, too much emphasis on the field you are leaving may give the impression that you are not truly committed to your new chosen field. However, many skills are transferable.

Several years ago, one of the authors was asked by a mutual friend to counsel a neophyte to the library field who was having a crisis of confidence as she tried to launch her new career. As she told the story, a family emergency had forced her out of the employment market just as she had completed her library degree. A year and a half later, she was sure employers would doubt her level of commitment and wonder whether she had been in jail or homeless during the gap in her resume.

Further conversation revealed that her father-in-law died just before she graduated. He had been running a large dairy farm in Wisconsin. She and her husband had put their careers on hold and moved to the farm so that they could manage a liquidation of the property and its assets. It took 18 months to sell the farm, its equipment, and its herd at a time when the market was advantageous and also to resettle her mother-in-law into a new home. During this period, her husband ran the dairy side of the operation and she had handled the business side, including keeping all of the records. Hundreds of thousands of dollars were involved. Can you think of any knowledge and skills that she demonstrated that would be useful in a library setting? After thinking the situation through, she decided that she had demonstrated many useful and marketable skills during her stint as the business manager of a family enterprise during its orderly liquidation.

As you progress through your vocational self-analysis, you will be ready to start drafting a resume. The purpose of the resume is to sketch an honest picture of the person you are trying to market. Every phrase in the resume should be another brush stroke portraying the professional knowledge and skills you want to apply in your new job. Facts about you that do not add to this persona—however proud of them you are—have no place in the resume. At the same time, some of the images you paint can be subtle. For example, one of the qualities employers need on the job is teamwork. If possible, you should list something on your resume that indicates that you have demonstrated teamwork in the workplace. However, if you have not yet had an opportunity to document this in a job setting, then perhaps success in community organizations, sports teams, or student clubs will suffice. This is but one example of the myriad of small impressions that can be conveyed with a well-constructed resume.

Common attributes that employers look for in employees are listed at the end of this chapter. The checklist can serve as a tool to evaluate whether you have included something to spark the interest of a potential boss about the kinds of skills you are prepared to bring to their organization.

Resume Formatting

Books on resume preparation provide differing advice about the sequence of the sections of your resume. Sometimes it makes sense to decide on the particular area in which you are likely to have an advantage over your competitors for the position. Again, the point is not to prove that you are qualified for the position. Several others may also be qualified. Your goal is to show that you are the *most qualified* person for the job. Ask yourself, are you likely to have more work experience than your fellow job applicants? If so, then your job history should be the lead item in your resume. If your advantage is education, that section should come first. If your expertise is computer skills or a foreign language, make sure these are prominently displayed. Arrange your resume so that employers can look it over and quickly zero in on whatever item interests them most.

A good resume should showcase your skills, education, and relevant work experience and echo the qualifications spelled out in the job advertisement. Regardless of the method you choose for compiling a resume or the finished format, experts recommend starting with a personal data list. You will need to gather the pertinent facts and dates about your prior job history, education, and training before you can start organizing these data into a selling tool.

Computer screening of resumes is becoming more popular, especially in the high-tech industry. A resume is electronically submitted by the candidate, then searched for the number and occurrence of key vocabulary and phrases relevant to the employer's job description. Based on the ranking from this keyword analysis, a candidate may or may not warrant an interview.

Many Web sites, software, and books exist to help you format or lay out your resume. Some of the best have hundreds of samples to illustrate good and bad resumes. Your college career center or local public library is likely to stock many titles. We have provided several Web site addresses and recommended titles in the resources section at the end of this chapter. In addition, here are some basic tips that apply to all resumes:

- Check spelling in the document and show it to at least one other person before sending it out. Neatness and spelling should be impeccable.

- Never submit a typed or handwritten resume; use a word processor.

- Choose a standard business font, not an artsy or hard-to-read typeface.

- Clearly present contact information (i.e., home, work, or fax telephone numbers, e-mail address).

- Leave out personal information about hobbies, age, marital status, health, and religion.

- Use action words and phrases throughout the resume.

- Ask a professional in the field to review it and make comments on your draft.

Cover Letter

A cover letter with your resume provides an opportunity to highlight in narrative form the most important items from the application and the resume. It also serves as a sample of your written communication skills and lets you demonstrate that you know something about the agency or company. The purpose is to make a connection between the job opening and the person described in the resume. The letter should be brief—normally less than one page. Your intent should be to guide a reader through the cover letter as quickly as possible and urge him or her to be eager to read your resume to learn more about you.

The first sentence should indicate very clearly for which job you are applying. Remember that the first person to read it will most likely be a human resources clerk. That person may not care about your wonderful qualifications, but you do want the clerk to place your packet into the correct file. Organizations often recruit simultaneously for many positions. In addition, such offices receive a high volume of mail every day.

Your next task is to demonstrate to the personnel who screen applications that you have thoughtfully and thoroughly read their job posting. Veteran library personnel officers often get cover letters that appear to have been sent to them by mistake or to have been recycled, without modification, from a very different job search. Be enthusiastic, but remain professional. One of the authors received, over the course of a year and a half, two separate applications from the same person for two very different jobs. Each letter claimed that the advertised vacancy was exactly the one for which the applicant had patterned all of his education and years of experience. If you are inclined to such hyperbole, be careful not to send it to the same employer twice.

Next, show that you have carefully analyzed your skills. Use a few key phrases from the actual posting as you highlight a couple of the most important areas in which you meet or exceed the requirements. Suggest that, as they read the enclosed resume, they will see additional areas in which your knowledge and skills are appropriate to meet their needs.

Close by stating your eagerness (within reason) to discuss further with them how you are prepared to solve the problem that led them to post this opening, and, as a result, support their efforts to provide quality services to their customers. Keep the entire letter to a single page.

Application Form

This is a tool used to screen applicants and to narrow the pool to those who merit an interview. Especially for civil service-type jobs, such as public libraries, schools districts, and public colleges and universities, be sure to follow application instructions *precisely*. If you omit some information or a required part of the packet, this alone can disqualify you, regardless of how wonderful your skills are.

Often, application forms are generic, gathering the most basic employment history and background information from applicants at all levels within an organization. This is where the importance of a resume as a personalized statement comes into play.

In summary, the purpose of the cover letter is to stimulate the reader to carefully examine the resume. The purpose of the resume is to procure an interview. It is the primary tool of the job search, and you should expect to work through several drafts before arriving at a finished product.

References and Letters of Recommendation

Most application forms request a list of employment-related references. That is, names and contact information of people who can vouch for your work experience, job performance, education, or all three. As a courtesy to your reference person and as a safeguard for yourself, always ask first before listing someone as a job reference. Be sure that your reference person is comfortable about giving you a positive endorsement. If asking for a letter of recommendation, allow adequate lead time for its preparation. (Contacting a potential reference for a letter the night before the application deadline is not a smart idea.) Although not always required, an appropriate, well-written letter of recommendation from a former employer, an intern supervisor, or an instructor can be another asset in your application packet.

Interviewing Skills

Once selected for an interview, the wise candidate takes time to prepare for that day. Be aware that you are likely to be involved in a group interview where several staff members will ask you questions in turn. The crux of the interview is to persuade the panel or group that you are the best person for the job in question. You can affect this persuasion in several ways: using your appearance, demeanor, presentation, and interpersonal skills and crafting thoughtful responses to the questions posed. From the panel's perspective, there is much more going on than just hearing a right or wrong answer. This is a chance for them to evaluate how you think on your feet, your personality, your job philosophy, as well as your technical knowledge. This holds true whether you are interviewing for a civil service list, with a private sector employer, or with an outsourcing agency.

There are many books, videos, and Web sites available on interviewing skills. A few resources are listed in the resources section; public libraries, college career centers, or local bookstores should carry many representative titles on this topic. Although every job interview is different, there are some standard questions candidates can expect to be asked, and, for which thoughtful, appropriate answers can be prepared. Some typical interview questions include the following:

- Describe your qualifications for this job.

- Why are you interested in this position?

- Describe your strengths.

- Describe your weaknesses.

- What are your career goals; where do you see yourself in five years?

- How would you deal with the following situation? (Usually a scenario where you need to solve a problem, assist customers, enforce a policy, demonstrate sensitivity to patrons or staff, and so on.)

- What accomplishment in your work life are you the most proud of and why?

- Describe a difficult situation and how you handled it.

- Skills demonstration questions to test candidate's knowledge of library technology, information science, Internet skills, and so on.

- Computer and technology expertise questions to determine proficiency with various software programs, library-specific systems and products, and Internet use, among others.

Although many interviews will be structured in such a way as to make this impossible, the book *The Five Minute Interview* outlines a method for beginning an interview in a positive way. The strategy is for the candidate to ask the first significant question. That question would be worded something like: "It would help me to focus my responses to your questions if you could take just a minute and share with me your key expectations for the successful candidate." Don't try to force this question if the opening is not there. It can be asked at the end of the interview. However, the earlier it is asked and answered, the more advantageous the information will be.[6]

Do take advantage of any final opportunity to pose questions to your interviewers. Come prepared with a list of questions about the job, the library, and the parent organization. Also, be prepared to sum up your key qualifications, reaffirming your enthusiasm and interest for the position. This represents a last chance to make an impression on the interviewers and is all too often overlooked by applicants.

If you think you need practice with interviews, consider applying for a job opening or two that you may be only slightly interested in, just to experience the application process and the interview session. Such practice will provide you exposure to the process and can serve as a dry run for any future interview situations.

Questions about a candidate's personal life, sexual orientation, ethnicity, age, health, religion, and so on, are all examples of illegal interview questions. Be tactful in your response; try steering the conversation to another topic. If this happens to you, report suspect questions to the personnel analyst or board after your interview.

If you are not the chosen candidate, you may want to call the human services or personnel department and ask for feedback on your interview performance. Constructive comments noted by the panel may help you improve in your next interview. At the same time, be understanding if local policy does not allow them to provide this information to you.

The following lists include interview tips that can help you accomplish a successful interview:

Interview do's:

- Dress professionally. This may vary from organization to organization. As a rule of thumb, you should dress a half step more conservatively than you would if you were already working in the job.

- Be on time (or early) for the interview. Aside from the rudeness of being late, the interview committee may be on a tight schedule and may not have the opportunity to make up the time. Also, arrive early enough to allow a visit to the restroom for any last-minute grooming needs.

- Answer questions concisely, using specific illustrations or examples to make your point.

- If asked a complex or multipart question, attempt to answer it. Do not hesitate to look straight at the person who posed the question and inquire as to whether you covered all parts of it.

- Be attentive and polite.

- Be confident

Interview don'ts:

- Don't drink too much caffeine prior to the interview. Your natural adrenaline flow will be sufficient stimulation.

- Don't ramble on. Answer the question efficiently and move on.

- Don't make negative comments about yourself or any former employers.

- Don't focus on any health or personal problems you may have.

- Don't chew gum.

- Don't wear overly strong perfume, cologne, or aftershave.

- Don't initiate a conversation about salary at this point.

For further consideration, realize that potential employers have a problem finding staff members who:

- can learn quickly;
- can organize work and time;
- can set priorities and focus on what is important;
- can analyze complicated problems;
- can generate several potential solutions;
- can concentrate on complex details;
- can interact well with all kinds of people and meet the public well;
- can perform their jobs in a manner that makes it easier for co-workers, superiors, and sub-ordinates to do their own jobs well;
- can follow through on long, complex procedures;
- can think linearly;
- can write well;
- can work independently;
- can see the big picture;
- can balance many activities simultaneously;
- can teach others, train others, or both;
- can think well on their feet;
- can "listen" well with both their ears and their eyes;
- can speak well;

- can understand the environment in which they work;
- can keep focused on the customer;
- are goal oriented;
- are responsible;
- are looking for better ways to do things;
- are computer literate;
- are intellectually curious;
- are service oriented;
- are emotionally secure;
- are intelligent;
- are creative;
- are team players;
- are not "binary brained";
- are dependable;
- are self-starters;
- are flexible;
- are fast workers;
- are accurate;
- are honest;
- actively seek opportunities to grow both personally and professionally;
- have a thorough knowledge of their profession in general and their specialty in particular;
- have high professional standards; and
- enjoy learning new things.

Study Questions

1. Why is it important to keep your job hunting skills updated?

2. What are some of the trends predicted for the library and information center workforce? What trends do you see in your region?

3. What is outsourcing? Can you find examples of outsourcing companies in your state? Do contract jobs appeal to you?

4. How do the resume, cover letter, and application form differ in the information they present about a candidate?

5. Divide up your class into small groups of four. Choose one person to be the interview candidate and have the other three role play as the interview panel. Have the panel devise several typical questions and pose them to the candidate in a mock interview situation. Afterward give feedback to the interviewee on their performance.

6. Why is networking important to a job hunter? Describe some opportunities for networking in the library and information science field. Have you developed a network of contacts yet?

Resources

Print

American Libraries. January 1998. (Entire issue devoted to discussion of outsourcing.)

Bolles, Richard Nelson. *What Color Is Your Parachute: A Practical Manual for Job Hunters and Career-Changers.* Berkeley, CA: Ten Speed Press, 2000. (Online supplement available: http://www.bookwire.com/bookinfo.publisher)

Kuntz, Tom. "Next Time, Eat the Pizza After the Interview." *New York Times* (24 January 1999): sec 4, p. 2.

Newlen, Robert R. *Writing Resumes That Work: A How-To-Do-It Manual for Librarians.* New York: Neal-Schuman Publishers, 1998. (Table of Contents available: http://www.neal-schuman.com)

Sellen, Betty-Carol, ed. *What Else You Can Do with a Library Degree: Career Options for the 90's and Beyond.* New York: Neal-Schuman, 1997. (Table of Contents available: http://www.neal-schuman.com)

Web Sites

- American Library Association
  http://www.ala.org/
  (Accessed November 30, 2001)
       ALA maintains an extensive, up-to-date Web site featuring news releases, conference dates, legislation updates, and job listings from several months' worth of its *American Libraries* magazine.

- Archeus's Work Search
  http://www.garywill.com/worksearch/
  (Accessed November 30, 2001)
       This site is sponsored by Gary Will, a consultant and speaker who works with clients on job search and recruitment. The sections on resume preparation and job interviewing are especially good.

- Chronicle of Higher Education
  http://chronicle.merit.edu/jobs/
  (Accessed November 30, 2001)
       The leading weekly paper (available in print and on the Web) for news and trends in academia also features a jobs listing that includes professional librarian openings. Basic searching of job database is free; premier searching requires a subscription fee.

- Council on Library/Media Technicians
  http://library.ucr.edu/COLT/
  (Accessed November 30, 2001)
       Council on Library/Media Technicians (COLT) is an organization specifically devoted to library technicians and library support staff. The Web site lists upcoming conferences, COLT publications, posts regional job openings from selected chapters, and has links to many national and international job lines.

- JobWeb
  http://www.jobweb.org
  (Accessed November 30, 2001)
       The JobWeb site is full of career postings as well as how-to information on resumes, interviews, and so forth. Produced by the National Association of Colleges and Employers, "America's bridge between higher education and the world of work." The site is well-organized and frequently updated.

- Library Job Postings on the Internet
  http://webhost.bridgew.edu/~snesbeitt/libraryjobs.htm
  (Accessed November 30, 2001)
       Sarah L. Nesbeitt's Library Job Postings on the Internet is one of the Web's most comprehensive guides to library-related jobs, including over 250 links to library employers. A librarian at Bridgewater State College, Massachusetts, she maintains this service for free. Organized by job type (e.g., archives and records management, academic) or by geographic region.

- Special Libraries Association
  http://www.sla.org/
  (Accessed November 30, 2001)
  SLA features listings and other job search services, most of which are available to members only. A personal resume evaluation service is available to all for a fee.

Notes

1. "Job Prospecting: Tools & Techniques," *AIM News: The Newsletter for Library and Information Professionals* (Fall 1996): 2.

2. Bureau of Labor Statistics, "Occupational Outlook Handbook, 2000/01," *Occupational Outlook Handbook, 2000/01*. Available: http://stats.bls.gov/ocohome.htm (Accessed November 30, 2001).

3. Renee Olson, "Hawaii Librarians Poised to Take Back Materials Selection," *School Library Journal* (August 1997): 18.

4. George M. Eberhart, "Hawaii Terminates Outsourcing Contract," *American Libraries* (August 1997): 15.

5. Rob Seitz, "Outsourcing Helps Library Meet Demand," *American City & County* (May 1998): 72.

6. Richard H. Beatty, *The Five Minute Interview: A New and Powerful Approach to Interviewing*, 2d ed. New York: John Wiley & Sons, 1997.

Chapter 10

Impact of the Internet

Libraries were changed irreversibly by the flourishing of the remarkable tool known as the Internet. Although early Internet protocols, such as the endless menus of Gopher and the UNIX commands of Telnet, were "clunky" and limited in use primarily to academics and technical professionals, the advent of the World Wide Web in the mid-1990s brought the Internet to the masses.

Using hypertext transfer protocol (HTTP), the Web combines intuitive point-and-click technology to access visually appealing multimedia and hyperlinked documents. Its ease of use, graphical nature, and accessibility were an incredible improvement over past utilitarian protocols. Users can choose which hyperlinks to follow as they pursue research, or they can just "surf" to sample what is available. Hypertext Markup Language (HTML) is the coding that allows this document linkage to take place and is a relatively simple language to learn. With the added help of numerous HTML editing software programs, the ability to create a multimedia Web document is readily available to anyone with a little know-how, patience, computer access, and space with a Web hosting service for storing the files.

The Web has something for everyone. Colorful, interactive, kid-friendly sites attract children from an early age; seniors eagerly follow their investments online; students conduct research for papers from the comfort of their home; and business professionals market, buy, and sell products online. Among adults, information gathering and e-mail communication top the list of reasons for logging onto the Web.[1]

Web Usage

Tracking Internet statistics is a rather slippery pursuit because of the medium's ever-changing nature, but some usage milestones and trends can be ascertained. According to the *Computer Industry Almanac*, 9th edition, there were 147 million adults worldwide using the Internet by the end of 1998, as compared to 61 million in 1996. In 1998, more than half of these users—defined as those accessing it at least once a week—resided in the U.S.[2] By the summer of 2001, worldwide use numbers increased to 513.4 million, with 180.7 million residing in North America.[3]

Meanwhile, resource-poor Third World countries with limited access to technology are decidedly behind in Internet usage. In addition to the lack of computers and aging or nonexistent infrastructures in many poorer nations, freedom of information is not a universally embraced concept. Repressive government regimes actively restrict access to the Internet for their citizens.

In terms of gender, as of mid-1999, various studies indicated that women had made great strides and constituted half of American adult users of the Web. This contrasts sharply with early Internet use surveys in 1996 that showed a substantial gender gap, with males dominating Web usage by about a four-to-one ratio.[4]

Popularity of E-Mail

E-mail—a highly practical, efficient, and inexpensive means of communication—was embraced early on and continues to be an extremely popular and convenient tool, both for business and for personal purposes. In 1999, a report by consultants Frost & Sullivan indicates that e-mail has taken its place alongside the telephone and the fax as a primary means of business communication in the U.S. Their study placed the total number of e-mail accounts worldwide at more than 112 million in 1998; up from nearly 49 million in 1997.[5] In terms of volume of use, industry analysts at *eMarketer* noted that 766 billion e-mail messages were transmitted in 1998 within the U.S. (not including unsolicited "junk mail," commonly called "spam"), while only 107 billion pieces of U.S. postal service mail were delivered.[6]

E-mail habits have been a focus of several studies undertaken by the Pew Internet and American Life project. Research conducted in spring 2000 revealed that "on a typical day, 28% of all Americans and 60% of all Internet users go online to check email and engage in at least one activity on the Web. For the months of March and April, this represents 55 million Americans emailing on an average day. Overall, 84 million people, or 45% of all Americans, are email users."[7] The growing reliance upon e-mail as a standard means of communication will only increase as new Web products offer more ways to use this tool.

Effect on Libraries and Researchers

Not since the release of the Gutenberg Bible has the library field been enveloped in such dramatic change as that brought by the Internet revolution of the 1990s. Many of the long-touted promises of the information technology age that were heralded in earlier decades came true with the development of the World Wide Web. All aspects of library operations have been impacted, from daily staffing needs to the publishing industry to patron services. A librarian's job description is dramatically different from a decade ago, with computer proficiency and teaching skills both critical requirements. Duties of other library staff members have also been changed unalterably. Even the physical plant and the design of library and information center facilities have undergone major modification to reflect the reliance on online use.

Information Access and Publishing Trends

The world of publishing has been turned upside down as the old method of distributing information solely in paper format has been revolutionized by the Web delivery system. As a result, instant and often free access to all types of journals, magazines, newspapers, book reviews, and legal codes is now a reality for researchers. More hardcopy materials are being transferred to Web format every day, reaching wider audiences, and gaining greater exposure for the publisher. For periodicals, simultaneous publication in hardcopy and on the Web is commonplace for both scholarly journals and popular magazines, although the two versions may differ. The Web has also given birth to "e-zines" and "e-journals," publications found exclusively on the Web with no corresponding hardcopy edition.

For Free and For Fee

In the idealistic culture of the Web, the myth of free access to all information thrives. And from many users—especially those outside of a business or corporate environment—a commonly heard cry is, "You mean they are gonna charge me to get into their Web site?" Information is a sought-after commodity, and, no, it never has all been free; there is no reason to think the Web will alter that. Although numerous publishers do offer all or some of their online publications free of charge, many have access or subscriber fees, just as they do in hardcopy format. To researchers accustomed to libraries paying the subscription costs, direct access fees may come as a surprise. For example, searching the *Los Angeles Times* newspaper Web site is free, but retrieving an article from the online archives costs a couple of dollars per article or requires one to be a paid subscriber with an I.D. number. Customers are also often unaware of the true cost to libraries of commercial databases, such as *Ebscohost*, *ProQuest*, *Infotrac* or others that they are able to access while on a school campus, in a corporate library, or remotely with a special password.

Expect pricing for Web products—especially services targeted toward libraries—to vary widely as publishers and their customers continue to test the waters on pricing patterns.

From Breaking News to the Classics

Although the bulk of material published on the Web is in the English language, there is a wide diversity of foreign language materials available online, from daily newspapers to museum exhibits to scholarly papers to political manifestos. This virtual language lab opens up a whole new world of information for immigrants, business travelers, students, and tourists.

The Web provides an exciting new forum for current events reporting. Virtually all the major U.S. dailies and television news stations continually update their Web sites, offering breaking news as it happens "24/7" along with audio and video clips. The dynamic news environment is no longer only the realm of journalists with newspaper wire service access.

Another boon to researchers is the proliferation of full-text classics online. For the works of Jane Austen, William Shakespeare, Herman Melville, and many other titles in the public domain, readers can download or browse the texts on the Web thanks to the efforts of Project Gutenberg and others to make them digitally available for free.

Patron Services

The Web has opened up an enticing, multicolored smorgasbord of information to consumers. Although many sources now online, such as the *Occupational Outlook Handbook*, *The ThomCat*, various newspaper and proprietary databases, have long been familiar resources to librarians and serious researchers, to the novice student or casual searcher their accessibility on the Web makes them seem to be brand new.

The information search itself has become much easier for patrons. Ferreting out information from mysterious, bound books and indexes or "clunky" computer programs has been exchanged for the point-and-click ease, visual appeal, and 24-hour access of the Web. Published information—whether back issues of newspapers, stock quotes, job listings, or government reports—receives much greater exposure to consumers when mounted on the World Wide Web and is no longer a trade secret of librarians.

Emphasis on Convenience

In addition, many library-specific services are new, improved, and more convenient for the computer savvy patron. Remote searching of Web-based public access catalogs lets patrons browse for items and initiate holds on desired titles from the comfort of their home. The majority of libraries use e-mail to place interlibrary loan requests that allow for improved fill rates and speedier patron service.

Students and researchers with access to commercial databases locate journal articles online, then conveniently send them to their e-mail accounts. Many academic institutions offer e-mail-based "alert" services, which allow library users to receive notices of new publications in their interest area or research specialty.

Electronic reserve reading is becoming a reality for college students. Instructors' lecture notes, sample quizzes, along with articles and texts meeting copyright compliance can be viewed on the Web rather than only in the reserve reading room of the campus library.

Patrons with Disabilities

With the help of software to read text aloud, people with visual impairments also share in the benefits of the Internet and are no longer dependent solely on Braille editions or books-on-tape. Homebound individuals formerly reliant on library shut-in services can now have access in their homes to an enormous global resource with an Internet-ready computer.

Family Historians

Samplings of the largest, richest library and archival collections of American historical records are beginning to show up on the Web. With major funding often from private industry, pilot digitization projects are underway at repositories such as the Library of Congress and the National Archives. Portions of George Washington's and Thomas Jefferson's letters and diaries are online, both in facsimile and as transcriptions. The digitization of historical photographs and images from major archives opens up unpublished, historical treasures to schoolchildren, genealogists, and scholars.

The world's largest repository for family history records, The Church of Jesus Christ of Latter-day Saints' Family History Library in Salt Lake City, Utah, is currently conducting pilot tests for the transfer of some of their voluminous holdings to the Web. Now stored in a specially outfitted underground vault, the Mormon collection contains more than 2 million rolls of microfilm, 700,000 microfiche, and 280,000 books.[8] Meanwhile, their popular Web site serves as a powerful index to the microform and print collection.[9]

From the smallest to the largest library, and for all categories of researchers, the Internet revolution has resulted in a tremendous increase of available resources. Gone are the days of strolling through a library's book stacks and thinking, "I guess that's all they have." Collections now extend beyond the physical shelves to the virtual warehouse.

Impact on Staff

For library and information center staffers at all levels, the Internet has brought fundamental change to "business as usual." Acquisitions operations have been streamlined with online ordering from vendors' and publishers' Web sites. Staff training possibilities have been made richer and more relevant with the growth in teleconferencing; burgeoning continuing education offerings emphasize distance-learning delivery of courses.

Electronic discussion groups, or listservs, provide a convenient venue for making contacts for problem solving and for information-sharing among colleagues. These tools provide fresh avenues for discussion among library and information center employees on a global basis. Because e-mail is not geographically bound, responses to a query are just as likely to come from an online colleague in Australia or Europe as from a local librarian. In addition, e-mail extends opportunities for such international exchanges to staff who previously would not have had access to them because of limited travel funds to attend faraway conferences.

Staff can also go online for the latest industry news and reporting. Many library trade periodicals have sprouted Web versions and there are numerous specialty e-journals catering to areas of the field, such as the pioneering *Associates* newsletter, which is dedicated to library support staff issues (see http://www.ukans.edu/~assoc/).

The rise of the Internet and reliance on digital information has created new job classifications within library and information center environments. The need for digital librarians—those who create and manage digital library services and collections—is on the rise. Knowledge of imaging technologies, markup languages, Web technology, and more go hand in hand with customer service orientation, knowledge of key sources, and collection development.

In government, private industry, and nonprofit sectors, Web masters are a growth job category; graduate library/information science schools are a fertile training ground for these prospective Web masters, with entry level jobs garnering as much as $45,000.[10] In schools and colleges, librarians and technicians now work with instructors to identify and create multimedia resources for classroom presentations or distance education, which is increasingly using the Web as the mechanism for delivering instruction to students.

This leads again to the critical need for ongoing retraining and skills updating for all library personnel—from seasoned staffers now on the job to new recruits just entering the library and information science field. The new developments and creative energy brought to the field by the Internet and technological change require staff committed to growth and a parallel commitment of libraries to provide opportunities for staff development.

Modern Services Demand New Floor Plans

For many libraries, existing floor plans are often incompatible with a twenty-first century concept of service delivery. Information centers and libraries are rapidly evolving from the more static role of a book depository to dynamic high-tech information centers. This is a major cause for librarians to rethink their facility's layout. Today there is a need for greater numbers of computer workstations; in many cases, open access labs of 30 computers are typical in schools, colleges, and public libraries. If separate from existing reference service points, these areas require additional staffed counters.

Older audiovisual centers, which focused on the now obsolete 16-mm films and older media, are being converted to teleconference areas or multimedia labs. New uses for old spaces may require remodeling, expansion, or at least a reworked floor plan. Heavy-duty cabling for electricity and data connections can be difficult and costly to provide in older buildings. This may lead to incorporation of wireless networks and appliances to serve the needs of customers and staff.

Study carrels and cozy chairs need to be interspersed with suitable furniture and outlets for patrons' laptop computers and accessible terminals with appropriate adaptive features for patrons with disabilities. All service desks must be Internet-ready and proximate to patron computer banks, whereas large stack areas need OPACs at convenient locations throughout. Some of the physical plant issues range from the critical upgrading of high-speed cabling to partitioning off quiet reading or study areas from heavily trafficked, noise-intensive computer areas.

Librarians Are Now Teachers

Information managers, librarians, and library technicians have always drawn from their teaching skills as they walk individual patrons through the mysteries of the card catalog, call numbers, periodical indexes, shelf locations, and other tools essential to locating information. In the Internet era, add to that basic skill set the need to train users in keyboarding, computer basics, Web use, e-mail access, and specific programs, along with the ability to differentiate between reliable and spurious information sources.

The greatest challenge of the twenty-first century will be attempting to provide our customers with critical thinking skills in how to sort out the proverbial "wheat from the chaff." Often, electronic information available through libraries has not passed through the filtering process to which information published on paper is subjected. What is a welcome gain in timely distribution is often more than offset by loss in quality control. Accuracy is not checked to the same degree. Authority and reliability of the author is not pre-verified for the consumer. We will continue to be challenged as to how to best help our patrons learn how to locate reliable information on the Web.

Instructional presentations to small groups, entire classrooms, or computer labs are a daily duty that require competency in public speaking and teaching, along with knowledge of diverse learning styles. In addition, strong computer skills, patience, and an ability to problem solve are all a must. Those contemplating a career in the field need to carefully ponder these requirements and consider their comfort level with public speaking, instructing, and computer usage, in addition to a love for books.

As mentioned previously, the need for staff to continually update themselves is overarching. Newer professional certification and training programs that cater to updating librarians and educators in high technology competencies are flourishing, with many courses available in a distance learning mode.

Future Happenings

The ever-increasing traffic on the Web, the need for improved connectivity, and the growth in "e-commerce" with its multimedia advertisements and banners have led some pioneer users of the Internet to look for an alternate route for their data. Begun in late 1996 by a consortium of U.S. universities, Internet2 is an effort by the research and academic communities to build upon and improve the technology of the highly popular original Internet. Internet2 combines the financial support and advanced research efforts of academia and the private sector, along with North American, Asian, and European government partners.

Feeling that the current network is too clogged by commercial and personal users, the Internet2 members are committed to paying for the research, upgrading of technologies, and organizational structure needed to provide a more reliable, faster network for sophisticated, serious research use. They also expect that the newer network applications they pioneer will eventually benefit all levels of Internet users.

To long-term Internet veterans, it may seem as if, to paraphrase the inimitable Yogi Berra, "It's beginning to look like déjà vu all over again." The original Internet started in a very similar manner. Much of the impetus for the original Internet came from the need of faculty and graduate students at major research universities to have access to one of the handful of super computers that had been funded by the National Science Foundation (NSF). NSF couldn't afford to fund super computers on every campus, so they facilitated researchers, whose projects they sponsored, to have what were at that time considered high-speed connections to the nearest NSF-supported super computer. However, the transmission speeds achieved then would be considered intolerable even to home modem connections today.

At that time the Internet was only a dedicated wire from the super computer center to the next major research university, which was then connected to the next major research university, and so on. Other universities, colleges, and entities were not connected, nor were they considered in the planning. So far, this sounds very similar to the evolution of Internet2.

What happened next with the original Internet will also probably happen with Internet2. High-technology companies are already starting to participate. Other universities, beyond the elite few initially included, will want to have access to the greater bandwidth and speed of Internet2. Is anyone already starting to consider those needs for Internet3? But even our current Internet system is a tangled maze of information providers that is often impenetrable to the novice.

In terms of library-specific developments, leading institutions are making serious attempts at "taming the Web" by applying familiar principles of information organization to cyberspace. By creating and maintaining sophisticated portals or indexes to recommended Web and electronic resources, these digital projects facilitate Internet research by librarians, students, and serious researchers. The Librarian's Index to the Internet (http://www.lii.org/) has become a standard tool for reference librarians across the nation.

Just as libraries have banded together in networks and consortia to share physical collections and resources, the trend now is in developing cooperative interfaces to their collective Web resources. Good examples are the California Digital Library (http://www.cdlib.org), touted as the tenth campus of the University of California state system, and the Colorado Virtual Libraries site (http://www.aclin.org/). Led by the extant consortium, New York Comprehensive Research Libraries, the state of New York is undertaking a major effort to build a state digital library. See their Web site (http://www.nysl.nysed.gov/nycrl) for updates on the project.

As was alluded to previously, no one owns the Internet; it just "grew up." After the major research universities were connected, other institutions arranged to pay for dedicated communications lines to connect to the nearest organization that was already connected; and so it went. Likewise, no one organization maintains the Internet either. If there is a problem, it's often unclear to the user who should be responsible for fixing it. Similarly, no one entity, either nationally or internationally, makes rules that apply to all things in all places. What a tangled Web we weave! Although this lack of definition is often frustrating, it is one of the features that has allowed it to develop and permeate our lives so quickly.

Getting Comfortable with a New Technology

So is there a downside to this remarkable global network, the Internet, that has so transformed our lives? Any new technology is invariably accompanied by new issues and unforeseen problems as it evolves and as diverse users continue to interact with it. In the meantime, the many controversial aspects of the Internet provide plenty of fodder for public discussion among the media, educators, scientists, and futurists.

Haves Versus the Have-Nots

A familiar societal concern about the proliferation of the Internet is how the phenomenon affects those with no access to or understanding of computers. Commonly referred to as the "have-nots," this encompasses the disadvantaged, disabled, low-income, poorly educated, immigrant, and elderly groups. These people are being bypassed as information publishers assume that the Web is the standard tool and that every office and home is equipped with a contemporary, high bandwidth, multimedia personal computer. Is the burgeoning reliance on online information and entertainment catering to the wealthier, better-educated population, and leaving the poor even farther behind? If so, how can equitable access be ensured and what is the role for libraries and information centers in this regard?

Information Credibility and Research Habits

In the fervor to publish around the clock, editorial and reporting standards can fall by the wayside as each media outlet rushes to "scoop" its competitors. The old editorial consideration of "Should we go to press with this?" can be lost in the rush to be first, leaving the Web fertile ground for gossip, innuendo, and inaccuracies. As with any information source, Internet data requires novice and experienced researchers alike to apply scrutiny to what they find. And because of its self-publishing nature, Web-based information bears a need for an extra measure of evaluation. Spurious descriptions of whales in the Minnesota River (there aren't any) and "world history" accounts that no Nazi concentration camps existed, can be found on legitimate-looking sites.[11]

Researchers—especially younger students—have a tendency to think exclusively in terms of the Internet as a source. In many cases, they are unaware of reference books, CD-ROM products, or other sources and are forsaking tools that may be better suited to their task. A corollary of this sole reliance on Web resources is that novice researchers have less tolerance for using text-based resources and are more in need of a photo fix or a sound bite to summarize complex ideas.

The technology of the Web also encourages plagiarism. Just cut and paste and, voilà, you have a term paper. Some professors claim to see a rise in highly fragmented, choppy term papers, and amalgams of paragraphs cobbled together from the many Web sites critiquing popular study topics, such as Shakespeare's plays or current political issues. Although plagiarism is as old as the hills and will always be a temptation, the Web makes it easier to substitute original thought with snippets of someone else's comments (no matter what their credentials may or may not be).[12]

The Internet As a Reliable Archive

The Internet is still young, but the emphasis is very clearly on current and contemporary information. Owners of Web publishing ventures may reach different conclusions as they answer questions like the following: Is it a profitable venture to convert older magazines, newspapers, journals, and public domain works to the Web? Will people pay for access to archival files as they will for the latest issues? Publishers are still determining pricing and packaging of access to their holdings.

A library-specific corollary issue is that of perpetual access to periodicals. Will an online commercial database always maintain access to archival issues? Or will they suddenly drop or omit the older files, leaving a huge gap of back issues within the library collection. For any research institution, this issue is critical as they decide whether to become more dependent on the many Web-based periodical indexes and databases. Professors, students, scholars, and researchers expect libraries to be repositories for non-current periodicals, books, government documents, and the like. As library networks or consortia negotiate contracts with commercial publishers of online products, perpetual access is a major point of negotiation.

Health Effects

Science has yet to thoroughly document the mental and physical health effects from the increasing amount of time humans now spend in front of computer screens, some days logging more hours in cyberspace than in the real world. But certain trends are apparent. Carpal tunnel syndrome and repetitive-use injuries have long been commonplace among data entry operators, and are on the rise among youth who have grown up with substantial keyboarding use.

Carnegie Mellon University conducted a study in 1998 suggesting that using the Internet can cause isolation, loneliness, and depression. In a two-year survey of 169 Pittsburgh residents, researchers found that using the Internet for as little as one hour per week resulted in an average increase of 1 percent on a depression scale; 0.04 percent on a loneliness scale; and a loss of 2.7

members of the user's social group.[13] This seems logical to some but counterintuitive to others, who feel that computers help them connect with others. Clearly, more study is needed.

As the Internet encourages us to replace interpersonal transactions, such as in-person banking and shopping, with virtual commerce, it remains to be seen whether there will be an increased sense of isolation or frustration. Will virtual commerce dead-ends frustrate like the endless voicemail loop, leaving us longing to speak to a live person? Of course, this issue did not first appear with the Internet. All forms of automation, including telephone answering machines, have contributed to this phenomenon.

Current health trends indicate that obesity is on the rise among Americans, with 55 percent of adults and 13 percent of children being overweight.[14] Obesity is often linked to a sedentary lifestyle, with many leisure hours spent camped in front of a television and a lack of regular physical exercise. Increased reliance on computer monitors—whether for work or for pleasure—can't help but further compete for discretionary time and make it that much harder to engage in exercise or physical fitness activities.

And there is the issue of technology overload. The proliferation of newer, faster, cheaper, more convenient electronic tools is an amazing convenience from which we all benefit, but it can also be a mixed blessing. In a business environment that assumes that one is always available by e-mail, pager, cellular telephone, fax, or other invention, where are the boundaries between privacy and access in our personal lives? Is the virtual reference librarian available to answer a patron query 24 hours a day, seven days a week (24/7)? Managing the use of modern communication tools and technology to prevent psychological stress from the constant pressure to be on duty is an important contemporary issue.

As the phenomenon of the Internet continues to mature, future inventions will help resolve some of these current pressing issues while simultaneously ushering in a host of new challenges. Count on the Internet to spark discussion among old and young, and technological gurus and novices as to its virtues and vices. But the changes ushered in by the Internet, and particularly by the World Wide Web, will not go away. Nor will the pace of change abate. In fact, it is likely to accelerate.

Summary

If the dynamic environment described in the preceding chapters seems attractive to you, then you may have a future in library science. If you are over thirty and contemplating a career change, you will not be alone. In the twentieth century, librarians and library technicians alike typically chose their careers after spending some time in other endeavors.

Students in graduate library schools had an average age of 30. The men were likely to be bunched between 27–33. Women, on the other hand, were distributed from 22–55. Students in library technology programs historically have been primarily female and "fortyish." This latter demographic has been encouraged because most library/information technology course work predominantly has been scheduled at night. It remains to be seen if the increasing need for Web development skills will result in younger, "geekier" males being attracted to the career pathways within librarianship.

Whatever the gender and age demographics of those employed in the library business turn out to be, their mission will be to solve information problems for their clients. In this quest, the only predictable constant appears to be change. The cascading development of technology and the resulting explosion of both formats and quantity of information will make problem-solving skills in this field more necessary than ever.

Study Questions

1. Describe how you use the Web in your personal life and in your coursework. What is your favorite Web portal page?

2. Do you pay for access to any Web-based databases or services? Why or why not?

3. What attributes of e-mail have made it so accepted and popular? How often do you use e-mail?

4. How does your public library differ now from when you were a high school student? Has the building been remodeled or redesigned to accommodate changes?

5. Has the burgeoning of the Internet left libraries obsolete? Why or why not?

6. Pretend that you've just had a book published and are now looking forward to collecting your royalties on each copy sold to reward you for all of your hard work. How would you feel about having a Web version of your work made accessible free of charge?

Resources

Articles

Collins, Sarah. "Austen in Cyberspace," *New York Times Book Review* (5 May 1996): 35.

Guernsey, Lisa. "Library Groups, Decrying 'Excessive Pricing,' Demand New Policies on Electronic Journals," *Chronicle of Higher Education* (10 April 1998): A33–34.

Herring, Mark Y. "10 Reasons Why the Internet is No Substitute for a Library," *American Libraries* (April 2001): 76–78.

Jost, Kenneth. "Libraries and the Internet," *CQ Researcher9* (1 June 2001): 467–87.

Simon, Eric J. "Are E-Books Ready for the Classroom?" *Syllabus* (September 2001): 28, 29.

Stebelman, Scott. "Cybercheating: Dishonesty Goes Digital," *American Libraries* (September 1998): 48–50.

Books

Burke, John J. *Neal-Schuman Library Technology Companion: A Basic Guide for Library Staff.* New York: Neal-Schuman, 2000.

Ensor, Pat, ed. *Cybrarian's Manual 2.* Chicago: American Library Association, 2000.

Gordon, Rachel Singer. *Teaching the Internet in Libraries.* Chicago: American Library Association, 2001.

Horton, Sarah. *Web Teaching Guide: A Practical Approach to Creating Course Web Sites.* New Haven, CT: Yale University Press, 2000.

Janes, Joseph, et al. *The Internet Public Library Handbook.* New York: Neal-Schuman, 1999.

Murray, Laura K. *Basic Internet for Busy Librarians: A Quick Course for Catching Up.* Chicago: American Library Association, 1998.

Videos

Best of the Internet Inside Libraries. (28 min.). Towson, MD: American Library Association/ Library Video Network, 1997.
Showcases innovative library-sponsored Internet projects from 1995 to 1997.

Searching the Web: Introduction to Search Techniques on the Web. (20 min.). Towson, MD: American Library Association/Library Video Network, 1997.
A beginner's overview of how search engines work, how to make effective use of them, how to evaluate Web resources, and how to use reference techniques for the Web.

Pacific Bell and the UCLA Graduate School of Education and Information Studies. *E-literate?* (9 min.). Los Angeles: University of California Regents, 2000. An introduction to the issues of evaluating online information.

Web Sites

* *Associates: The Electronic Library Support Staff Journal*
  http://www.ukans.edu/~assoc/
  (Accessed December 2, 2001)
      Founded in 1994, this well-written electronic journal deals with all issues concerning library support staff. Published three times a year, the journal's Web site also maintains an easily accessed archive of back issues.

* *Falling Through the Net: Defining the Digital Divide*
  http://www.ntia.doc.gov/ntiahome/digitaldivide
  (Accessed December 2, 2001)
      A report released by the Department of Commerce's National Tele-communications Administration in their ongoing efforts to study American telephone, computer, and Internet usage. Specifically, the report documents the increasing gap along ethnic lines between those with access to computers and those without.

* *Human Deployment Report*
  http://www.undp.org/hdro/99.htm
  (Accessed December 2, 2001)
      This lengthy United Nations report includes a discussion about U.S. dominance in the use of computers and of the parallel dominant use of the English language on the Web, despite the fact that less than 1 percent of the global population can read the English language.

* *Internet Index*
  http://www.openmarket.com/intindex/index.cfm
  (Accessed December 2, 2001)
      Interesting newsletter published two or three times annually and packed with facts and figures tracking Internet usage. Home page gives access to the current edition as well as to previous issues and also cites original source data.

* *Internet2 Project*
  http://www.internet2.edu/
  (Accessed December 2, 2001)
      For background and updates on the progress of this project, visit the home page of the Internet2 consortium.

* *Librarians' Index to the Internet*
  http://www.lii.org
  (Accessed December 2, 2001)
      Highly regarded and popular among reference librarians throughout the United States, this Internet-ready reference tool is extensive and regularly maintained.

- *Pew Internet & American Life Project.*
  http://www.pewinternet.org/reports/toc.asp?Report=39
  "The Internet and Education: Findings of the Pew Internet & American
  Life Project: Our Reports."
  (Accessed December 9, 2001)

- *Yale Style Manual*
  http://info.med.yale.edu/caim/manual/
  (Accessed December 2, 2001)
      Provides a well-written overview of Web page design and standards,
  which is also available in book format.

Notes

1.   "Usage Patterns: Reasons for Being Online." April 8, 1999. Reasons for Being
Online (or not). *eMarketer.* Available: http://www.emarketer.com/estats/usage_reason
_online.html (Accessed April 8, 1999).

2.   David Plotnikoff. "Honoring Internet's Best and Worst," *Telegram-Tribune*, San
Luis Obispo, California, 22 March 1999, B4, B5.

3.   Scope Communications Group. "NUA: Internet, How Many Online?" Available:
http://www.nua.net/surveys/how_many_online/index.html (Accessed November 26,
2001).

4.   "Women Equal Number of Men Online." April 4, 1999. *eMarketer.* Available:
http://www.emarketer .com/estats/040599_women.html (Accessed April 8, 1999).

5.   "email Becoming Mainstream Communications Tool." n.d. *eMarketer.* Available:
http://www.emarketer.com/estats/040599_women.html (Accessed April 8, 1999).

6.   Ibid.

7.   Pew Internet & American Life Project. "The Love Bug: Few Take an Online Sick Day
Due to Virus." Pew Internet Project: Our Reports. Available: http://www.pewinternet
.org/reports/reports.asp?Report=13&Sectiion=ReportLevel1&Field=Level1ID&ID=12
(Accessed December 17, 2001).

8.   Kristen Moulton. "Mormons Offer Online Family Tree: New Mormon Web Site
Lists and Charts More than 400 Million Names," *AOL*, May 24, 1999, The Associated
Press.

9.   The Church of Jesus Christ of Latter-day Saints. "Family Search Internet Genealogy
Service." Available: http://www.familysearch.org/ (Accessed December 15, 2001).

10.   Marissa Melton. "The Modern M.L.S. Degree: Library Schools Today Are
Turning Out Webmasters," *Online U.S. News.* Available: http://www.usnews.com
/usnews/edu/beyond/grad/gbmls.htm (Accessed May 12, 1999).

11.   Tina Kelley. "Whales in the Minnesota River? Only on the Web, Where Skepticism Is a Required Navigational Aid," *New York Times* (4 March 1999): D1, D8–D9.

12.   David Rothenberg. "How the Web Destroys the Quality of Students' Research Papers," *Chronicle of Higher Education* (14 August 1997): A44.

13.   Joshua Quittner. "Bummed Like Me," *Time* (14 September 1998): 84.

14.   Associated Press. "Kids Pedal to Pay for View," *Los Angeles Times* (19 April 1999): A-13.

APPENDIX A

LIBRARY AND INFORMATION STUDIES EDUCATION AND HUMAN RESOURCE UTILIZATION A STATEMENT OF POLICY

EXECUTIVE SUMMARY

In 1999 the 1st Congress on Professional Education created four task forces. Task Force #4, Personnel Stratification, now Library Career Pathways, was charged with the review of the means, methods, and expectations for entry into the library professions.

Initially, the Task Force reviewed a policy statement entitled, "Library Education and Personnel Utilization" which the Council of the American Library Association had adopted on June 30, 1970. This ALA policy document appeared in need of some (but remarkably little) revision, given its age. The Library Career Pathways Task Force updated the statement, incorporating a more current view of librarianship and its partner professions. Feedback is encouraged on the draft document that is below. You may send comments to the Task Force Chair, Julie G. Huiskamp or any member of the Library Career Pathways Task Force.

* *

Major revisions to the document include:

- The substitution of library and information studies and the inclusion of the title Specialist where the terms library education, library science, librarianship, and Library Assistant/Technical Assistant have previously appeared;

- The recognition that the library and information studies realm of practice includes several professions at various levels of entry;

- The acknowledgment of support staff as integral contributors to and participants in the library professions;

- A statement encouraging professional preparation which would include a broad educational background for study in the humanities, the sciences, and the social sciences, over preference to a narrowly defined, specialized field of study.

267

The document continues to demonstrate several points of career entry at levels from high school graduation through the Masters level, considered the terminal degree for professional practice. Qualifications and expectations at all levels are described in narrative form, and through the means of a graphic "Career Lattice".

The statement on career development and continuous learning draws a distinct difference between the individual responsibility for professional development expected of librarians and specialists, and the library managers' responsibility for providing access to continuous learning for support staff contributors.

Library and Information Studies and Human Resource Utilization*

A Statement of Policy adopted by the Council of the American Library Association, January 23, 2002**

1. The purpose of the policy statement is to recommend categories of library personnel, and levels of training and education appropriate to the preparation of personnel for these categories, which will support the highest standards of library service for all kinds of libraries and the most effective use of the variety of skills and qualifications needed to provide it.

2. The phrase "library and information studies" is understood to be concerned with recordable information and knowledge and the services and technologies to facilitate their management and use. Library and information studies encompasses information and knowledge creation, communication, identification, selection, acquisition, organization and description, storage and retrieval, preservation, analysis, interpretation, evaluation, synthesis, dissemination, and management.

---

*The policy statement adopted by ALA with the title Library Education and Manpower. In the spring of 1976, the Office for Library Personnel Resources Advisory Committee edited this statement to remove sexist terminology. This version of the statement includes changes adopted by the ALA Council at the 2002 Midwinter meeting.

**Throughout this statement, wherever the term "librarianship" is used, it is meant to be read in its broadest sense as encompassing the relevant concepts of information science and documentation; wherever the term "libraries" is used, the term refers to public, academic, corporate, medical and other special libraries; current models of media centers, learning centers, educational resources centers, information, documentation, and referral centers are also assumed. To avoid the necessity of repeating the entire gamut of variations and expansions, the traditional library terminology is employed in its most inclusive meaning.

3. To meet the goals of library service, both professional and supportive staff are needed in libraries. Thus, the library occupation is much broader than that segment of it which is the library profession, but the library profession has responsibility for defining the training and education required for the preparation of personnel who work in libraries at any level, supportive or professional.

4. Skills other than those of librarianship also have an important contribution to make to the achievement of superior library service. There should be equal recognition in both the professional and supportive ranks for those individuals whose expertise contributes to the effective performance of the library.

5. A constant effort must be made to promote the most effective utilization of personnel at all levels, both professional and supportive. The tables in Figure 1 suggest a set of categories which illustrate a means for achieving this end.

Figure 1.

CATEGORIES OF LIBRARY PERSONNEL—PROFESSIONAL

Library-Related Qualifications	Non-Library Related Qualifications	Basic Requirements	Nature of Responsibilities
Senior Librarian	Senior Specialist	In addition to the requirements for Librarian/Specialist—relevant experience and continued professional development.	Top-level responsibilities including but not limited to administration; superior knowledge of some aspect of librarianship; or of other subject fields of value to the library.
Librarian	Specialist	For Librarian: Master's degree For Specialist: Appropriate professional degree for the specialty.	Professional responsibilities which may include those of management and supervision requiring independent judgment; interpretation of rules and procedures; analysis of library problems; and formulation of original and creative solutions for them. (Normally utilizing knowledge of the subject field represented by the academic degree.)

CATEGORIES OF LIBRARY PERSONNEL—SUPPORTIVE

Library-Related Qualifications	Non-Library Related Qualifications	Basic Requirements	Nature of Responsibilities
LIS Associate	Associate Specialist	Bachelors degree (with preferred coursework in library and/or information science); OR bachelors degree, plus additional applicable academic work.	Associate is hired or promoted into the job based on previous library work experience; the library specialist has extensive experience, perhaps supplemented by job-sponsored training in a specialized area—e.g. Interlibrary borrowing/lending; preservation; book searching and replacement; second-tier reference; copy cataloging; etc.
LIS Assistant	Assistant Specialist	At least two years of college-level study; or AA degree, (with or without library technical assistant training) preferred; OR post-secondary school training and relevant skills; OR certificate program.	Tasks performed as supportive staff following established policies and procedures and may include supervision of such tasks.
Clerk (Exact titles vary depending on type of library circumstance.)	Clerk (Exact titles vary depending on type of library circumstance.)	High school diploma or equivalent.	Assignments as required by the individual library.

6. The titles recommended here represent categories or broad classifications, within which it is assumed that there will be several levels of promotional steps. Specific job titles may be used within any category: for example, catalogers, reference librarians, children's librarians would be included in either the "Librarian" or (depending upon the level of their responsibilities and qualifications) "Senior Librarian" categories; department heads, the director of the library, and certain specialists would

presumably have the additional qualifications and responsibilities which place them in the "Senior Librarian" category. In addition, the categories are not discreet, library staff members may actually be performing tasks in a number of categories. The categories are not static, but dynamic and are meant to provide a guide to assist in illustrating the wide range of job responsibilities and tasks performed in the library setting.

7. Where specific job titles dictated by local usage and tradition do not make clear the level of the staff member's qualification and responsibility, it is recommended that reference to the ALA category title be used parenthetically to provide the clarification desirable for communication and reciprocity. For example:

   REFERENCE ASSISTANT (LIS Associate)

   HEAD CATALOGER (Senior Librarian)

   LIBRARY AIDE (LIS Assistant)

8. The title "Librarian" carries with it the connotation of "professional" in the sense that professional tasks are those which require a special background and education on the basis of which library needs are identified, problems are analyzed, goals are set, and original and creative solutions are formulated for them, integrating theory into practice, and planning, organizing, communicating, and administering successful programs of service to users of the library's materials and services. In defining services to users, the professional person recognizes potential users as well as current ones, and designs services which will reach all who could benefit from them.

9. The title "Librarian" therefore should be used only to designate positions in libraries which utilize the qualifications and impose the responsibilities suggested above. Positions which are primarily devoted to the routine application of established rules and techniques, however useful and essential to the effective operation of a library's ongoing services, should not carry the word "Librarian" in the job title.

10. Libraries with limited staff would not need staff appointments in each of these categories. It is urged, however, that this basic scheme be introduced wherever possible to permit, where needed, the necessary flexibility in staffing.

11. The salaries for each category should offer a range of promotional steps sufficient to permit a career-in-rank. The top salary in any category should overlap the beginning salary in the next higher category, in order to give recognition to the value of experience and knowledge gained on the job.

12. Libraries should pay particular attention that stratification of personnel not occur along lines of race, ethnicity, or gender. If these patterns of stratification occur, steps should be taken to investigate and ameliorate

possible discrimination. Libraries should promote the full education, utilization, and promotion of all employees regardless of race, ethnic background, or gender. Libraries and programs of library and information studies should be particularly sensitive to discrimination patterns that reflect the prejudices of society and should take proactive measures to combat the effects of these influences.

13. Inadequately supported libraries or libraries too small to be able to afford professional staff should nevertheless have access to the services and supervision of a librarian. To obtain the professional guidance that they themselves cannot supply, such libraries should promote cooperative arrangements or join larger systems of cooperating libraries through which supervisory personnel can be supported. Smaller libraries which are part of such a system can often maintain the local service with building staff at the Associate level.

Library Career Lattice

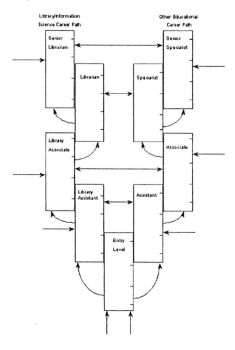

Figure 2.

If one thinks of Career Lattices rather than Career Ladders, the flexibility intended by the Policy Statement may be better visualized. The movement among staff responsibilities, for example, is not necessarily directly up, but often may be lateral to increased responsibilities of equal importance. Each category embodies a number of promotional steps within it, as indicated by the gradation markings on each bar. The top of any category overlaps in responsibility and salary the higher category.

Comments on the Categories

14. The Clerk classifications do not require formal academic training in library subjects. The assignments in these categories are based upon general clerical and secretarial proficiencies. Familiarity with basic library terminology and routines necessary to adapt clerical skills to the library's needs is best learned on the job.

15. The Assistant categories assume certain kinds of specific "technical" skills; they are not meant simply to accommodate advanced clerks. While clerical skills might well be part of a Assistant's equipment, the emphasis in an assignment should be on the special technical skill. For example, someone who is skilled in handling multimedia equipment, or at introductory data processing, or display art might well be hired in the Assistant Specialist category for these skills, related to librarianship only to the extent that they are employed in a library. An LIS Assistant is a person with certain specifically library-related skills—in preliminary bibliographic searching for example, or utilization of certain equipment or technology—the performance of whose duties seldom requires a background in general education.

16. The Associate categories assume a need for an educational background like that represented by a bachelor's degree from an accredited four-year institution of higher education (or foreign equivalent). Assignments may be such that library knowledge is less important than general education, and whether the title is LIS Associate or Associate Specialist depends upon the nature of the tasks and responsibilities assigned. Persons holding the B.A. degree, with or without a library science minor or practical experience in libraries, are eligible for employment in this category. Titles within the Associate category that are assigned to individuals will depend upon the relevance of their training and background to their specific assignments.

17. The Associate category also provides the opportunity for persons of promise and exceptional talent to begin library employment below the level of professional (as defined in this statement) and thus to combine employment in a library with course work at the graduate level. Where this kind of work/study arrangement is made, the combination of work and formal study should provide 1) increasing responsibility within the Associate ranks as the individual moves through the academic program, and 2) eligibility for promotion, upon completion of the master's degree (or appropriate professional degree for the specialty), to positions of professional responsibility and attendant reclassification to the professional category.

18. The first professional category—Librarian, or Specialist—assumes responsibilities that are professional in the sense described in paragraph #8 above. A well-rounded liberal education plus graduate-level

study in the field of specialization (either in librarianship or in a relevant field) are seen as the minimum preparation for the kinds of assignments implied. The title, however, is given for a position entailing professional responsibilities and not automatically upon achievement of the academic degree.

19. The Senior categories assume relevant professional experience as well as qualifications beyond those required for admission to the first professional ranks. Normally, it is assumed that such advanced qualification shall be held in some specialty, either in a particular aspect of librarianship or some relevant subject field. Subject specializations are as applicable in the Senior Librarian category as they are in the Senior Specialist category.

20. Administrative responsibilities entail high-level specialty, and appointment to positions in top administration should normally require the qualifications of Senior Librarian with a specialization in administration. This category, however, is not limited to administrators, whose specialty is only one of several specializations of value to the library service. There are many areas of specialized knowledge within librarianship which are equally important and to which equal recognition in prestige and salary should be given. Highly qualified persons with specialist responsibilities in some aspects of librarianship—archives, bibliography, reference, for example—should be eligible for advanced status and financial rewards without being forced to abandon for administrative responsibilities their areas of major competence.

Implications for Formal Education

21. The academic degree (or evidence of years of academic work completed) is recommended as the single best means for determining that the applicant has the background required for the position. If an ALA-recognized Master's degree or state or provincial certification is unavailable, examinations may be valid and reliable tests of equivalent qualification.

22. In the selection of applicants for positions at any level, and for admission to programs of library and information studies, attention should be paid to personal aptitudes and qualifications in addition to academic ones. The nature of the position or specialty, and particularly the degree to which it entails working with others, with the public, or with special audiences or materials should be taken into account in the evaluation of a prospective student or employee. Importance should be placed on the education and employment of individuals with diverse ethnic backgrounds who are multilingual and, additionally, on those who possess a multicultural perspective. When language translation is required in individual job assignments, the proper educational background to be able to write and communicate in a given language is necessary.

23. As library services and technologies change and expand, as new audiences are reached, as new media and technology take on greater importance in the communication process, and as new approaches to the handling of materials continue to be introduced, the kinds of preparation required of those who will be employed in libraries will become more varied. Degrees in fields other than librarianship will be needed in the Specialist categories. For many Senior Librarian positions, an advanced degree in another subject field rather than an additional degree in librarianship, may be desirable. Previous experience need not always have been in libraries to have pertinence for appointment in a library.

24. Because the principles of librarianship are applied to the materials of information and knowledge broader than any single field, and because they are related to subject matter outside of librarianship itself, responsible education in these principles should be built upon a broad background in education which includes the humanities, the sciences, and the social sciences, rather than a narrowly specialized background.

25. Emphasis in the two-year Technical Assistant programs should be more on skills training than on general library concepts and procedures. In many cases it would be better from the standpoint of the student to pursue more broadly-based vocational courses which will teach technical skills applicable in a variety of job situations rather than those limited solely to the library setting. These programs should combine a strong general education component, library technical specialty courses, and courses related to the library technical specialty program.

26. Undergraduate instruction in library science other than training courses for Library Technical Assistants should be primarily a contribution to liberal education rather than an opportunity to provide technological and methodological training. This does not preclude the inclusion of course work related to the basic skills of library practice, but it does affect teaching method and approach, and implies an emphasis on the principles that underlie practice rather than how-to-do-it, vocational training.

27. Certain practical skills and procedures at all levels are best learned on the job rather than in the academic classroom. These relate typically to details of operation which may vary from institution to institution, or to routines which require repetition and practice for their mastery. The responsibility for such in-service parts of the total preparation of both librarians and supportive staff rests with libraries and library systems rather than with the programs of library and information studies.

28. The objective of the master's programs in library and information studies should be to prepare librarians capable of anticipating and engineering the change and improvement required to move the profession constantly forward. The curriculum and teaching methods should be

designed to serve this kind of education for the future rather than to train for the practice of the present.

29. Certain interdisciplinary concepts are so intimately related to the basic concepts underlying library service that they properly become a part of the library and information studies curriculum rather than simply an outside specialty. Where such content is introduced into library and information studies it should be incorporated into the entire curriculum, enriching every course where it is pertinent. The stop-gap addition of individual courses in such a specialty, not integrated into the program as a whole, is an inadequate assimilation of the intellectual contribution of the new concept to library and information studies and thinking.

30. In recognition of the many areas of related subject matter of importance to library service, library and information studies should make knowledge in other fields readily available to students, either through the appointment of staff members from other disciplines or through permitting students to cross departmental, divisional, and institutional lines in reasoned programs in related fields. Intensive specializations at the graduate level, building upon strengths in the parent institution or the community, are a logical development in library and information studies.

31. Programs of library and information studies should be encouraged to experiment with new teaching methods, new learning devices, different patterns of scheduling and sequence, and other means, both traditional and nontraditional, that may increase the effectiveness of the students' educational experience.

32. Research has an important role to play in the educational process as a source of new knowledge both for the field of librarianship in general and for library and information studies in particular. In its planning, budgeting, and organizational design, programs of library and information studies should recognize research, both theoretical and applied, as an imperative responsibility.

Career Development and Continuous Learning

33. Career development and continuous learning is the shared responsibility of the individual, the employer, formal education providers, and professional associations. Continuous learning is essential for all library and information studies personnel, supportive and professional, whether or not they seek advancement.

34. Employers are responsible for providing training that supports the work of their organization. This can take the form of planned staff development activities or less formal activities such as committee assignments and special projects.

35. Employers are responsible for providing support for individual career development and continuous learning. Examples of support include release time, sabbaticals, tuition reimbursement, and mentoring programs. Such support is essential in hiring and retaining an excellent workforce.

36. Education providers are responsible for developing and making available learning opportunities that reflect the needs of the library and information studies profession. To address individual learning needs and styles, these must be available in multiple formats and in a variety of locations.

37. Professional associations are responsible for providing learning opportunities that meet the needs of their membership. These may take the form of workshops, conference programs and articles in professional journals. Workshops and conference programs should be planned to ensure adherence to the best practices of adult learning theory.

38. For the individual, career development and continuous learning includes both formal and informal learning situations and need not be limited to library and information studies. In some cases, post-masters and doctoral programs may be appropriate.

APPENDIX B

LIBRARY BILL OF RIGHTS

The American Library Association affirms that all libraries are forums for information and ideas, and that the following basic policies should guide their services.

I. Books and other library resources should be provided for the interest, information, and enlightenment of all people of the community the library serves. Materials should not be excluded because of the origin, background, or views of those contributing to their creation.

II. Libraries should provide materials and information presenting all points of view on current and historical issues. Materials should not be proscribed or removed because of partisan or doctrinal disapproval.

III. Libraries should challenge censorship in the fulfillment of their responsibility to provide information and enlightenment.

IV. Libraries should cooperate with all persons and groups concerned with resisting abridgment of free expression and free access to ideas.

V. A person's right to use a library should not be denied or abridged because of origin, age, background, or views.

VI. Libraries which make exhibit spaces and meeting rooms available to the public they serve should make such facilities available on an equitable basis, regardless of the beliefs or affiliations of individuals or groups requesting their use.

Adopted June 18, 1948.
Amended February 2, 1961, and January 23, 1980,
inclusion of "age" reaffirmed January 23, 1996,
by the ALA Council.

APPENDIX C

CODE OF ETHICS
OF THE
AMERICAN LIBRARY
ASSOCIATION

As members of the American Library Association, we recognize the importance of codifying and making known to the profession and to the general public the ethical principles that guide the work of librarians, other professionals providing information services, library trustees and library staffs.

Ethical dilemmas occur when values are in conflict. The American Library Association Code of Ethics states the values to which we are committed, and embodies the ethical responsibilities of the profession in this changing information environment.

We significantly influence or control the selection, organization, preservation, and dissemination of information. In a political system grounded in an informed citizenry, we are members of a profession explicitly committed to intellectual freedom and the freedom of access to information. We have a special obligation to ensure the free flow of information and ideas to present and future generations.

The principles of this Code are expressed in broad statements to guide ethical decision making. These statements provide a framework; they cannot and do not dictate conduct to cover particular situations.

I.   We provide the highest level of service to all library users through appropriate and usefully organized resources; equitable service policies; equitable access; and accurate, unbiased, and courteous responses to all requests.

II. We uphold the principles of intellectual freedom and resist all efforts to censor library resources.

III. We protect each library user's right to privacy and confidentiality with respect to information sought or received and resources consulted, borrowed, acquired or transmitted.

IV. We recognize and respect intellectual property rights.

V. We treat co-workers and other colleagues with respect, fairness and good faith, and advocate conditions of employment that safeguard the rights and welfare of all employees of our institutions.

VI. We do not advance private interests at the expense of library users, colleagues, or our employing institutions.

VII. We distinguish between our personal convictions and professional duties and do not allow our personal beliefs to interfere with fair representation of the aims of our institutions or the provision of access to their information resources.

VIII. We strive for excellence in the profession by maintaining and enhancing our own knowledge and skills, by encouraging the professional development of co-workers, and by fostering the aspirations of potential members of the profession.

Adopted by the ALA Council

June 28, 1995

APPENDIX D

THE FREEDOM TO READ STATEMENT

The freedom to read is essential to our democracy. It is continuously under attack. Private groups and public authorities in various parts of the country are working to remove or limit access to reading materials, to censor content in schools, to label "controversial" views, to distribute lists of "objectionable" books or authors, and to purge libraries. These actions apparently rise from a view that our national tradition of free expression is no longer valid; that censorship and suppression are needed to avoid the subversion of politics and the corruption of morals. We, as citizens devoted to reading and as librarians and publishers responsible for disseminating ideas, wish to assert the public interest in the preservation of the freedom to read.

Most attempts at suppression rest on a denial of the fundamental premise of democracy: that the ordinary citizen, by exercising critical judgment, will accept the good and reject the bad. The censors, public and private, assume that they should determine what is good and what is bad for their fellow citizens.

We trust Americans to recognize propaganda and misinformation, and to make their own decisions about what they read and believe. We do not believe they need the help of censors to assist them in this task. We do not believe they are prepared to sacrifice their heritage of a free press in order to be "protected" against what others think may be bad for them. We believe they still favor free enterprise in ideas and expression.

These efforts at suppression are related to a larger pattern of pressures being brought against education, the press, art and images, films, broadcast media, and the Internet. The problem is not only one of actual censorship. The shadow of fear cast by these pressures leads, we suspect, to an even larger voluntary curtailment of expression by those who seek to avoid controversy.

Such pressure toward conformity is perhaps natural to a time of accelerated change. And yet suppression is never more dangerous than in such a time of social tension. Freedom has given the United States the elasticity to endure strain. Freedom keeps open the path of novel and creative solutions, and enables change to come by choice. Every silencing of a heresy, every enforcement of an orthodoxy, diminishes the toughness and resilience of our society and leaves it the less able to deal with controversy and difference.

Now as always in our history, reading is among our greatest freedoms. The freedom to read and write is almost the only means for making generally available ideas or manners of expression that can initially command only a small audience. The written word is the natural medium for the new idea and the untried voice from which come the original contributions to social growth. It is essential to the extended discussion that serious thought requires, and to the accumulation of knowledge and ideas into organized collections.

We believe that free communication is essential to the preservation of a free society and a creative culture. We believe that these pressures toward conformity present the danger of limiting the range and variety of inquiry and expression on which our democracy and our culture depend. We believe that every American community must jealously guard the freedom to publish and to circulate, in order to preserve its own freedom to read. We believe that publishers and librarians have a profound responsibility to give validity to that freedom to read by making it possible for the readers to choose freely from a variety of offerings. The freedom to read is guaranteed by the Constitution. Those with faith in free people will stand firm on these constitutional guarantees of essential rights and will exercise the responsibilities that accompany these rights.

We therefore affirm these propositions:

1. *It is in the public interest for publishers and librarians to make available the widest diversity of views and expressions, including those that are unorthodox or unpopular with the majority.*

   Creative thought is by definition new, and what is new is different. The bearer of every new thought is a rebel until that idea is refined and tested. Totalitarian systems attempt to maintain themselves in power by the ruthless suppression of any concept that challenges the established orthodoxy. The power of a democratic system to adapt to change is vastly strengthened by the freedom of its citizens to choose widely from among conflicting opinions offered freely to them. To stifle every nonconformist idea at birth would mark the end of the democratic process. Furthermore, only through the constant activity of weighing and selecting can the democratic mind attain the strength demanded by times like these. We need to know not only what we believe but why we believe it.

2. *Publishers, librarians, and booksellers do not need to endorse every idea or presentation they make available. It would conflict with the public interest for them to establish their own political, moral, or aesthetic views as a standard for determining what should be published or circulated.*

Publishers and librarians serve the educational process by helping to make available knowledge and ideas required for the growth of the mind and the increase of learning. They do not foster education by imposing as mentors the patterns of their own thought. The people should have the freedom to read and consider a broader range of ideas than those that may be held by any single librarian or publisher or government or church. It is wrong that what one can read should be confined to what another thinks proper.

3. *It is contrary to the public interest for publishers or librarians to bar access to writings on the basis of the personal history or political affiliations of the author.*

No art or literature can flourish if it is to be measured by the political views or private lives of its creators. No society of free people can flourish that draws up lists of writers to whom it will not listen, whatever they may have to say.

4. *There is no place in our society for efforts to coerce the taste of others, to confine adults to the reading matter deemed suitable for adolescents, or to inhibit the efforts of writers to achieve artistic expression.*

To some, much of modern expression is shocking. But is not much of life itself shocking? We cut off literature at the source if we prevent writers from dealing with the stuff of life. Parents and teachers have a responsibility to prepare the young to meet the diversity of experiences in life to which they will be exposed, as they have a responsibility to help them learn to think critically for themselves. These are affirmative responsibilities, not to be discharged simply by preventing them from reading works for which they are not yet prepared. In these matters values differ, and values cannot be legislated; nor can machinery be devised that will suit the demands of one group without limiting the freedom of others.

5. *It is not in the public interest to force a reader to accept with any expression the prejudgment of a label characterizing it or its author as subversive or dangerous.*

The ideal of labeling presupposes the existence of individuals or groups with wisdom to determine by authority what is good or bad for the citizen. It presupposes that individuals must be directed in making up their minds about the ideas they examine. But Americans do not need others to do their thinking for them.

6. *It is the responsibility of publishers and librarians, as guardians of the people's freedom to read, to contest encroachments upon that freedom by individuals or groups seeking to impose their own standards or tastes upon the community at large.*

It is inevitable in the give and take of the democratic process that the political, the moral, or the aesthetic concepts of an individual or group will occasionally collide with those of another individual or group. In a free society individuals are free to determine for themselves what they wish to read, and each group is free to determine what it will recommend to its freely associated members. But no group has the right to take the law into its own hands, and to impose its own concept of politics or morality upon other members of a democratic society. Freedom is no freedom if it is accorded only to the accepted and the inoffensive.

7. *It is the responsibility of publishers and librarians to give full meaning to the freedom to read by providing books that enrich the quality and diversity of thought and expression. By the exercise of this affirmative responsibility, they can demonstrate that the answer to a "bad" book is a good one, the answer to a "bad" idea is a good one.*

The freedom to read is of little consequence when the reader cannot obtain matter fit for that reader's purpose. What is needed is not only the absence of restraint, but the positive provision of opportunity for the people to read the best that has been thought and said. Books are the major channel by which the intellectual inheritance is handed down, and the principal means of its testing and growth. The defense of the freedom to read requires of all publishers and librarians the utmost of their faculties, and deserves of all citizens the fullest of their support.

We state these propositions neither lightly nor as easy generalizations. We here stake out a lofty claim for the value of the written word. We do so because we believe that it is possessed of enormous variety and usefulness, worthy of cherishing and keeping free. We realize that the application of these propositions may mean the dissemination of ideas and manners of expression that are repugnant to many persons. We do not state these propositions in the comfortable belief that what people read is unimportant. We believe rather that what people read is deeply important; that ideas can be dangerous; but that the suppression of ideas is fatal to a democratic society. Freedom itself is a dangerous way of life, but it is ours.

This statement was originally issued in May of 1953 by the Westchester Conference of the American Library Association and the American Book Publishers Council, which in 1970 consolidated with the American Educational Publishers Institute to become the Association of American Publishers.

Adopted June 25, 1953; revised January 28, 1972, January 16, 1991, July 12, 2000, by the ALA Council and the AAP Freedom to Read Committee.

A Joint Statement by:
American Library Association and
Association of American Publishers

Subsequently Endorsed by:

- American Association of University Professors

- American Booksellers Foundation for Free Expression

- American Society of Journalists and Authors

- American Society of Newspaper Editors

- Anti-Defamation League of B'nai B'rith

- Association of American University Presses

- Center for Democracy & Technology

- The Children's Book Council

- The Electronic Frontier Foundation

- Feminists for Free Expression

- Freedom to Read Foundation

- International Reading Association

- The Media Institute

- National Coalition Against Censorship

- National PTA

- Parents, Families and Friends of Lesbians and Gays

- People for the American Way

- Student Press Law Center

- The Thomas Jefferson Center for the Protection of Free Expression

Author/Title Index

Subject Index